Persistent Disparity

Persistent Disparity

Race and Economic Inequality in
the United States since 1945

William A. Darity Jr

*Cary C. Boshamer Professor of Economics,
University of North Carolina, USA*

Samuel L. Myers Jr

*Roy Wilkins Professor of Human Relations and Social Justice,
University of Minnesota, USA*

Edward Elgar

Cheltenham, UK • Northampton, MA, USA

Published by
Edward Elgar Publishing Limited
Glensanda House
Montpellier Parade
Cheltenham
Glos GL50 1UA
UK

Edward Elgar Publishing Company
6 Market Street
Northampton
Massachusetts 01060
USA

A catalogue record for this book is available from the British Library

Library of Congress Cataloguing in Publication Data
Darity, William A., 1953–
    Persistent disparity: race and economic inequality in the United
States since 1945/William A. Darity Jr, Samuel L. Myers Jr.
    Includes bibliographical references and index.
    1. Discrimination in employment—United States. 2. Race
discrimination—Economic aspects—United States. 3. Afro-Americans—
Economic conditions. 4. Income distribution—United States.
5. United States—Economic conditions—1945–   I. Myers, Samuel L.
II. Title.
HD4903.5.U58D37   1998
331.13'3'097309045—dc21   97–30626
                                                        CIP

ISBN 1 85898 658 3
    1 85898 665 6 – paperback

Printed and bound in Great Britain by Biddles Ltd, Guildford and King's Lynn

Contents

v

List of figures

viii   *Persistent disparity*

List of tables

Foreword

For the past 40 years, economists have been grappling with the difficult topic of racial inequality in economic life. Their engagement with the issue was sparked by the publication of Gary Becker's pathbreaking book, *The Economics of Discrimination*.

Many economists welcomed Becker's analysis as a convenient application of economic theory to racial differences in income, which ostensibly showed that such differences were the result of differences in worker productivity rather than racial animus. Further, according to Becker, such income differences were unlikely to continue over time as open, competitive markets equalized wages and worker productivity.

But the Becker analysis of racial inequality in economic life was never satisfactory to economists who observed persistent, pervasive disparities between the economic status of African Americans and others in American labour markets. Even a cursory examination of employment status, wages and family incomes has long shown black Americans in a consistently inferior position compared with white Americans on almost every measure of economic well-being. Equally important, broad racial disparities in economic status persist despite a significant narrowing of productivity differences between population groups over the past three decades. Indeed, by some measures racial inequality in income has worsened in recent years, in clear contradiction with what might have been expected from the Beckerian view of the world.

William Darity and Samuel Myers address this major dilemma in economics through their careful, skilful, comprehensive analysis of the available data on individual and family income. The authors go beyond the conventional approach to the issue to reach a deeper level of analysis that recognizes the racial aspects of pre-labour market experience. Among other creative methodological devices, they take race into account as a factor influencing the measurement of statistical indices. Their approach offers a broader, richer perspective on the impact of race on the economic status of different population groups.

This book will challenge every economist interested in racial inequality, and will force scholars to approach the topic in a new, more illuminating way. In short, the Darity and Myers work is a major contribution to the economics profession.

It is not an accident that the authors are two of our nation's most outstanding African American economists. The excellence of their academic preparation, the seriousness of their purpose, and the uncompromising integrity of their intellectual values are all on brilliant display in this carefully written book. And the book comes none too soon.

Our nation is caught in the grip of a querulous debate over race relations. The agony of racism and racial inequality threatens to tear the social fabric asunder. Not since the civil rights movement more than 30 years ago have we, as a nation, been so exercised over the need for racial harmony and tolerance.

Now, as then, much of the issue turns on the realities and consequences of racial inequality in American economic life. Since 1993, the nation has produced more than 11 million new jobs. Still the unemployment rate of black Americans remains above 10 per cent, or twice the rate of unemployment among white workers. Young black men, one of the most disadvantaged groups in our society, are unemployed at a rate of more than 40 per cent.

When employed, black workers are still found disproportionately in the lowest-paying jobs, and black families still earn, on average, less than six dollars for every ten dollars available to white families. These indices of economic well-being reflect the dimensions of racial inequality in America.

There is an old Talmudic proverb that says, 'If you don't know where you're going, any road will take you there.' The burden of economists is to light the way towards the goal of economic opportunity. To do that requires a clear understanding of how the economy works; how it interacts with societal values, attitudes and behaviour to produce persistent inequality in economic life. Darity and Myers have turned up the lamp switch several notches to increase the wattage in the light bulb and illuminate the realities of racial inequality.

Their work provides compelling justification for affirmative action as a public policy to reduce economic inequality. As Supreme Court Justice Blackman said in his opinion on the *Bakke* case, 'In order to get beyond race, we must first take account of race.' In short, we cannot reduce, and eventually eliminate racial inequality until we understand precisely how race affects an individual's life changes – both before and after entering the labour market. The authors carefully dissect the issue, and untangle the knot which binds together education, job skills, occupational status, family structure, wage determination, technology, and even the tax code. Darity and Myers enrich our understanding of racial inequality, and lead the way towards policy prescriptions that might assure equal opportunity in American economic life. Few contributions by economists could be more valuable, and for that we are deeply in their debt.

Bernard E. Anderson

Acknowledgements

This volume was by no means the product of our efforts alone. At various stages of its development we have benefited heavily from the research assistance, the advice and the criticisms of many, many others. We would like to acknowledge their contributions here.

At the University of Maryland at College Park we received research help from: Tsze Chan, Lisa Cook, Norlisha Crawford, Jeannette Gibson-Murphy, Kevin Hart, Tammy A. Ray Jenkins, Anita Klalo-Baines, Russell Lamb, Ruby Taylor-Lewis and Sekai Turner. At the University of North Carolina at Chapel Hill, Ngina Chiteji, Darrick Hamilton and Alicia Robb provided valuable help. And the project could not have been brought to completion without the extraordinary efforts of Judy Leahy as well as Andrianna Abariotes, Julia Blount, Chanjin Chung, Kris Dalen, Lan Pham, Joe Stahl and David Waithaka at the University of Minnesota.

We must also acknowledge the financial support of the Upjohn Institute in Kalamazoo, Michigan, during the development of the manuscript. In particular, Jean Kimmel, H. Allan Hunt and Randall Eberts at Upjohn provided detailed criticisms of earlier drafts of the manuscript.

Other social scientists who have provided helpful commentary on various chapters of *Persistent Disparity* include Bernard Anderson, Douglas Glasgow, Robert Hill, Ronald Mincy, Llad Phillips, Margaret Simms, Belinda Tucker and Harold Votey.

Finally, we must mention the source of the most substantive and trenchant discussions and criticisms of the text – our colleagues in an ongoing endeavour to reconstruct the economic theory of discrimination – Patrick Mason, William Rodgers, William Spriggs and Rhonda Williams. They are our true compadres, and they keep our feet to the fire.

William Darity Jr, University of North Carolina at Chapel Hill
Samuel Myers Jr, University of Minnesota

1. The widening gap – increasing interracial and intraracial inequality

Affirmative action. Quotas. Race-based scholarships. Women- and minority-owned business set-asides. These and other policies were intended over the past quarter-century to remedy patterns of racial, ethnic, and gender inequality in the US economy.

The explosive issue of what to do about these remedies cannot be understood without reference to a broader pattern of widening economic inequality across all of American society. Widening group-specific disparity has gone hand in hand with widening general inequality. The attack on affirmative action in public and private employment as 'reverse discrimination' against white males must be understood within the context of declining real wages faced by many white males. The charge that policies aimed at improving the employment prospects of women and minorities are unfair to the majority in general and white men in particular is a charge that must be considered in the context of the evidence of narrowing job prospects for the middle class.

On the one hand, there is a mounting concern about the decline in the availability of good jobs for persons with less than a college education. This is a concern for the majority of Americans at the middle of the income distribution whose earnings have remained stagnant during a period of unprecedented shifts towards greater economic inequality in the United States. Many hard-working white Americans are falling behind because their income from labour, which accounts for a large share of their total family income, is not growing.

On the other hand, there is opposition to preferential treatment of special classes of Americans who undeniably have been deprived of the economic benefits of full participation in the economy in previous eras. The handicap that many disadvantaged racial minority groups face results from the cumulative effects of explicit state-enforced efforts to retard their progress. The damage lingers across generations, in part because the remedy for preferential treatment is inexact, benefiting some but not all members of racial minority groups. Thus the gap between the majority and the minority continues to widen.

A major policy dilemma looms as a consequence of two issues. The first issue is one of widening intragroup inequality: there is a widening of the gap between the top and the bottom; there is a squeezing of the middle. The second issue is

1

one of widening intergroup inequality: there is a widening of the gap between whites and blacks, even if some blacks are doing well financially.

The dilemma is that labour market policies designed to solve the second of these problems – widening intergroup inequality – become unpopular and divisive in a world where the first of these problems – widening intragroup inequality – is of mounting concern. Is it possible that there is a fundamental linkage between these two types of inequality? Are the factors that are driving a wedge between the top and the bottom – and thus squeezing the middle – also factors that are contributing to the widening gulf between whites and blacks?

In this monograph, we examine the intersection of the widening gaps between blacks and whites and widening gaps within races. We take the position that the whole debate on the widening gap between rich and poor (and the corresponding theme of the diminishing middle class) has been conducted without proper focus on the racial dynamics of widening inequality. It has not been just a matter of the rich getting richer and the poor getting poorer, but that while both affluent blacks and whites got richer, it was the *black* poor that got poorer. Moreover, the evidence of diminishing fortunes of the middle class derives primarily from focusing on families, and the overall deterioration in the condition of families is magnified when emphasis is placed on black families.

Two parallel discussions precede our empirical claims. We examine the standard reasons given for the widening of intraracial inequality – or inequality within groups – and those given for widening interracial inequality – or inequality between groups. We contend that much of the widening racial inequality is attributable to conditions and policies that have contributed to exacerbating general inequality.

At the same time, some policy shifts directed towards interracial inequality – weakening US government support for affirmative action and the dismantling of race preferences in hiring, contracting and university admissions – are implicated in the evidence on widening intraracial inequality. Because blacks are found disproportionately at the bottom of the income distribution, and because public policies themselves are often hostile *de facto* toward racial minority groups, the overall growth in general inequality has contributed to increased racial inequality.

Of course, some policies seemingly unrelated to race have had adverse consequences for all poor Americans, and especially poor non-whites. These include educational policies that have favoured the middle class and resulted in the neglect of inner-city schools. Other policies, such as affirmative action in employment, have had limited impact on persons who do not work, who are outside the mainstream economy, or who are marginalized. Policies that focus on persons who are employed or who have the necessary skills to be hired have limited impact on those at the very bottom of the social and economic ladder.

Regardless, such policies – which favour some over others – may have a limited impact on racial inequality.

A conventional argument that the two phenomena of widening interracial and intraracial inequality largely operate independently is embodied in the claim that labour market trends have moved against rewarding low-skilled workers. Since blacks are disproportionately concentrated among low-skilled labourers, there has been no alteration in the degree of discrimination. Blacks are simply 'victims' of a shift that has had an unfortunate impact on all low-skilled workers, regardless of race.

We demonstrate in this monograph that the skill shift argument does not adequately explain the renewed divergence between black and white earnings in the 1980s. Indeed, a skills mismatch effect does not adequately explain the widening general gap in earnings across all Americans. Therefore we seek a different answer. We recommend that researchers move towards an analysis that fully recognizes the endogenous character of the practice of discrimination. Job losses and earnings losses for white males who are the 'victims' of the unequalizing spiral will lead them to intensify their efforts to preserve their remaining occupational turf and to squeeze black workers further down the occupational ladder.

To provide policy makers with better tools for grappling with both forms of widening inequality, this monograph examines the stylized facts about the patterns and trends and the many explanations for the two patterns of inequality observed in recent years. It details many of the most important trends and patterns that underscore changes in incomes, earnings and wages in the past decades. It sketches and critiques the conventional wisdom concerning these patterns and trends, while offering a broad catalogue of explanations for both the widening of intragroup inequality and of intergroup inequality. New evidence on the position of families shows how conventional wisdom is not only misleading, but can also be dead wrong. Our conclusions suggest a need for substantially improved tools and data to assist policy makers in crafting sound strategies to reverse the momentum toward greater inequality in American life.

WIDENING INTRARACIAL INEQUALITY

For most of the post-World War II period, the distribution of income in the United States remained fairly stable. There has been wide variation between the incomes of families at the top of the distribution and those at the bottom, but the variation remained largely the same for 40 years (Levy, 1987). This stability ended in the last decade.

There is a substantial academic literature debating both the existence and the causes of this turnaround (Danziger and Gottschalk, 1993). Initially, when

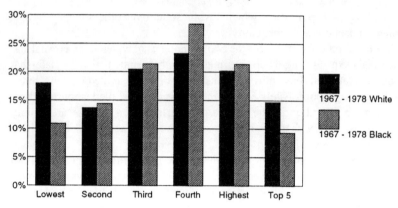

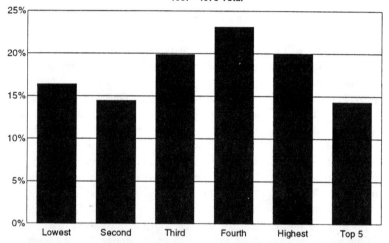

1967 - 1978 Total

evidence showed the sharp reversal in the fortunes of families in the middle class and below, Reagan Administration officials objected fiercely to findings of a 'big U-turn' in income inequality. They argued that there were numerous data problems so severe that there had to be strong doubts as to whether the United States had made a 'U-turn' in its traditional path towards a stable income distribution. It is politically unpopular to admit that the middle class is suffering, so the tendency is to deny the evidence upon which the claim is made. But as the empirical evidence accumulated throughout the 1980s, such denials became much more difficult to sustain.

Figure 1.1 reveals the story that made the headlines. The four panels of the figure document percentage changes in mean incomes between 1967 and 1978 and again between 1979 and 1992. The first two panels show these changes for black and white families separately. The latter two panels show the percentage

67-78
largest income growth
in 3-5th quintile

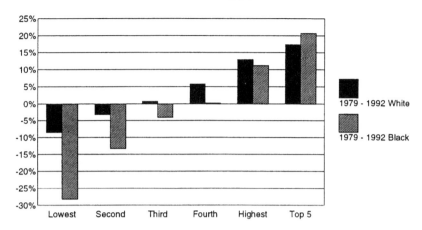

1979 - 1992 Total

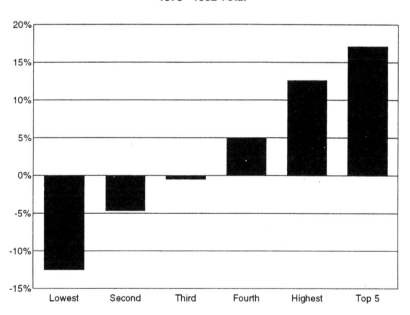

Source: US Bureau of the Census, Current Population Reports, Series P-60, No. 184, *Money Income of Households, Families, and Persons in the United States: 1992*, US Government Printing Office, Washington DC, 1993.

Figure 1.1   Change (%) in mean income in each quintile between 1967–78 and 1979–92

79-92
income losses for
bottom 3 quitiles

changes in incomes for the two time periods for all families. The first and third panels show the changes for 1967 to 1978; the second and fourth panels show changes for 1979 to 1992. The clear message of the figure is: all incomes were rising between 1967 and 1978; thereafter, incomes at the middle and below were falling, especially among black families.

Between 1967 and 1978, in every income quintile (or fifth of the income distribution), families saw real increases in their incomes. Whether a family was in the bottom fifth of the distribution or the top fifth, whether in the next highest fifth above the bottom or the next lowest below the top, and particularly at the middle fifth, incomes increased in the period before the late 1970s. Thus, if we were to rank all families by income from the top to the bottom, divide the ranked families into five equal groups, and find the average family income in each group, we would find that each group or income quintile experienced impressive improvements before the 1980s.

Figure 1.1 also shows the stability of the American income distribution. But when attention is drawn to more recent years, for example, a comparison between 1979 and 1992, evidence of a stable income distribution evaporates. Indeed, in more recent years only the wealthiest American families have improved their standing; middle class families and those at the bottom of the income distribution have slipped considerably.

Figure 1.1 reveals that there has been a widening between the top and the bottom and a 'squeezing' out of the middle class. This conclusion has generated significant alarm among policy makers and the public in general.

One salient aspect of the 'squeezing' out of the middle class is the putative decline in good jobs. To get a glimpse at rudimentary evidence of this and of the widening gap between the educated and less well educated, consider Figure 1.2, showing the ratio of median weekly earnings among young white men to median weekly earnings among older white men.

The figure shows a decline in young white men's earnings during the 1980s. Young white men could expect to earn 62 cents for every dollar earned per week by older white men in 1979. This amount, computed for full-time, year-round employees, dropped to 51 cents in 1992. Since full-time, year-round employees 16–24 years old are disproportionately those with little or no education beyond high school, analysts look at these disparities as confirmation of the widening gulf between the educated and less well educated. But these numbers mask yet another gulf: the gulf between the current generation for whom 'good jobs' are scarce and a previous generation that could count on wage premia from working in unionized sectors of the economy now in decline.

In Chapter 2 we outline the array of explanations offered for this widening gap in American society. As others have shown in comprehensive reviews, the evidence is far from conclusive. Each new study provides seemingly contradictory findings concerning the effects of 1) the entry of the baby boom generation into

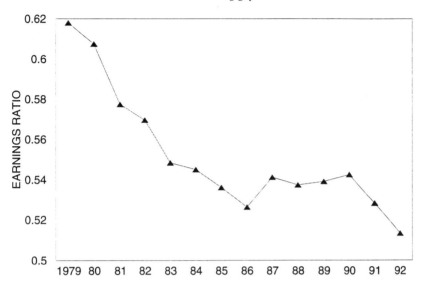

Source: US Bureau of the Census, *Statistical Abstract of the United States: 1993*, Washington, DC, 1993.

Figure 1.2   Median weekly earnings ratio, 1979–92, white men 16–24/white men 25–54

the labour market; 2) the restructuring of the labour market and the loss of middle-class jobs; 3) the effects of technological change; 4) the changing price of skills; 5) business cycle effects; 6) changes in tax codes; and 7) other demographic changes in the population. These explanations, however, are episode-specific and focus on changes in earnings inequality. They ignore long-run patterns of changing income inequality.

WIDENING INTERRACIAL INEQUALITY

Simultaneous with the rise in general inequality has been a worsening of the relative income position of black families in America. The black–white disparity in family incomes has widened over the past decades. As Figure 1.3 graphically demonstrates, the family income ratio – ranging between 0.61 and 0.62 – in 1989 and 1990 was below what it was for *every single year from 1967 to 1980*. The ratio rose from 0.625 in 1967 to almost 0.65 in 1970. It declined during the early 1970s, falling to a little more than 0.62 in 1973. It rebounded in the mid-1970s, reaching about 0.645 in 1976.

However, by the early 1980s that changed. The sharp nose-dive in the ratio of black–white family incomes reached a decades-low point during the 1982

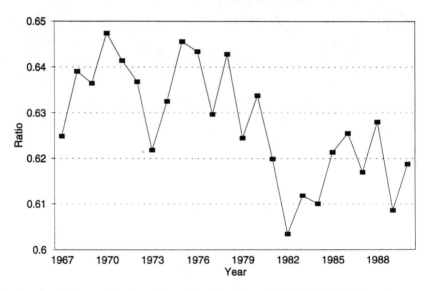

Source: US Bureau of the Census, Current Population Reports, Series P-60, No. 184, *Money Income of Households, Families and Persons in the United States: 1996*, US Government Printing Office, Washington, DC, 1992.

Figure 1. 3   Black–white family income, 1967–90

recession when black families received less than 60½ cents in income for every dollar that white families received. Even though the ratio climbed back after the recession, black families have never fully recovered. They still had incomes in 1990 that were relatively below their position in 1970.

Chapter 3 provides a summary of the explanations for the widening of the racial income gaps, with most of the emphasis placed on earnings. Other comprehensive reviews examine the supply and demand factors that have contributed to the decline in earnings of blacks (Moss and Tilly, 1991). Going beyond that literature requires an examination of the problem of the changing status of family heads with particular reference to the impact of schooling quality, years of education and cohort of family heads. This examination is undertaken in Chapter 4.

FAMILY STRUCTURE AND INEQUALITY

The most obvious explanation for the decline in black family incomes is the rise in the share of black families headed by females. We demonstrate in Chapter 5, however, that the evidence is far from clear that the causal factor contributing

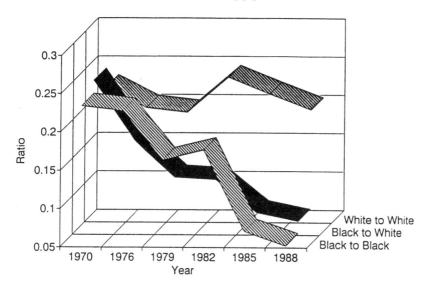

Source: Authors' computations from 1976, 1985 and 1993 IRP Family Extract Files (CPS March Supplements Tapes).

Figure 1.4   Earnings disparities among young men, 1970–88, high-school drop-outs vs college graduates

to the widening earnings gap between black and white family heads is the increased presence of female family heads among blacks. Even among male-headed families, there are substantial differences in earnings that are linked inextricably to age and education. Although the formal demonstration of this requires a technical econometric analysis relegated to an appendix, the kernel of truth rests in the observation from Figure 1.4, displaying the earnings gaps between young black and white family heads between 1970 and 1988. This figure maps the ratio of annual wage and salary incomes of high-school drop-outs to the annual wage and salary incomes of college graduates among 16- to 24-year-olds. The figure shows the ratios among blacks, among whites and between blacks and whites. For all pairings, of course, the earnings of young uneducated heads of families are lower than the earnings of young college graduates, revealing, on the face of it, the conventional skills gap effect.

But for white heads of families these differentials largely remained stable from 1970 to 1988. While young white uneducated heads of families only earned about 25 cents for every dollar that young white educated family heads earned, the wage premium for having a college degree remained largely stable throughout the nearly two decades among whites.

Among blacks, however, the wage premium grew. Whereas young uneducated black male heads of families earned 25 cents for every dollar that young educated black male heads of families earned in 1970, by 1988 they only earned 5 cents for every dollar that young educated black male heads of families earned. Thus, when a comparison is made between the earnings of young uneducated black male heads of families and those of young educated white male heads of families, a sizeable increase in disparity is evident from 1970 to 1988. This suggests that the widening of the income gaps between black and white families may not be just a simple result of the growth of female-headed families among blacks – families whose heads earn less – but a more complex effect of changing returns to skills that differs between blacks and whites.

As we explain more fully in Chapters 4 and 5, if the only effect were an overall decline in the returns to skills among young, uneducated family heads, the technological factors contributing to the rise in wage premia for highly educated workers would explain the rise in the racial earnings gaps because of the high concentration of black family heads among the young and uneducated. But more must be at work when there is, as we find, a divergence between the earnings of family heads who are black male college graduates and those who are black male high-school drop-outs, but no change in the gap between college graduates and high-school drop-outs among white male family heads.

If anything, the differences between the races in the impact of changing returns to skills or education must be attributable to continuing labour market discrimination – a market that consistently values a black male high-school drop-out differently from a similarly uneducated white – or to aspects of pre-labour market discrimination that lower the value of the black high-school drop-out's education below that of a similarly situated white. In short, either equally uneducated blacks and whites with identical skills have unequal returns to those skills or equally uneducated blacks and whites have unequal skills because of disparities that originate outside the labour market.

PERSISTENCE OF PRE-LABOUR MARKET DISCRIMINATION

The evidence in Chapter 5 points both to ongoing pre-market and in-market discrimination as contributing to the widening racial gap in family incomes. Indeed, the distinction between the two types of discrimination potentially becomes less and less sharp. Chapter 6 presents forecasts on the likely path of racial inequality in the absence of direct market interventions designed to remedy racial income inequality. The prognosis is pessimistic. Given the existing trends, even the most positive assessment has relative black family incomes levelling off by the year 2000 at a point below that reached in 1970.

If the long-term negative trend of the entire period from 1967 to 1990 were to prevail into the next millennium, by the year 2000 the ratio of black–white family incomes would be below the level it reached at the lowest point of the recession of 1982. Furthermore, if the most optimistic evidence were marshalled, showing relatively increased black per capita incomes over the past decades, then the forecasts show that black and white per capita money incomes would not converge until 2303 or nearly 12 generations from now! To provide perspective, African-Americans are now a mere five generations from the era of US slavery.

Thus, in the absence of direct remedies, racial earnings inequality is likely to persist for generations to come. There are substantive policy problems associated with past and projected attempts to remedy racial inequality in the US economy. The context of these problems is detailed in Chapter 7. We point out that race-based remedies are under attack but non-race-based remedies do not work. Is there a middle ground? Are there race-based remedies that are acceptable to the political majority? The answer is 'perhaps'.

WHAT CAN BE DONE?

Our ambiguous answer to the question of what can be done to reverse the downward spiral in black–white inequality is a product of our assessment of the relationship between overall inequality and racial inequality. We point out that the economic fortunes of blacks are linked to the degree of economic distress felt by whites. That linkage is manifest in the endogenous nature of discrimination. When whites feel no economic threat from racial minorities there is little opposition to 'diversity', 'affirmative action' and similar efforts to promote the interests of the minority. When whites are threatened, as they are now with the shrinking middle class and the loss of working-class jobs, there is every reason to believe that policies designed to remedy racial inequality will be targeted for elimination. The solution, then, is to see the connection between the effectiveness of policies designed to reduce racial inequality and the evolution of policies designed to reduce intragroup inequality.

The empirical evidence shows, however, that even if policies can be implemented to address current inequality, there remains the problem of intergenerational inequality. Much of the earnings gap between blacks and whites can be attributed to unequal opportunities that are rooted in past inequalities. Policies that have no impact on redressing historic inequalities – particularly inequalities in wealth – are unlikely to succeed in permanently reducing racial earnings inequality. The answer to the question, 'How long must affirmative action programmes be in place?' may have to be 'Forever', if policies fail to address intergenerational inequities.

To reiterate: growing racial disparity in earnings poses serious policy questions. Two important dimensions concern (1) the widening gap in general inequality between the top and the bottom of the income distribution and the consequent squeeze on the middle and (2) the widening gap in racial inequality between blacks and whites. Policies such as affirmative action, that address current market discrimination and disparities, may fail to win political support when there is a widening of general inequality. Yet even those policies may be less than fully effective if some or most current labour market inequality rests on historic disparities transmitted from one generation to the next.

The problem we address in this monograph is the evidence that the gap has grown between the top and the bottom of the overall income distribution in the US. This change is unprecedented in the twentieth century. For example, between World War II and 1979, when real median incomes peaked, every quintile of families experienced income improvements. But from 1979 to 1993 only the top two quintiles improved. The relative position of the bottom quintiles deteriorated and the middle quintile was stagnant. This issue was at the centre of the 1988 and 1992 presidential debates – or at least the issue of the middle quintile remaining stagnant. The rallying cry of President Clinton's 1995 economic address, of course, was tax policies ostensibly designed to improve the well-being of this middle-income quintile, known popularly as the 'middle class'.

There has also been a growth in the earnings gap between college-educated workers and those with equivalent experience but without college degrees. While it has nearly always been the case that college graduates earn more than high-school drop-outs, the earnings premium for having graduated from college expanded greatly during the 1980s. Economists are not settled on the reasons for this, but a widening skill gap appears to be the leading explanation. Our assessment is that there is indeed a widening skills gap. But there is a clear racial dimension to this gap, leading to a different policy interpretation of what can be done about it.

The decline in the real wages of white males is certainly one of the most alarming findings that economists have uncovered in recent years. It has particular importance with respect to the political feasibility of policies designed to address increasing racial inequality: gaps between white and non-white earnings and between income and employment widened during the 1980s at the same time that the relative earnings of white males declined. While there is ample evidence that some non-whites gained during the period, it is hardly reassuring to the majority that the overall decline in their incomes was matched by some improvements in minority incomes.

Therefore a policy agenda designed to address the problem of general economic inequality has direct relevance to the issue of growing racial inequality. We urge consideration of a sustained research effort to underscore the connection between the worsening condition of white males in the economy and the significant deterioration of the relative position of blacks. That effort will enhance our ability to discover and implement strategies that arrest the shrinking of the middle class and simultaneously curb the growing racial economic divide in American society.

Ultimately, we conclude that the long-run goal of achieving racial economic equality will require honest debate and assessment of the viability of wealth transfers. In the concluding chapters we evaluate the merits of alternative strategies for achieving racial equality and conclude that wealth transfers must be included in any systematic effort to end once and for all persistent racial economic inequality in America. The political stakes will undoubtedly be high in adopting this strategy. But the political stakes are already high for adopting alternatives that offer far less hope of permanently eradicating inequality. The argument in favour of *wealth redistribution*, then, must rest on the view that other remedies for racial economic inequality such as affirmative action or general human capital efforts are just as objectionable to the majority but yield far fewer long-run gains.

Only wealth Redistribution will work because much inequality results from intergenerational transfers

2. General inequality in American society and the widening of the gap within races

The conventional wisdom about general inequality is that for much of the post-World War II period the distribution of income has remained fairly constant. There are wide variations between the incomes of families at the top of the distribution and families at the bottom of the distribution, but those variations remain largely stable through time (Levy, 1987).

Two implications can be drawn from this evidence of a stable income distribution, a distribution where income growth is shared among all persons coupled with little apparent mobility from the bottom to the top. The first of these implications is the suggestion that during the 1950s and 1960s economic growth, expanding job opportunities, improved education and the like benefited all. The second of these implications is that the benefits were not strictly redistributive; while families at the bottom of the distribution may have been better off in an absolute sense, they were still at the bottom.

THE WIDENING OF THE INCOME GAP

The conventional wisdom about the stability of the income distribution was challenged by data from the late 1970s and 1980s showing a sharp reversal in the fortunes of families in the middle class and below. Unlike previous eras, when all family incomes seemed to rise as the average increased, in recent years the top parts of the distribution saw dramatic improvements while the bottom parts of the distribution experienced falling shares (Danziger, Gottschalk and Smolensky, 1989). The fierce objections during the Reagan Administration to findings showing a 'big U-turn' in income inequality have subsided in the 1990s. These objections were based on concerns that the data used failed to account for differing labour force participation rates, differing non-cash benefits, differing methods of top coding of data across data sets, and differing notions of what constituted a 'U-turn.' (Mattera, 1990).

Figure 1.1 (see page 4) revealed that there has been a widening of the gap between the top and the bottom and a 'squeezing' out of the middle class. Two important qualifications are pertinent. First, although the language suggests that the data are comparing individual families at particular points in time, this is not the case. The data used in most analyses of changes in family income inequality constitute annual snapshots of different families. A specific family at the bottom of the income distribution in 1980 may have moved up the ladder by 1990. The change in average incomes in a particular quintile does not require that each family remain in the same quintile from year to year. To assess such movements a longitudinal data set on families would be required.

A second qualification is that the data do not make adjustments for the size of families. Per capita real incomes continued to grow throughout a period when family incomes declined. To reconcile falling median family incomes with rising per capita income, we have to recognize that family size is falling and fewer traditional (husband, wife and children) family units are being formed. An additional technical issue concerns the choice of price deflator. The negative trend in median family incomes can be altered sharply by the use of an alternative price deflator (Congressional Budget Office, *Trends in Family Incomes*, 1988).

These income distribution changes in recent years can also be documented using summary measures of inequality such as the Gini coefficient, which is an index of income concentration. The higher the value of this index, the greater the concentration of income in the hands of a few individuals or families at the top of the distribution; the lower the value of this index, the lesser the concentration of income and the greater the evenness of the distribution of income across all income classes.

Figure 2.1 shows that income concentration declined and then remained relatively stable from the 1940s to the early to mid-1970s. Among white families in particular even up to 1982, income concentration was lower than it was in the late 1940s. This changed in the 1980s when there was a sharp increase in the concentration of income, reaching record highs by the late 1980s and early 1990s.

Figure 2.1 also shows that the income distribution among blacks, Hispanics, and non-whites is more uneven than it is among whites. For the years since the late 1960s when the data have been disaggregated to distinguish blacks from other non-whites, and from the early 1970s when the data have been disaggregated to distinguish Hispanics (of any race), the evidence shows continued dispersions in the incomes of these minority group members. In short, the widening of the income gap among non-whites predates that of whites. The unmistakable rise in the Gini coefficient for blacks and Hispanics dates to at least the late 1960s and early 1970s.

However, these figures show the relative position of families as measured by their incomes and not by unrelated individuals or by earnings. The patterns of income inequality among individuals have not paralleled those of families. As Figure 2.2 shows, there has been a general decline in income concentration among

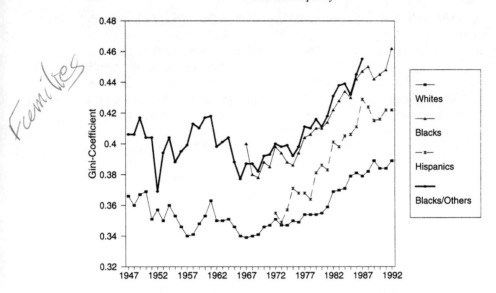

Source: U.S. Bureau of the Census, Current Population Reports, Series P-60, No. 184, *Money Income of Households, Families and Persons in the United States: 1992*, U.S. Government Printing Office, Washington, DC, 1993.

Figure 2.1   Family income concentration, 1947–92

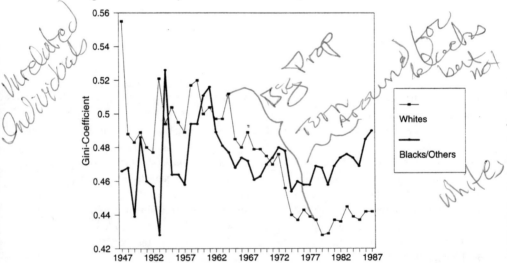

Source: U.S. Bureau of the Census, Current Population Reports, Series P-60, No. 184, *Money Income of Households, Families and Persons in the United States: 1987*, U.S. Government Printing Office, Washington, DC, 1989.

Figure 2.2   Unrelated individual income inequality, 1947–87

unrelated individuals since the mid-1950s, with particularly sharp reductions in income concentration among white unrelated individuals from 1964 to 1979, largely attributable to anti-poverty programmes assisting the elderly. Although inequality began to rise again among white unrelated individuals in the 1980s, it still was far from the high levels of the late 1940s. Figure 2.2 reveals, in contrast, that non-white unrelated individuals have faced generally rising income inequality since 1973, with higher levels in the late 1980s than in the mid-1960s. This is largely attributable to those at the top gaining and those at the bottom losing.

THE RICH GET RICHER AND THE *BLACK* POOR GET POORER

A more vivid way of viewing the widening gap between the top and the bottom is to consider the percentage of families with incomes below $5000 and above $100 000. Figure 2.3b shows that the percentage of white and black families with incomes below $5000 declined from the late 1960s to the mid-1970s. In 1967 about 3 per cent of white families had incomes below $5000; about 9 per cent of black families were at the very bottom. By 1976, these numbers had fallen to 2 per cent and 6 per cent. A steep rise in the percentage of black families with incomes below $5000 is seen since 1976. A smaller increase is seen for white families. The percentage of these families with incomes below $5000 was a little higher in 1990 than it was in 1980, levelling off at 2.5 per cent.

This contrasts sharply with the dramatic growth in the percentage of white families with incomes above $100 000. This upper reach of the income distribution increased from 1.8 per cent in 1967 to 3.6 per cent in 1979 to 6.1 per cent in 1989. These figures come from recent Current Population Reports (CPR) and are not directly comparable to earlier versions of the CPR series because of changes in the method used to adjust income for inflation (US Bureau of the Census, 1991). Nevertheless, the patterns of change remain the same: sharp increases in the percentage of white families with incomes above $100 000. There also has been a sharp increase in the percentage of black families with incomes above $100 000. The numbers grew from 0.4 per cent in 1967 to 0.5 per cent in 1979 to 1.4 per cent in 1989, small absolute proportions but huge relative increases.

The interpretation of these increases at the very bottom and the very top is clear. The rich got richer, but it was the black poor in particular that got poorer. The widening of the gap between the top and the bottom reveals considerable racial division at the bottom. And even at the top there remain significant racial inequalities.

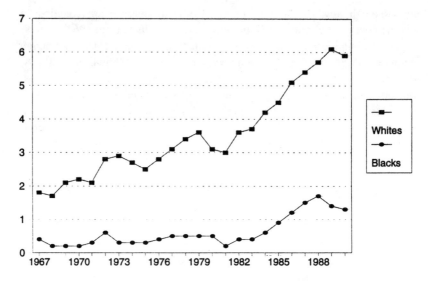

Source: U.S. Bureau of the Census, *Money Income in the United States: 1990.*

Figure 2.3a   Distribution of family incomes, 1967–90, percentage over $100k

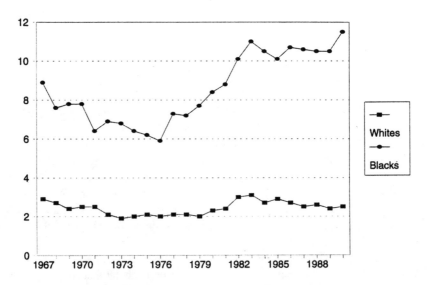

Source: U.S. Bureau of the Census, *Money Income in the United States: 1990.*

Figure 2.3b   Distribution of family incomes, 1967–90, percentage below $5k

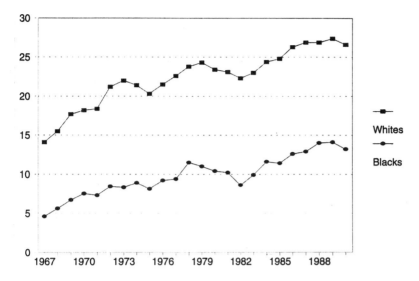

Source: U.S. Bureau of the Census, *Money Income in the United States: 1990.*

Figure 2.4a   Distribution of family incomes, 1967–90, percentage $50–100k

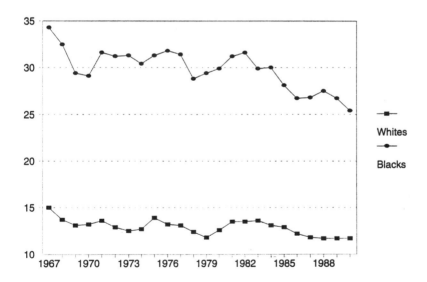

Source: U.S. Bureau of the Census, *Money Income in the United States: 1990.*

Figure 2.4b   Distribution of family incomes, 1967–90, percentage $5–15k

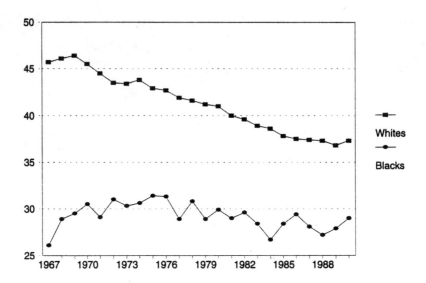

Source: U.S. Bureau of the Census, *Money Income in the United States: 1990.*

Figure 2.5a   Distribution of family incomes, 1967–90, percentage $25–50k

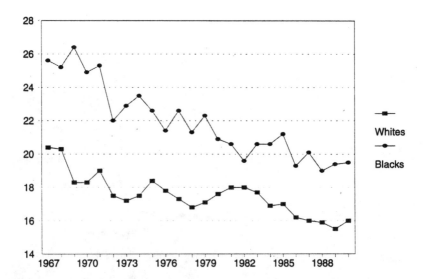

Source: U.S. Bureau of the Census, *Money Income in the United States: 1990.*

Figure 2.5b   Distribution of family incomes, 1967–90, percentage $15–25k

Figure 2.4 reveals another aspect of this widening gap when focus is placed on the 'near poor' and the 'near rich'. The percentage of black families with incomes from $5000 to $15 000 dropped from 35 per cent to 25 per cent from 1967 to 1990. In 1990, the percentage of white families in this income range remained about the same, at 12 per cent, after falling from 15 per cent in 1967 to 13 per cent in the 1970s. The percentage of black and white families with incomes between $50 000 and $100 000 rose steadily from 5 and 15 per cent in 1967 to 13 and 26 per cent in 1990. Thus the ranks of the 'near rich' grew and the black 'near poor' shrank.

What was happening to the middle? The percentage of white families with incomes between $25 000 and $50 000 was on the decline. Whereas more than 45 per cent of white families received incomes in this middle range (expressed in 1990 dollars) in the late 1960s, only about 37 per cent did in the late 1980s. The black proportion remained stable at just below 30 per cent. Just below the middle, incomes between $15 000 and $25 000 (1990 dollars), there was steady decline for both blacks and whites. Figure 2.5 reveals that the middle, measured variously from $15 000 to $25 000 or $25 000 to $50 000, was shrinking.

INEQUALITY IN LABOUR INCOMES

Labour income accounts for a considerable share of total family income. To understand the rise in inequality in family incomes we need to understand changes occurring in the earnings of individuals and changes in family composition.

Rand economist Lynn Karoly (1994) has undertaken an extensive examination of the changing labour earnings distributions by race and gender. She has computed real weekly wage and salary earnings by race and gender using the US Department of Commerce *Current Population Survey* with corrections for various well-known data problems affecting the comparability of *CPS* calculations across years. One such problem is changes in the top coding of income data during the 1980s.

Figures 2.6 to 2.9 reproduce Karoly's calculations with computations of the rate of change in weekly wage and salary incomes between 1970 and 1979 and between 1979 and 1987 for each quintile. Figure 2.6 clearly shows that in the lower quintiles white males' wage and salary incomes on average fell in real terms in the latter period. But their earnings were falling even earlier. Thus, although the family income data reveal that the white middle-class squeeze is a phenomenon of recent origin, the decline in wages of white males in the lower reaches of the wage distribution began earlier. Researchers point to the rise in labour force participation rates and the rise in earnings of white women as the explanation for maintenance of white family incomes despite the fall in white male earnings.

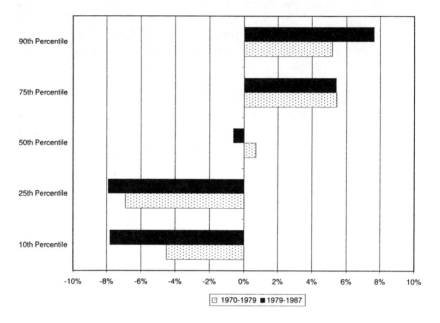

90th Percentile

Source: Karoly, Lynn A. 'The Trend in Inequality Among Families, Individuals, and Workers in the United States: A Twenty-Five Year Perspective,' *Uneven Tides: Rising Inequality in America*. (Sheldon Danziger and Peter Gottschalk, eds, New York: The Russell Sage Foundation, 1994)

Figure 2.6   Change (%) in weekly wage and salary income, 1970–79 and 1979–87, white non-Hispanic males

Figure 2.7 sheds further light on what must have been happening within white families. The picture shows that white female earnings were increasing in virtually every quintile in the earlier and the latter periods. The improvements, while more pronounced in the earlier periods, were sustained in more recent years.

Figures 2.8 and 2.9 show that the fortunes faced by black males and black females have not always paralleled those of whites. Weekly wages of black males grew in every quartile from 1970 to 1979. The largest gains were in the highest quartile. At the top 10 per cent, black men saw their earnings rise by an impressive 16 per cent from 1970 to 1979. Even black men in the lowest decile realized increases in their wages of more than 12 per cent during that period. The years between 1979 and 1987 saw sharp reversals of those positive trends. In every quartile there were declines in the real incomes of black men. Only the highest 10 per cent of black men had incomes that did not decline during the 1980s. And for them, the increases in weekly wages were only about 2 per cent. Thus for black men there were sharp reversals of the progress of the 1970s during the 1980s.

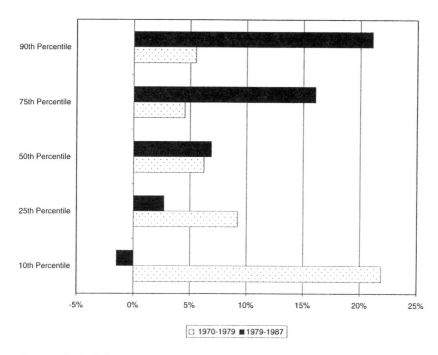

Source: As Fig. 2.6.

Figure 2.7   Change (%) in weekly wage and salary income, 1970–79 and 1979–87, white non-Hispanic females

In contrast, weekly wages of black females generally rose both during the 1970s and during the 1980s. For example, the top quartile among black females saw weekly wages rise 20 per cent during the 1970s. That same group realized increases in weekly wages of more than 10 per cent during the 1980s. For the bottom decile there were increases in wages of more than 50 per cent during the 1970s. Even though this improvement ceased during the 1980s, there were no substantial losses in real earnings for black women as there were for black men.

Lynn Karoly's research provides confirmation of the growth in earnings disparity between the top and the bottom of the distribution among individuals and the shrinking of the middle. Nevertheless, her computations do not show in direct fashion the implications for families. For that, information on the earnings of family heads must be examined.

The Institute for Research on Poverty's Family Extract Tapes permit such an analysis. These tapes reconfigure the *CPS* March Supplement Tapes to match

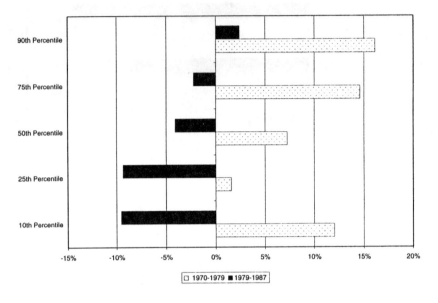

Source: As Fig. 2.6.

Figure 2.8   Change (%) in weekly wage and salary income, 1970–79 and 1979–87, black non-Hispanic males

information on family householders with all other variables that are related to persons. Thus it is possible to isolate the wage and salary earnings of family heads. The analysis below focuses on all family heads excluding 'one-person families' or unrelated individuals with positive wage and salary earnings in the years preceding 1976, 1985 and 1993.

Additional analyses can also be performed on those in the labour force. One such includes positive weeks for persons who worked or were looking for work in the past year. An alternative analysis focuses on 'potential labour force participants'. These are persons who did not work but whose principal reasons for not working were that they could not find a job or they were on layoff. The effect of including zero earners in the sample is to lower substantially the median wage and salary earnings of those at the bottom of the earnings distribution. The vast majority of the zero earners across the entire distribution are female heads of families.

Table 2.1 presents the results of computing the real median wage and salary incomes for each quintile of the earnings distribution (expressed in constant

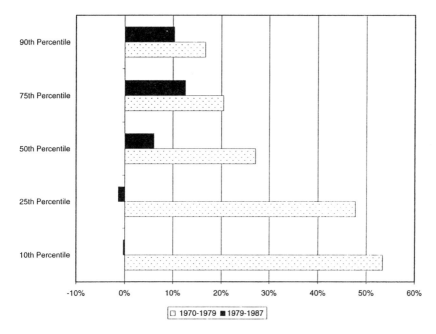

Source: As Fig. 2.6.

Figure 2.9   Change (%) in weekly wage and salary income, 1970–79 and 1979–87, black non-Hispanic females

1982–84 dollars). At the very top of the distribution the median rose by 17 per cent from 1976 to 1993. At the very bottom of the distribution the median fell by 8 per cent from 1976 to 1985 and 5 per cent from 1976 to 1993.

In stark terms, this table shows a 'shrinking middle'. Other authors (for example, Bluestone and Harrison) have detected this pattern but have been faulted for reliance on data that includes persons who worked part-time or part-year. Since we are focusing on family heads, we consider it particularly relevant to include all workers, to produce a more accurate picture of the economic status of earnings inequality across families.

When measured this way, the middle clearly shrank. Real median wage and salary incomes expressed in 1982–84 dollars for persons who worked or who were looking for work any time in the previous year dropped from $18 519 to $17 993 among the middle quintile of family heads between 1976 and 1993. This shrinking of the labour earnings of those in the middle represented a drop of about 3 per cent of the real median wage and salary incomes.

Table 2.1   Percentage of family heads within income quintiles by sex and race, 1976, 1985 and 1993, median income and percentage change for each quintile (positive income – total sample)

	Male				Female			
	White	Black	Other	Total	White	Black	Other	Total
1976								
Highest fifth	95.85	2.10	1.22	99.17	0.64	0.18	0.00	0.82
Fourth fifth	91.18	5.32	0.95	97.45	2.11	0.38	0.06	2.55
Third fifth	85.01	7.66	1.16	93.83	4.89	1.23	0.06	6.18
Second fifth	74.73	9.57	1.61	85.91	10.74	3.19	0.15	14.08
Lowest fifth	61.22	9.45	1.29	71.96	19.49	8.21	0.34	28.04
1985								
Highest fifth	93.26	2.67	2.71	98.64	1.24	0.10	0.02	1.36
Fourth fifth	88.61	4.67	2.05	95.33	3.59	0.95	0.13	4.67
Third fifth	79.16	6.83	2.44	88.43	8.76	2.55	0.28	11.59
Second fifth	66.77	9.53	2.29	78.59	15.62	5.30	0.49	21.41
Lowest fifth	57.27	8.37	1.80	67.44	21.75	10.20	0.61	32.56
1993								
Highest fifth	90.58	2.96	3.42	96.96	2.21	0.53	0.29	3.03
Fourth fifth	83.19	5.92	2.74	91.85	6.13	1.75	0.27	8.15
Third fifth	75.10	7.20	3.09	85.39	10.33	3.92	0.35	14.6
Second fifth	65.25	8.91	3.01	77.17	15.87	6.11	0.85	22.8
Lowest fifth	55.70	7.14	3.01	65.85	22.22	10.84	1.10	34.16

Median income					
				% change	
	1976	1985	1993	1976–85	1976–93
Highest fifth	34 007	37 175	40 183	9.32	18.16
Fourth fifth	24 242	26 022	25 606	7.34	5.63
Third fifth	18 519	18 587	17 993	0.37	–2.84
Second fifth	13 131	12 081	11 765	–8.00	–10.40
Lowest fifth	5 051	4 647	4 775	–8.00	5.46
Original obs.	48 245	63 633	63 763		
Subsample	26 355	30 862	29 181		

Source: Authors' computations, IRP Family Extract Tapes, 1976, 1985 and 1993 supplements. *CPS* data.

How is the middle divided by family type and race? The share of the middle quintile represented by white male-headed families dropped from 85 per cent in 1976 to 79 per cent in 1985 and then to 75 per cent in 1993. In contrast, the share of the middle accounted for by white female-headed families increased from less than 5 per cent in 1976 to more than 10 per cent in 1993. Black male-headed families maintained a share of about 7 per cent of the middle; black female-headed families more than tripled their share from 1.23 per cent in 1976 to 3.92 per cent in 1993. Most of the rest of the redistribution of the middle went to male-headed families of other races.

In other words, the middle was shifting away from the white male-headed family and more towards female-headed families and male-headed families of other races. Does this mean that the traditional white male-headed family was losing ground by falling into the lower rungs of the earnings distribution? Or does it mean that the squeezing out of the middle merely meant that white male-headed families moved up the income distribution?

Table 2.1 shows that neither of these conclusions holds. At the top of the distribution, white male-headed families saw their share drop from almost 96 per cent to 91 per cent from 1976 to 1993. At the bottom of the distribution, white male-headed families saw their share drop from 61 per cent to 56 per cent. The overall 'loss' in the white male-headed family's share of earnings in each distribution is due to the rise in the presence of female-headed families and of male-headed families of other races. The 'loss' in reality is a shift in the underlying demographics of the population; more and more labour force participants are persons other than white males.

To underscore this, we note the dramatic increase in the share of the top fifth of wage and salary incomes among white family heads accruing to white female heads of families. White females' share of the top more than tripled from 0.64 per cent in 1976 to 2.21 per cent in 1993. White females' share of the middle and bottom also increased. White females accounted for 4.89 per cent of the middle of the white distribution in 1976; they accounted for 10.33 per cent in 1993. They accounted for 19.49 per cent of the bottom in 1976; their share of the bottom fifth rose to 22.22 per cent in 1993.

Thus, even within the white distribution, there was a substantial shift in the entire wage and salary distribution of family heads away from white male heads of families toward female heads of families. The shrinking of the middle class wage, then, must be understood within the context of the demographic shift away from the traditional white male-headed family earner towards a more diverse population of families.

GOOD JOBS VERSUS BAD JOBS

But the change in family composition definitely does not tell the entire story. Table 2.2 shows that there was a shift from 1976 to 1993 in the distribution of

Table 2.2   Earnings ratios and percentage distribution of good jobs vs bad jobs of all earners by race, 1976, 1985 and 1993

Black–white mean earnings and ratios by good jobs vs bad jobs, family heads in 1976, 1985 and 1993

	1976			1985			1993			% change in black–white ratio, 1976–93
	Black	White	Ratio, black–white	Black	White	Ratio, black–white	Black	White	Ratio, black–white	
Top fifth	19 436	25 499	0.762	20 155	28 432	0.709	21 664	27 835	0.778	2.11
Next top fifth	17 339	24 146	0.718	16 944	25 184	0.673	18 682	25 154	0.743	3.43
Middle fifth	13 839	20 378	0.679	13 972	20 535	0.680	15 039	20 582	0.731	7.60
Next bottom fifth	11 184	17 344	0.645	11 412	17 921	0.637	11 544	17 504	0.660	2.28
Bottom fifth	7 125	10 534	0.676	2 436	4 539	0.537	1 949	3 599	0.542	–19.90

Percentage shares and ratios of good jobs vs bad jobs by race in 1976, 1985 and 1993

	1976			1985			1993			% change in black–white ratio, 1976–93
	% black	% white	Ratio, black–white	% black	% white	Ratio, black–white	% black	% white	Ratio, black–white	
Top fifth	11.20	10.60	1.057	6.38	7.66	0.833	4.69	6.34	0.740	–29.99
Next top fifth	26.12	26.81	0.974	16.57	19.49	0.850	16.92	22.74	0.744	–23.61
Middle fifth	23.15	28.08	0.824	15.47	22.42	0.690	14.23	19.02	0.748	–9.92
Next bottom fifth	23.72	22.94	1.034	19.59	18.11	1.082	20.93	20.60	1.016	–1.17
Bottom fifth	15.79	11.57	1.365	42.03	32.31	1.301	43.23	31.31	1.381	1.17

Notes: Earnings are for the previous year and percentage shares are for the current year. Primary family heads only.

Source: As Table 2.1.

28

good versus bad jobs held by family heads. The share of good jobs declined; the share of bad jobs increased. The earnings from good jobs increased; the earnings from bad jobs declined.

To see this, consider what we mean by a 'good job'. For 1976 we computed the median weekly wage and salary incomes of full-time, year-round employees in each of more than 50 industry classifications. We ranked the resulting wages from highest to lowest. The top fifth of those jobs were considered to be 'good jobs'; the bottom fifth could be designated 'bad jobs'. These are jobs in industries ranked well or poorly in relation to all other industry jobs. The computation uses two-digit industry codes.

'Good jobs' in this ranking included those in the following industries: petroleum and chemicals, aircraft and automobile manufacturing, mining and primary metals, communications, and professional and photographic equipment manufacturing. 'Bad jobs' included: textiles, repairs, leather and leather products, medical except hospitals, apparel and other finished products, personal services and private household services and agriculture.

Now suppose that this same ranking persisted throughout the 1980s and through the early 1990s. Suppose that a good job in 1976 was also a good job in 1993. That is, the designated category of the top fifth remains unchanged – even though it is entirely possible for the mean wage in that category to change.

We computed the mean wage and salary incomes for family heads for 1976, 1985 and 1993. And, indeed, the mean wage and salary incomes of black and white family heads did change in most of the designated categories. The top part of Table 2.2 shows that the good jobs in 1976 yielded increased real incomes in 1993; the bad jobs yielded declines in real incomes in 1993. For white family heads, the middle category of jobs yielded stagnant wages.

For black family heads, the middle category of jobs revealed sizeable increases. Specifically, the average annual real wage and salary income of white family heads was $20 378 in 1976. By 1993 it was $20 582. The average for black family heads in 1976 was $13 839. In 1993 it increased to $15 039. Moreover, the ratio of black–white earnings increased for the middle and higher categories of jobs, but the ratio declined for the lowest ranking of jobs. The decline in the earnings ratio among persons holding bad jobs is attributable in part to the increase in the share of black family heads who have never worked.

Even though there were some improvements in the earnings of black family heads who held middle category jobs, the share of black family heads who held such jobs dropped sharply. In 1976, 23 per cent of black family heads held middle-category jobs. In 1985, only 15 per cent of families held such jobs. By 1993, the percentage had fallen to 14 per cent. The decline in the share of family heads holding middle-category jobs was not restricted to blacks. The white share declined from 28 per cent in 1976 to 19 per cent in 1993.

Moreover, both white and black family heads saw dramatic reductions in the share of 'good jobs' they held. In 1976, 4 and 10 per cent of black and white family heads held jobs ranked among the top 20 per cent of all jobs. By 1993, only 5 and 6 per cent of black and white family heads held such jobs, based on these jobs' 1976 rankings. At the bottom end, black and white shares of bad jobs increased. While 16 and 12 per cent of black and white family heads held the lowest ranked jobs in 1976, an astonishing 43 and 31 per cent of black and white family heads held these bad jobs by 1993.

Since the increase in the share of bad jobs was larger for blacks than for whites and since the reduction in the share of good jobs was smaller for whites than for blacks, the effect was that the black–white ratio of the share of bad jobs increased and the black–white ratio of the share of good jobs fell. Blacks lost larger shares of good jobs than whites, and they gained larger shares of bad jobs than whites. There was a negative 30 per cent change in the ratio of black–white shares of good jobs from 1976 to 1993 and a positive 1 per cent change in the ratio of black–white shares of bad jobs from 1976 to 1993.

In other words, at least part of the story about the shrinking middle comes from a shift in the job base of the economy. Jobs ranked by industry yielding weekly earnings in the middle of the distribution of jobs constituted a declining share of all jobs, even if the real earnings associated with these jobs remained constant or drifted slightly upwards. Among family heads, at least, changing fortunes are not due to changing family composition alone.

FAMILY COMPOSITION

Nevertheless, changing family composition is not irrelevant. For blacks in particular the dramatic increase in the incidence of female headship over the past 20 years is tied closely to the precipitous decline in the relative availability of marriageable black males and that decline is linked to the economic marginalization of black males (Darity and Myers, 1995). By the mid-1980s, for every 100 unmarried black women there were only 32 black 'marriageable men' (unmarried men in the labour force or in school) down from 46 in the mid-1970s. For whites, the proportion actually rose to 49 men per 100 women from 46 men per 100 women a decade earlier (Darity, Myers, Carson and Sabol, 1994, pp. 155–61).

Figures 2.10 and 2.11 also reveal that the patterns of shifting inequality depend on how one measures 'family'. In Figure 2.10 the changes in wage and salary incomes of family heads are graphed. In Figure 2.11 the changes in the wage and salary incomes of household heads are graphed. Family heads refers to householders living in units where there are two or more persons related by marriage, birth or adoption. Household heads includes family householders and unrelated householders. In other words, the sample of household heads includes 'single-person householders', persons 'living together' as well as traditional families. Whereas Figure 2.10, relating to family heads, reveals a collapse of

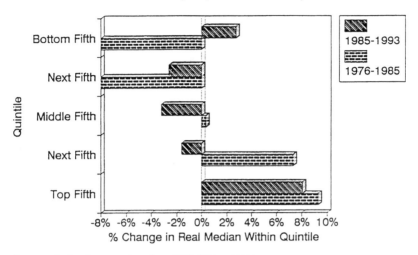

Source: Authors' computations from 1976, 1985 and 1993 IRP Family Extract Files (CPS March Supplements Tapes).

Note: Family heads include: primary families, secondary families and subfamilies. Quintile medians computed for family heads' wage and salary income in previous year for persons with positive wage and salary incomes.

Figure 2.10   Change (%) in wage and salary incomes, 1985–93 and 1976–85, positive earners among family heads

the middle quintiles during the late 1980s and a rise at the top fifth of the distribution, Figure 2.11, relating to householders, shows only a slight drop in the middle and considerably less growth in income at the top of the distribution during the late 1980s.

Put differently, the conclusions about the decline of middle-class jobs are most pertinent to *families*. Middle-class family heads are losing ground and their incomes have dropped in recent years.

How have black middle-class families fared relative to white middle-class families? After a drop in the ratio of black–white median incomes for the respective middle-income quintiles from 1976 to 1985, there was an increase in the ratios from 1985 to 1993. As shown in Figure 2.12, black and white family heads' wage and salary incomes at the middle were closer to equal than in any other quintile by 1993. This figure does not contradict evidence of continuing divergence of family incomes, which include more than just a) the wages of the head and b) wage incomes. The total family income includes the wages and salaries of other members of the family, and in particular for two-parent families, the wages of the spouse and the income from rents, dividends, interest and royalties. Black families fare less well than white on both accounts: they

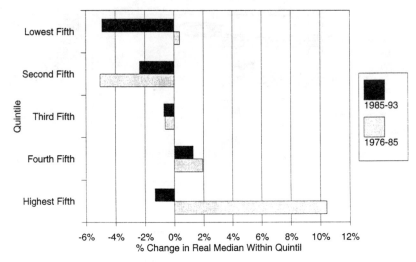

Source: Authors' computations from 1976, 1985 and 1993 IRP Family Extract Files (CPS March Supplements Tapes).

Note: Family heads include: primary families, secondary families and subfamilies. Quintile medians computed for family heads' wage and salary income in previous year for persons with positive wage and salary incomes.

Figure 2.11   Change (%) in wage and salary incomes, 1985–93 and 1976–85, positive earners among householders

are less likely to have two earners and less likely to have non-earned income than are white families.

A further qualification to the optimistic finding that the wages of black and white family heads at the middle are moving toward parity is the fact that the middle is different for blacks and whites. Each distribution is ranked from top to bottom and the medians refer to the middle of the middle fifth of the respective distributions. Regrettably, the appearance of convergence of wage and salary incomes between black family heads and white family heads at the middle quintile is due principally to the reduction in real earnings of white family heads at the middle!

Indeed, the appearance of improvement in relative earnings of black family heads between 1985 and 1993 rests primarily on the diminished real earnings of white family heads. This takes us back to our original finding of the decline in earnings among white men.

The patterns and trends documented above reveal a widening of the gap in wage and salary earnings both between the top and the bottom and between whites and non-whites. The widening of both gaps is related to the narrowing of the middle.

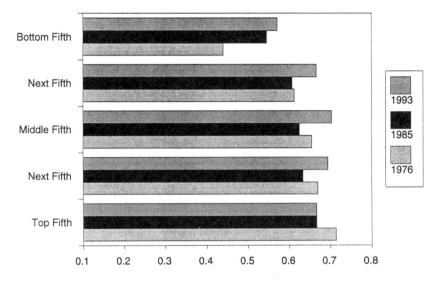

Source: Authors' computations from 1976, 1985 and 1993 IRP Family Extract Files (CPS March Supplements Tapes).

Note: Family heads include: primary families, secondary families and subfamilies. Quintile medians computed for family heads' wage and salary income in previous year for persons with positive wage and salary incomes.

Figure 2.12   Black–white earnings ratios, 1976, 1985 and 1993, family heads by quintiles

EXPLANATIONS FOR WIDENING INEQUALITY

There are various explanations for this widening of inequality. Before exploring them in depth it is useful to document some of the correlated changes in the labour force and the economy that suggest possible explanations. These are the decline in unionization, changes in tax laws, a shift in production away from manufacturing, and in~~~   market competition due to immigration. F: been a continuing decline of unionized w(r the past decade. This decline extends a p   , in particular, whose unionization rates exc   drops in their membership in unions duri   e 2.13 shows that there has been a rise in th   with the sharpest increases occurring durir   unionization.

(a)   **Immigration**

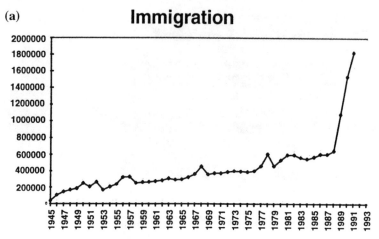

Annual numbers of legal immigrants, 1945 - 1991.

(c)   **Operatives**

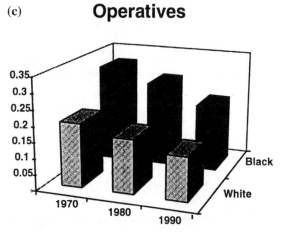

Percentage of workers employed as operatives, 1970-1990

There also has been a reduction in the share of jobs held by blacks and by whites in the occupational category of 'operatives', representing a historically highly unionized sector of the economy. The various panels of Figure 2.14 show, moreover, substantial declines in employment in manufacturing industries. No matter what measurement is used, non-farm employees in manufacturing or percentage of workers in manufacturing, annual *Current Population Surveys* or decennial censuses, or figures computed for blacks or for whites, the evidence is clear: employment in manufacturing diminished after the 1960s.

During this period of sharp reversals in the nature of employment in the US economy, there was also an important shift in the role of taxes as a redistributive

(b)
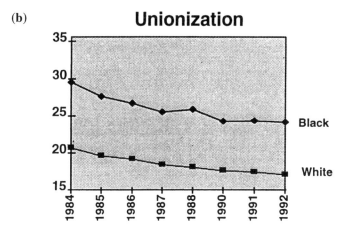

Annual percentage of employees represented by Unions, 1983-1992.

(d)
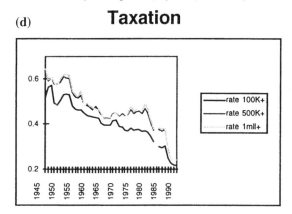

Effective tax rate (tax after credits/adjusted gross income)
on individuals, 1945-1990.

Sources: Immigration: US Immigration and Naturalization Service, *1992 Statistical Yearbook*; Unionization: US Bureau of Labor Statistics, *Employment and Earnings*, January issues, 1984–93; Operatives: US Bureau of the Census, *Census of Population, General Social and Economic Characteristic U.S. Summary*, 1980 and 1990; Taxation: US Department of the Treasury, *Statistics of Income, Individual Tax Returns*, 1954–90.

Figure 2.13   Trends in immigration, unionization, operatives and taxation, various years

device. The effective tax rates on incomes over $100 000, over $500 000, and over $1 million declined. The effective rate on the highest incomes exceeded 60 per cent in 1945. The rate declined to about 43 per cent in 1970, rose to a

(a)

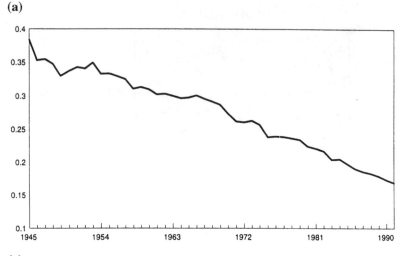

(c)

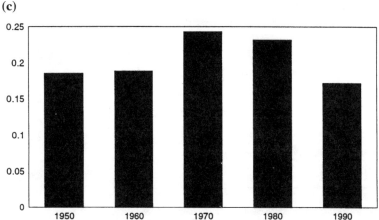

new plateau of around 48 per cent in the late 1970s, and fell sharply to 24 per cent in 1989.

These are some of the stylized facts that underlie various explanations for the widening earnings gaps in America: the decline in unionization, the rise in immigration, the drop in the effective tax rates on the highest incomes, the decline in operatives and the demise of manufacturing. Along with increases in trade deficits, the export of good, unionized jobs to other nations and the threat of international competition, these factors are among the various candidates for explaining the increased inequality in America.

The pattern of increasing inequality in the United States across a variety of economic categories disrupts the conventional wisdom concerning the relationship

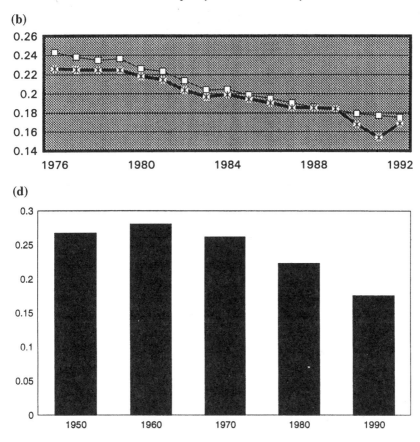

Sources: Non-farm employees: US Bureau of Labor Statistics, *Employment and Earnings*, January 1992; Employees black employees and white employees: US Bureau of Labor Statistics, labour force statistics derived from the *Current Population Survey*, 1982: US Census 1950, 1960, 1970, 1980 and 1990.

Figure 2.14   Declines (%) in employment in manufacturing industries: (a) non-farm employees 1945–90, (b) employees 1976–91, (c) black employees 1950–90 and (d) white employees, various years 1950–90

between national affluence and income dispersion across individuals or households. Embodied in Simon Kuznets's (1955) famous inverted U-curve hypothesis, the conventional wisdom contends that countries experiencing growth from low levels of income will also experience a deterioration in their income distribution, then at a certain threshold of per capita income the deterioration will be arrested, and beyond that threshold – or turning point – the income distribution will gradually improve.

Any estimated value of the threshold of per capita income places the United States well beyond the Kuznets turning point. Rising per capita income, even rising at a slow rate, should be associated with an improved or at least a stable distribution of income. This did not occur in the United States during the 1980s when a sharp downward break occurred in the comparative stability of the US income distribution that had prevailed for nearly thirty years from the early 1950s to the late 1970s (Levy and Murnane, 1992).

There had been a previous twentieth century episode of deterioration in the US income distribution, which might have given pause to those believing in the secular universality of Kuznets's hypothesis. For two decades following the 1929 Crash of the New York Stock Exchange, income disparity in the US began what Levy and Murnane (1992, p. 1340) describe as 'its own golden age'. The inconsistency with the Kuznets hypothesis may have been masked by the break with the previous period of movement towards greater equality that began with the Great Depression. Since per capita income actually declined at the start of the 1930s, it was convenient to interpret the United States as moving leftwards along the negatively sloped portion of the inverted U-curve, the portion to the right of the turning point. But the deterioration of the income distribution persisted into the 1940s, when per capita income surpassed pre-Great Depression era levels.

Consider this critical point: unlike the presumption of the Kuznets hypothesis, episodes of significant declines in economic equality are not limited to developing countries. On the contrary, the United States in particular demonstrates that income inequality can rise episodically in the world's most affluent nations.

Because the Kuznets framework offers the only comprehensive hypothesis about secular movements in the income distribution widely utilized and investigated by economists, and because recent US experience is inconsistent with the Kuznets hypothesis, economists have resorted to a patchwork of short run explanations for the rise in economic inequality in the 1980s. There is no unified theoretical framework that economists are now using to provide a long-run view of income distribution that would explain the historical record of the US. Consequently, each change in the pattern of income distribution is given a unique, episode-specific explanation.

Moreover, economists have narrowed their focus of explanation to earnings inequality, particularly earnings disparity among males rather than total income or wealth. In turn, the episode-specific explanations have been given over to the labour economists. The result has been an endeavour, to a greater or to a lesser degree, to massage the supply and demand framework applied to an aggregate national labour market and to intersectoral labour markets. This approach has generated the following catalogue of explanations for increasing inequality in the United States: (see especially Danziger and Gottschalk, 1993; Levy and Murnane, 1992, Tilly, 1991):

1. The impact of the entry of the baby boom generation into the labour market
2. The restructuring of the US labour market ('loss of middle class jobs')
3. Effects of biased technological change
4. Changes in returns to skills
5. Effects of the recession of the early 1980s (business cycle effects)
6. Changes in the US tax code
7. Other demographic changes in the population
8. Shifting wage norms.

1. Baby Boom Effect

This is a pure labour supply shift argument: a well educated baby boom generation enters the labour market and 'overcrowds' it, leading to a widening earnings gap between young and middle-aged white men. In conjunction with the technological change (demand-side) argument, this is the preferred position of Levy (1987). As Tilly (1991, p. 740) puts it, this argument invokes 'transitory "bad times"'. Note that for this argument to work the 'boomers' are not sufficiently well educated, on average, to benefit sufficiently from the alleged rising premium associated with advanced education to offset the adverse effect of their numbers on their relative earnings. Plus, as Levy and Murnane (1992, pp. 1351–2) themselves point out, by the mid-1980s the baby boom generation was turning 40, hardly new labour market entrants; yet inequality was continuing to rise.

2. Loss of Middle-class Jobs

After much debate it is now accepted that a stylized fact related to the rise in inequality in the 1980s was the compression of the number of jobs available offering a middle-class lifestyle (Levy and Murnane, 1992, pp. 1346–7). There was a growing polarization in the wage structure and in annual earnings. As Levy and Murnane (p. 1349) put it, there was a 'hollowing out' of the earnings distribution 'for year round, full time male workers'. But why did this occur? The controversial but powerful argument made by Harrison and Bluestone in the context of their 'great U-turn' hypothesis (1988) involved the deindustrialization of the US economy, the evaporation of well paid blue-collar employment, the shift to a service-based economy with a bifurcation between well paid professional employment and low-paid work requiring few educational credentials.

A shortcoming of this explanation is that this rising inequality occurred within manufacturing and service sectors, not just between them. Thus this cannot be the whole story. It is plainly an important part of the story – a critical category of well paid jobs no longer available in the US economy.

3.   Effects of Biased Technological Change

This story could explain rising inequality within the sectors. It is a somewhat similar story to the vanishing middle-class jobs effect, but this effect could occur within sectors as well. The argument is that technical change favours highly skilled employment and creates disadvantage for low-skilled employment – a demand shift argument again. This can also be labelled the skills mismatch hypothesis. It too has a transitory flavour. Skills will eventually adapt to the requirements of a restructured economy and the polarization in earnings will ease when that occurs. Government action could bring about a reduction in inequality by assisting workers in acquiring the skills needed in the evolving occupational structure.

There are difficulties with this explanation as well – more difficulties than with the loss of middle-class jobs explanation:

- The empirical support here is not based on any direct measures of skill requirements in occupations. For example, Berman, Bound and Griliches (1994, pp. 367–97) infer that a relative skill requirement altered in favour of highly skilled labour is based on changes in occupational distributions, not a direct investigation of the tasks involved in performing specific jobs. It could be that instead of all jobs across the economy being upgraded in terms of skill requirements, there is a growing bifurcation in job types in both the service and manufacturing sectors.

- Technical change is typically treated as an exogenous phenomenon in these studies, so that the fact that the direction of technical change is biased in favour of skilled employment is left unexplained. An exception would be a story where technical change is carried by human capital accumulation (for example Lucas, 1988). But then the assertion that the bias in technological change favours skilled employment becomes tautological, especially if one accepts in lock-step fashion a connection between education, skill acquisition and productivity.

- As Berman, Bound and Griliches (1994) acknowledge, technical change is virtually 'implicated by default' since alternative explanations for a skills mismatch effect – defence build-up or the shift to microelectronics production in response to competition in international trade – do not account for much of a phenomenon of 'skill upgrading' (again, measured by changes in occupational distribution). Moreover, while Howell and Wieler (1995, p. 5) report that 'while the effects of new production technology on skills varies by sector and occupation group, it is fair to say that overall, it tends to raise the demand for high cognitive skill workers and reduce the demand for low cognitive skill workers', they also point out that there 'is no support for the view that skill restructuring took place at a faster rate in the 1980s, when the greatest increases in inequality occurred...'

4. Changes in Returns to Skills

Here the idea is that there has been a change in premia going to differentially skilled workers. There is obviously a potential link with explanations 2 and 3. But here, rather than necessarily requiring the occupational structure to have altered, this explanation merely asserts that, for whatever reason, returns to more highly skilled workers have risen relative to less skilled workers (Murphy and Welch, 1994). The key is merely the marshalling of evidence to show that premia for the possession of more skills have risen.

The empirical case is problematic here. First, this explanation must presuppose, given a fixed occupational structure, that skilled workers have become comparatively more scarce. If skills are associated with education, measured by years of schooling, the skilled labour scarcity proposition runs directly counter to the 'baby boom effect' explanation of the deterioration of the income distribution.

But the use of years of schooling as the measure of skill acquisition is also unsatisfactory. In the burgeoning literature on the role of schooling quality differentials in explaining black–white income disparity it has now become the norm to use Armed Forces Qualification Test (AFQT) scores from a routine of NLSY as an index of skill accumulation (O'Neill, 1990; Maxwell, 1994; Neal and Johnson, 1995; Ferguson, 1995). Ironically, the AFQT scores, so ubiquitous in recent black–white economic disparity research, do not appear in studies of general inequality or inequality between white male earners. The studies on general earnings inequality estimate differential returns to years of schooling but call this 'returns to skills'.

Furthermore, even the use of AFQT scores discounts the question of the difference between the importance of general and specific skill requirements for jobs. If specific skill requirements are more important, then job experience rather than schooling becomes the critical source of skills.

5. Effects of the recession

The recession, it can be argued, adversely affected the distribution of income by disproportionately harming the earnings position of males at the low end of the distribution. There is little doubt that such an adverse effect was present.

None the less, the cyclical downturn explanation for increasing inequality does not wash as a complete answer to why inequality declined unless a long lag is invoked, since the decline in equality continued well after the early 1980s, when the economy was growing again (Levy and Murnane, 1992). Indeed, it is arguable that deterioration in the US income distribution dates from 1981, before the complete onset of recession.

6. Changes in the US Tax Code

This is a more interesting explanation (Gramlich, Kasten and Sammartino, 1994). Here the chronology makes sense, since the tax reform was adopted in 1981 and maintained thereafter. But measures of inequality based on pre-tax earnings and income also display evidence of deterioration. A more subtle explanation would be required: there was an indirect effect of the tax reform on earnings that led to a more unequal distribution of income. The tax reform had the effect of reducing relative pre-tax earnings for those at either the low end of the middle of the income distribution and/or raising relative pre-tax earnings for those at the high end of the income distribution.

7. Other Demographic Changes in the Population

If inequality across groups becomes more pronounced, it could lead to an overall downward change in the measured degree of equality. The problem with this line of argument is that within-group equality also decreased with the slide in the general degree of equality. For example, Cecilia Conrad (1994) has demonstrated that intraracial inequality for blacks worsened as early as the 1970s and continued in the 1980s. Levy and Murnane (1992) examine several groups demarcated in a variety of ways – including age, gender, poverty or income status – and reach similar conclusions about the path of intragroup disparity.

8. Shifting Wage Norms

Perhaps the most convincing explanation to date is advanced by David Howell (1994). He proposes a 'shifting wage norms' hypothesis in place of the 'skills mismatch' hypothesis. He opts to emphasize a systematic and successful assault on the wage standard by business management reinforced by public policy, leading to a decline in union strength, wage concessions, plant relocations, outsourcing and greater reliance on 'contingent workers'. In Howell's words, 'traditional wage-setting institutions' are in decline; simultaneously, 'middle-class jobs' are in decline. Howell's hypothesis suggests a potentially unified, secular alternative to the Kuznets hypothesis – variations in the structure of wage-setting arrangements lead to income distribution changes.

3. Inequality and the widening gap between the races

The debate about the reversal in the pattern of movement towards racial economic parity comes after several decades of research on the causes of the alleged movement towards parity. To appreciate fully the complexity of the current debate, one must understand the earlier body of research. Below, we summarize the main contours of the 'black–white convergence' dispute, the dispute when economists and other social scientists debated the existence and causes of the narrowing of the earnings gap between blacks and whites.

The main explanations offered for the alleged narrowing of the earnings gap were: the improvement in black human capital, especially as a result of migration from the South and desegregation of Southern schools (Smith and Welch, 1977) and the passage and enforcement of civil rights laws (Freeman, 1973; Leonard, 1990). An agnostic perspective held that there was no real narrowing, only an illusion of progress (Butler and Heckman, 1977; Lazear, 1979; Darity and Myers, 1980). The reasons for the 'illusion' of progress differed among authors but one popular explanation was that the lowest earners were drawn out of the labour force, causing the mean earnings of the positive earners to rise.

Subsequent research has indicated that the labour force drop-out effect accounts partially but not fully for the change (Brown, 1984; Vroman, 1986); the first two arguments remained contenders. Presumably, then, the more recent widening of the earnings gap must either be the result of a) the reversal of the positive effects of human capital gains during the 1960s and 1970s and the declining enforcement of affirmative action; or, b) new demand or supply factors not operating during the earlier era.

THE NARROWING OF THE RACIAL EARNINGS GAPS: 1948–75

The evidence used to support the convergence hypothesis was drawn from aggregate data on relative earnings and income for blacks and whites. The mean income ratio for black males and white males rose from about 55 per cent for all workers in 1950 to 66 per cent by 1975 (Smith and Welch, 1977; Smith and

Welch, 1978). The mean income ratio for black females and white females rose
from 61 per cent in 1950 to 95 per cent by 1975, close to parity (Smith,
'Convergence', 1978).

Figures 3.1 and 3.2 show these upward trends. Figure 3.1 plots the ratio of
black–white mean incomes for all male workers and for full-time, year-round
male workers. The steady increase in the earnings ratio is sharpest for year-round,
full-time employees after 1964, the year of the passage of the most comprehensive
US civil rights law since the Reconstruction period had passed. Thereafter, and
into the 1980s, the ratio levels off for all workers but maintains a slight positive
slope for year-round, full-time workers. Figure 3.2 reveals a sharper upward trend
in the ratio of black–white mean incomes among females, a trend that began its
upward climb well before enactment of the 1964 Civil Rights Bill and one that
levels off and even turns downward by the late 1970s.

The data from these two figures are the source of the claims during the late
1970s and early 1980s that black–white earnings were converging. The upward
trends were extrapolated forward in time to conjure the prospect of closing the
gap. The debate then turned to how to explain the change in the economic status
of blacks. What accounted for the improvement?

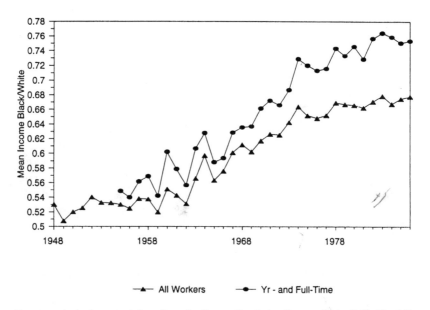

—▲— All Workers   —●— Yr - and Full-Time

Sources: Author's computations from the Current Population Reports, Series P-60, No. 162,
Money Income of Households, Families, and Persons in the United States: 1987, US Department
of Commerce, Bureau of the Census.

*Figure 3.1   Ratio of black–white mean income, males, 1948–86 (all workers
and year-round, full-time workers)*

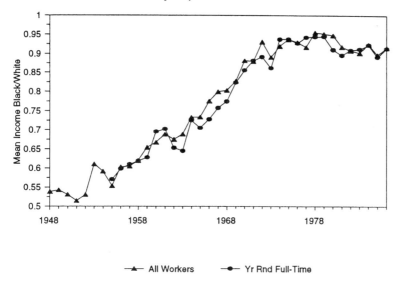

Sources: Author's computations from the Current Population Reports, Series P-60, No. 162, *Money Income of Households, Families, and Persons in the United States*: 1987, US Department of Commerce, Bureau of the Census.

Figure 3.2   Ratio of black–white mean income, females, 1948–86 (all workers and year-round full-time workers)

Two major competing hypotheses were advanced. The first was the position taken by James Smith and Finis Welch at RAND and UCLA respectively. They argued that the improved quantity and quality of black education, combined with South–North and rural–urban migration of blacks during the 1940s, 1950s and 1960s, led to a decline in the average productivity differential between blacks and whites. This in turn led to a decline in the earnings gap. At the core of the Smith and Welch view was the decisive role they gave to 'human capital' differences (which they associated largely with years of formal schooling in explaining average racial wage differences). The human capital gap was being closed as black schooling improved, ostensibly due to the rising quality of Southern schools attended by blacks as well as the beneficial effects of black migration to other regions where schools were superior.

Smith and Welch argued that there was a 'vintage effect', claiming that younger cohorts of blacks had educational experiences more similar to comparably aged whites, and therefore had more similar human capital endowments and more similar labour market experiences. The earnings gap for younger blacks, then, would be expected to be narrower than the earnings gap for older blacks.

In general, Smith concluded, 'Blacks are becoming less distinguishable from whites in at least one relevant index of performance – market earnings' (Smith, 'Status', 1978). The underlying reason, for Smith and Welch, was the closing of the gap between blacks and whites in terms of human capital acquisition.[1]

Smith and Welch's Panglossian vision of black economic progress evolves from a perspective that downplays any significant role for discrimination in labour markets as the source of racial economic inequality. Discrimination was, in their estimation, an important factor in the historical disparity in schooling opportunities for black and white youths. In the Smith and Welch view this was a type of pre-market or extra-market discrimination; they perceive the labour market as generally processing all individuals with reasonable fairness (or *market* fairness) based on the individual's productivity-linked characteristics. Thus, as the historical differential in schooling opportunities apparently declined, so the fundamental basis for earnings inequality declined as well.[2]

The Smith and Welch perspective leads to the conclusion that the labour market generally affords equal opportunity. As the pre-market environment comes to provide equal opportunity as well, Smith and Welch's analysis suggests that equal results will be the outcome. For Smith and Welch there is no necessary inconsistency between equal opportunity and equal results as articulated aims of racial equality.

Furthermore, there is no need for any special programmatic intervention for blacks, aside from continuing to ensure that educational opportunities for blacks move toward matching those available for whites. The labour market works and needs no corrective measures such as affirmative action or anti-discrimination measures.[3]

An alternative explanation was given by Harvard economist Richard Freeman, who argued that the trend towards economic convergence was attributable to a decline in labour market discrimination engineered by government anti-discrimination enforcement measures. In short, Freeman also took the position that equal opportunity would lead to equal results, but for equal opportunity to prevail government intervention would be required in employment markets.[4]

Although disagreeing on the causes, Freeman and Smith and Welch agreed on the 'fact' of a positive trajectory for black economic progress in the 1960s and 1970s. But there were dissenters, especially the authors of this monograph, who argued that the evidence used to make the case for convergence was misleading at best.[5]

An initial basis for the dissent was our discovery that the data on which Smith and Welch and Freeman based their findings did not account for zero earners – persons continuously unemployed or out of the labour force during the year. Black experience of long duration joblessness is much higher than that for whites. Consequently earnings and income ratios calculated exclusively from data on working persons will be biased by the selection effect. The bias tends to work by raising unduly the black–white earnings ratios.

For males, black labour force drop-outs are disproportionately from the lower end of the income spectrum, while white labour force drop-outs are disproportionately from the higher end of the wage spectrum.[6] When the earnings time series is corrected to account for males with no earnings in a given year, the change in the non-white–white ratio vanishes during the decade 1967 through 1977. Indeed the black–white earnings ratio for males was slightly lower in 1977 (55 per cent) than in 1967 (57 per cent) after the correction (Darity, 1980, p. 164). By 1990 the black–white male earnings ratio for full-time, year-round workers was 70 per cent, but for all males, with or without earnings, it was only 60 per cent (US Bureau of the Census, 1992, Table 11, p. 57).

For females, the Freeman and Smith and Welch black–white earnings and income ratios were biased by the dramatic growth in the entry of white women into the labour force after the 1950s. Black women had long had high labour force participation rates [Darity, 1980, pp. 159–67). The time series data from 1953 through 1977, unadjusted for zero income recipients among females, gives the impression that the earnings ratio of black–white females soared remarkably from 55 per cent in 1955 to 94 per cent by 1975.

When the series is adjusted to account for women with no incomes in a given year it flattens significantly; the ratio was 84 per cent as early as 1953, never dips below 70 per cent during the interval, and was at 94 per cent by 1977. Again, by 1990 the black–white female earnings ratio for full-time year-round workers was 90 per cent, and for all women it was a slightly lower 87 per cent (US Bureau of the Census, 1992, Table 11, p. 57). If anything, both types of time series now indicate evidence of a decline. To extrapolate on the basis of current trends would lead one to conclude that divergence, not convergence, is the trend for the future.

Per capita income ratios certainly do not show comparable evidence of dramatic economic progress for blacks. In two excellent recent studies, Jeremiah Cotton (1989, 1994) has shown that between 1963 and 1975 the per capita racial income ratio held steady at the 55 to 56 per cent range. Cotton also has examined the tenuous labour market status of large numbers of black males. He observes that between 1970 and 1985 there was a decrease in blue-collar employment among blacks – primarily in the operatives category. During the same period there was an increase in white-collar employment for black males, primarily in the sales category. Paradoxically, the shift involved movement from occupations with average earnings of $16 220 to jobs where average earnings were $14 114 in 1985.

For white males a similar shift had dissimilar economic effects. The change from blue-collar to white-collar employment meant going from a salary of $18 526 as an operative to a salary of $25 292 in sales. Moreover, the black–white earnings ratio in blue-collar occupations generally was 79 per cent in 1985, but it was only 67 per cent in white-collar occupations for the same year (Cotton, 1989, pp. 803–19 and 1994, pp. 6–11).

An additional basis for scepticism about the convergence hypothesis is the fact that data on black family incomes have never displayed the same pattern of gap closure as have the data on individual earnings or on income for persons with earnings or income. Between the mid-1960s and 1980 the black–white family income ratio stayed in a rather narrow range between 61 and 64 per cent. During the 1982 recession the ratio dipped below 60 per cent. By 1990 the mean black–white family income ratio was 62 per cent and the median black–white family income ratio was only 58 per cent (US Bureau of the Census, 1992, Table 10, p. 56).

In 1980 one of the authors of this monograph made the following observation suggesting the superiority of relative family income as a gauge of relative racial well-being:

> Although neither income nor earnings inequality between black and white women measured in per capita terms have been great in the postwar era, inequality in living conditions is probably quite substantial. This is a consequence of one of the shortcomings of per capita income as an index of relative well being. It ignores how people come together socially and hence economically. White women combine their incomes with white men far more frequently than black women combine their incomes with white men. In fact, the large proportion of single parent, female-headed black families indicates that black women combine their incomes with those of black men less often than white women combine theirs with white men. (Darity, 1980, p. 176)

The incidence of females heading black families underwent a sharp upturn in the 1970s, accelerating throughout the 1980s, with no evidence of a peak in sight. We computed comparative estimates of the percentage of black families headed by women from the Census Bureau's *Current Population Survey* for 1976 and 1985. Nationally, the incidence of female-headed families rose from 36 per cent to 45 per cent of all black families. Particularly dramatic increases took place in the West and North Central regions. In the West the incidence rose from 25 per cent to 47 per cent and in the North Central region the incidence rose from 39 per cent to 52 per cent. For white families, the direction of movement was the same but the magnitude was not the same. White families headed by females rose from 11 per cent in 1976 to 13 per cent in 1985.

Data from the *Current Population Survey* (see US Department of Commerce, 1992, p. 56) indicate that the racial income disparity is much narrower among married couple families. In 1991, the black–white ratio of mean income for married couple families was 80 per cent; the ratio of medians was 83 per cent. However, less than half of all black families, 47 per cent (3.57 million out of 7.47 million) were married couple families. Since a near majority of black families are now female-headed, evidence about approaching parity in relative incomes between black and white two parent families is misleading.

The growing incidence of female-headed black families signals the effects of a process we refer to as the marginalization of black males. This process bears an intimate relationship to the fragile status of the entire black population in the United States, whether male or female. Economic manifestations of the marginalization process are plentiful.

Consider the absolute decline in labour force participation rates (LFPRs) for males of both races that began in the early 1960s and the relative decline that occurred after the mid 1960s. Between 1954 and 1966 the ratio of black–white male LFPRs held fairly constant at 98 per cent. But over the course of the next decade LFPRs fell much faster for black males than white males. As a result, despite the fact that after 1976 LFPRs for black males seem to have bottomed out while white male rates continued to fall, a wide gap persists because of the sharp difference in rates of decline between 1966 and 1976 – the very period that Freeman and Smith and Welch have touted as the period of 'dramatic progress' for blacks.

By 1985 the employment–population ratio for adult black males was only 55 per cent, while it was 70 per cent for adult white males. Almost one out of every six black men between the ages of 25 and 54 reported zero earnings for 1984. By 1990 one out of every three black men 15 years old and over reported no earnings (US Bureau of the Census, 1992, Table 11, p. 57).

There also appears to be a bifurcation among black males based on credentials – between those with a college education or better and those with a high school education or less. The former group has far more earnings experience in the labour market than the latter. Pecuniary prospects are dim for young black males with a high-school education or less.

In a very interesting and revealing study, Bluestone, Stevenson and Tilly (1991) have provided a typology of Metropolitan Statistical Areas (MSAs) based on growth rates of total non-agricultural employment and total manufacturing employment in the 1980s. They classify (1,1) cities as those with the slowest growth rates in overall and manufacturing employment, (2,2) cities as those with mid-range growth rates in both categories, and (3,3) cities as the fastest-growing in both categories. They then compare unemployment rates by race for males 20 years of age with less than a college education in each type of city.

The results that they report are provisional because the sample cell sizes become relatively small for black males. But in the (1,1) cities they find that among 20-year-olds the black male unemployment rate was 42 per cent while the white male unemployment rate was 4.1 per cent. In (2,2) cities the black male unemployment rate was 26.5 per cent while the white male unemployment rate was 3.5 per cent for the same age group. Finally, in (3,3) cities the black male unemployment rate was 17.9 per cent while the white male unemployment rate was only 1.5 per cent, 17 times lower than the black rate! (Bluestone, Stevenson and Tilly, 1991).

Conditions have become so patently bleak that even Richard Freeman has done a complete flip-flop on his research agenda. In the 1970s Freeman sought to explain what he labelled the 'dramatic economic progress' of black Americans. Today he asks in collaboration with John Bound, 'What went wrong? Why have relative earnings and employment fallen for young black males?' (Bound and Freeman, 1992).

Exposure to college education does not alter conditions substantially for black males. Black males 25 years of age or older with one to three years of college education and with positive earnings received, on average, $22 979 in 1990. White males 25 years of age or older with earnings, who had dropped out of high school, had mean earnings of $19 270, about $3700 less. White males who completed high school earned more than $3000 more than black males with some college education.

Nor does completing college close the gap. A black male with four years of college and positive earnings in 1990 would have received mean earnings of $32 259, more than $10 000 below the mean of $43 919 earned by white male college graduates with positive earnings (Bureau of the Census, 1992, Table 12, pp. 46, 52).

Convergence in educational characteristics need not translate into convergence in earnings. In their 1992 paper, Bound and Freeman acknowledge that the increasingly depressed labour market experience for young black males is not due to a corresponding deterioration in their relative quality as potential employees:

> We find little support for the hypothesis that deteriorated labor market skills of young blacks due, say, to poor schooling, worsened family background resources, or increased drug use explains their declining economic position. The notion that the school skills of young blacks deteriorated runs into an immediate problem: standardized test scores show that on average their achievements rose modestly relative to those of whites in the period [1978 through 1986]. While this does not rule out the possibility that the skills of dropouts deteriorated as the dropout share of the population declined, it creates a hurdle for such a story, as selectivity would have to dominate changes in the mean for the population. Even if the gap in scores among dropouts rose, however, the modest link of standardized test to earnings conditioned on education would make this a weak strand on which to base a falling skills argument. The hypothesis that declining family background resources accounts for the erosion fails because: the cohorts suffering erosion were brought up *prior* to the big growth in single parenting and widening family income differentials at a time when the number of siblings among blacks fell and parental education increased ...; and because family background's primary influence is on education, which is controlled in our regressions. The hypothesis that increased drug use underlies the erosion founders on evidence that blacks are no more likely to use dangerous drugs (East and West) and that drug use declined among youths in the 1980s (National Institute of Drug Abuse). The likelihood that

the CPS [Current Population Survey] undercounts persons with drug problems also makes this explanation of erosion untenable: serious drug users are unlikely to appear in CPS data. (Bound and Freeman, 1992, p. 16)

Two key points need to be made. First, the Bound–Freeman (1992) discussion implies that the current trajectory will only worsen as more and more black males come into the labour market from younger cohorts that are now experiencing even greater resource deprivation. Second, and more fundamental, independent of the relative quality black males present to the labour market, processes persist that exclude them from comparable participation with non-black males with similar productivity-linked characteristics. To put it bluntly, discrimination in a comprehensive sense lies at the core of matters, not just at the point of employment but throughout an entire range of stages that affect labour market outcomes. American society is quite distant from attaining a pure equal opportunity environment, never mind correcting for historically inherited inequalities.

Current discrimination, while creating a disadvantage for the group against which it is directed, necessarily creates a corresponding advantage for another group. In 1991 the Urban Institute conducted an audit study of entry level job access in the cities of Chicago and Washington DC. The researchers paired young black and white males (19–24 years of age) with fake, identical credentials and had them apply for the same jobs. The subjects applied for a total of 1052 jobs. Treatment of the applicants appeared to be neutral 73 per cent of the time, but black males faced discriminatory treatment 20 per cent of the time while white males faced discriminatory treatment only 7 per cent of the time. Therefore black males were three times as likely to face job bias. There were also higher rates of discrimination against black males in white-collar jobs or jobs involving direct client contact (Lawlor and Pitts, 1991, 1A, 11A).

Gerald Jaynes has written, 'The heralded recovery of the mid 1980s apparently improved the position of white low-skilled men but not black. Why? We do not know' (Jaynes, 1990, p. 24). But we can make a highly educated guess. The changing structure of the US economy was narrowing the availability of well-paid blue-collar jobs – jobs that pay well without requiring advanced educational credentials. White labour's discriminatory behaviour would naturally intensify under such conditions, particularly if the 'heralded recovery of the mid 1980s' did not mean a sharp reversal of the deindustrialization of the US economy. It was simply a classic case of protecting one's occupational turf from darker rivals, and it revealed the endogeneity of discriminatory practices. While much economic research proceeds as if discrimination operates at a constant level of intensity or does not exist at all, a more plausible analysis would indicate that the degree of discrimination fluctuates with the nature of aggregate conditions of employment, while never disappearing altogether.

The omission of the continuously unemployed from the earlier Freeman and Smith–Welch studies was reflective of a general failure on the part of the black economic progress optimists to assess the internal distribution of income among blacks. There was a segment of the black population in the United States that experienced rapid income growth in the 1960s and 1970s, markedly after 1964 or so.

This was not because of affirmative action *per se*, since, arguably, affirmative action has rarely been intensively applied on behalf of blacks. The increase in the numbers of professional status blacks during that period was due primarily to the growth in public sector employment opportunities in social welfare agencies attributable to the Johnson Administration's Great Society programmes.

Simultaneously, there was a segment of the black population – frequently the clients of the same social welfare agencies – experiencing perpetual deprivation and poverty (Brown and Erie, 1981, pp. 308–9). That segment now is identified with the urban 'underclass'. The aggregate statistics marshalled by Freeman and Smith and Welch highlighted the experiences of comparatively élite blacks and neglected the experiences of those being left behind.

By the late 1980s, explaining black economic progress was no longer a reasonable intellectual pursuit! Even the indicators used by Freeman and Smith and Welch in the 1970s – earnings and income ratios for those with earnings and income – showed evidence of slippage (Cotton, 1989). Even the position of 'élite' blacks may be softening, although their position is not yet in the free-fall state confronting the black masses.

Jaynes, in analysing developments from World War II to the mid-1980s, asserts that there are three major empirical findings: 1) after three decades of improvement there have been two decades of relative stagnation in the economic status of black Americans; 2) employment has progressively declined for black males; 3) there is greater inequality within the black community (Jaynes, 1990, p. 24).

THE WIDENING OF THE RACIAL EARNINGS GAPS

More recent studies on black–white economic inequality have focused on the reversal in the pattern of alleged convergence in earnings between black and white males in the 1980s. The puzzle is: why is there now evidence of a renewed widening of the gap in black and white male earnings?

The thrust of a substantial portion of recent work on black–white economic inequality is to explain divergence in the 1980s by restoring the pure human capital explanation of racial economic disparity. Correspondingly, the operation of the labour market is immunized from playing a role in directly producing racial economic inequality. The upshot is the claim that the persistent black male lag in earnings is due to deficiencies in productivity characteristics of black males, rather than a failure of the market to offer them rewards parallel to those of white males with equivalent productivity characteristics.

The skills mismatch hypothesis is used in this context. According to this line of argument black males possess significantly fewer skills on average than white males. In the 1980s relative rewards for highly skilled workers rose *vis-à-vis* less-skilled workers. Since black males are disproportionately represented among less-skilled workers, their earnings have fallen relative to white males as relative rewards for skills have moved in favour of those with higher levels of skill acquisition.[7]

Skills are measured in many of these studies by AFQT scores available in the 1980 routine of the National Longitudinal Survey of Youth (NLSY). Inclusion of these scores in regression analyses that seek to examine racial earnings differences virtually eliminates unexplained residual differences in earnings between blacks and whites. Studies by O'Neill (1990), Maxwell (1994), Neal and Johnson (1995), and Ferguson (1995) all reproduce this same result: skill differentials (or, for O'Neill and for Maxwell, 'schooling quality' differentials) obviate any important role for discrimination in labour markets as an explanation for earnings gaps.

The 'returns to skills' explanation for widening earnings gaps has received prominent attention. According to this line of argument, black males possess significantly fewer skills on average than white males. Part of the reason for the focus on black and white males is that these groups show the largest earnings disparities. Black–white disparities among females are considerably less evident (Darity, 1980).

Support for the argument is not unequivocal. Using the Panel Study of Income Dynamics (PSID) data, Card and Lemieux (1994) estimate the returns to unobserved and observed skills for males with earnings from 1979 to 1985. Their hypothesis is that if the cause of the widening racial wage gap between blacks and whites in recent years is due to the increase in returns to skills, then one would expect to find that the black–white wage gap is proportional to the returns to skills across various years for a common cohort of workers. Therefore they conclude that the racial wage gap cannot be due to productivity differences because in their sample they estimate little change in the wage gap even in an era when returns to skills were increasing from 5 to 10 per cent.

The fact that Card and Lemieux do not find an increase in the wage gap for a common cohort of workers suggests that the observed increase in the wage gap among different cohorts of workers must be attributable to the differing experiences of younger black workers. This issue is addressed explicitly by Holzer (1995), who examines a variety of explanations for the deterioration of earnings among young blacks. He concludes that productivity-related or skills explanations are insufficient to account for the rising racial wage gaps and points at least in part to discriminatory processes (via networks) that must be at play.

The reversal in the narrowing trends in racial earnings gaps has brought forth new efforts to explain the phenomenon. Explanations include shifting industry and regional employment, a decline in the real minimum wage, deunionization, a growing supply of black educated workers relative to white workers, and increased criminal activities among school drop-outs (Bound and Freeman, 1992). Another explanation, the skills mismatch hypothesis, flows from the ghetto dispersal versus ghetto development debate of the 1960s (Kain, 1968; Harrison, 1972).

The question for the 1960s was whether residential segregation or employment discrimination caused the low incomes of blacks. The question for the 1990s is whether concentration in inner cities and/or industries where there are job losses or supply-side factors, such as high reservation wages and/or the inducements of crime, is the cause. The spatial mismatch debate has many of the features of the black underclass debate where the issues of contention are structural/demand-side factors versus behavioural/supply-side factors (Fainstain, 1987; Darity, Myers et al., 1995).

The key piece of evidence underlying the spatial mismatch hypothesis is the apparent loss of inner-city, low-wage jobs as employment expands in the suburbs (Kasarda, 1985; Wilson, 1987). David Ellwood tested the hypothesis and concluded: 'the problem is not space. It's race' (Ellwood, 1986, p. 181). Ihlanfeldt and Sjoquist (1990) do find a positive effect of proximity to a job on black and white youth employment rates. They find that 33 per cent to 54 per cent of the racial gap in youth employment rates can be explained by spatial separation from jobs. They conclude: 'poor job access is a significant contributor to the joblessness of black youth' (Ihlanfeldt and Sjoquist, 1990, p. 268).

Still, a comprehensive review of the recent evidence provides mixed support for the spatial mismatch hypothesis (Moss and Tilly, 1991). In contrast, the evidence against the *skills* mismatch hypothesis is more compelling. This hypothesis states that technological change has been biased against low-skilled workers, suggesting a decline in the demand for young blacks, who are disproportionately low-skilled. However, the greatest shifts in demand away from low-skilled workers occurred during the period when racial earnings gaps were narrowing. In more recent years, while racial earnings gaps continue to widen, the pace of skill restructuring has slowed markedly (Howell, 1994; Gittleman and Howell, forthcoming).

An incidental finding of many of the human capital-based studies of racial earnings inequality is that factors such as neighbourhood or census tract characteristics, percentage black, or degree of segregation enter as statistically significant variables in earnings regressions. The justification for inclusion of measures of segregation or concentration of minorities appeals to the social isolation conjecture of Wilson and/or the residential segregation thesis of Massey. Because the effects of concentrations of blacks on employment or earnings tend to be negative, the *ex-post* theory about the signs obtained relates to the various alleged disutilities associated with living in segregated or predominantly black neighbourhoods.

Clearly, there are numerous unresolved issues in the labour econometrics literature concerning the reasons for the increase in racial inequality in recent years. Five stand out prominently, on which we comment on below:

1. Skills Mismatch and General Inequality

Is the skills mismatch hypothesis valid as an explanation for changes in general inequality? If not, then it cannot motivate the analysis of black–white male earnings disparity in the 1980s. In particular, if a shift towards the demand for skills did take place, given the claim of these researchers that there was convergence before the 1980s, the shift must be timed precisely with the 1980s.

2. Times Series and Test Scores

There is an anomaly in time series results in contrast with cross section results. Time series data indicate that black standardized test scores rose relative to white scores in the 1980s, but earnings did not do so. The regression results that appear to vanquish the effects of discrimination all are based on cross section data.

3. Test Scores as Proxies for Race

Take any standardized test on which blacks do worse on average than whites. One suspicion is that any of these scores included in a regression analysis would have the effect of eliminating evidence of discriminatory residuals. But if, for example, AFQT scores are endogenous outcomes generated by processes similar to those generating earnings, these models are misspecified (just like models that use IQ as a proxy for 'ability'). Rodgers and Spriggs (1996) demonstrate how powerfully results are altered by recognizing the endogeneity of AFQT scores.

4. Unmeasured Effort

Patrick Mason (1994) argues that a previously unobserved variable that had been excluded from wage equations is effort. He attempts to demonstrate that black effort is greater for attainment of given characteristics because blacks face greater obstacles. The obstacles are embodied in disadvantageous 'social capital', not in the narrow neoclassical sense in which the term is construed by Glenn Loury, but in a broader sense.

For Mason, 'social capital' should be understood as 'The importance of having access by individuals embedded ... in positions of power and authority ...'. Consequently, equivalent scores between black and white males may actually correspond to *greater* black male personal productivity-linked skills.

Indeed Rodgers and Spriggs (1996) show that there is a systematic racial difference in the capacity of AFQT scores to predict earnings when they estimate separate structural equations for AFQT for blacks and whites with education, age, school quality, and family background measures as the independent variables. AFQT is a much weaker predictor of earnings outcomes for blacks than whites. This is consistent with the general observation that most standardized tests are weaker predictors of black than white performance in a variety of areas. Previous research has been predicated on the assumption that there is no racial difference in the predictive power of AFQT scores.

Coupled with the fact that employers would not observe the AFQT scores in the NLSY, Rodgers and Spriggs (1996) argue that AFQT is a biased predictor of black skills, since the coefficients in the black AFQT equation tend to generate lower scores for given education, age, school quality, and family background characteristics. They propose that a nondiscriminatory weighting of African–American characteristics would involve generating hypothetical black scores on AFQT by using the coeffecients from the white equation. When the hypothetical scores are inserted in the wage or earnings equation racial wage gaps re-emerge that point towards indirect statistical evidence of discrimination against blacks (see also Maume, Cancio and Evans, 1996, for a similar finding). Rodgers and Spriggs (1996) also point out that the military itself 'does not use the AFQT score as the only indicator in placing military personnel in different occupations' because it is a far from comprehensive predictor of performance.

5.   Wealth as an Omitted Variable

We remain curious about what results would be generated in earnings equations that decompose racial earnings differentials if another omitted variable entered into the analysis: wealth. However, oddly enough, in a case where reported wealth from the 1978 NLSY is included in a simultaneous equation model of wages and psychological well-being, the wealth variable is grossly insignificant (Goldsmith, Veum and Darity, 1996). It remains to be seen if that result holds with an older cohort with self-reports on wealth.

6.   Skills Premia in Earlier Eras

If there was not a strong pattern of convergence before the 1980s, then there is a puzzle about the role of skills during that period. If skills did not receive a higher premium during the period before 1980 and the difference in years of schooling was narrowing, then what happened? It is obviously important to the O'Neill–Maxwell–Ferguson case to establish that convergence was underway before the 1980s.

But we have argued that the ostensible pattern of convergence was largely illusory due to a labour force drop-out effect. If black male labour force drop-outs had lower earnings than white male labour force drop-outs, measures of black–white earnings ratios based on males with employment will overstate the black–white ratio. Finis Welch (1990) has tried to squash the proposition that the 'progress' of the 1970s was illusory by undertaking a selection correction for labour force drop-outs to demonstrate that the drop-out effect has little consequence for estimates of black–white earnings ratios.

But Welch's selection correction is not satisfactory. The selection correction is hypersensitive to the specification of the process that leads to inclusion or exclusion (Manski, 1989) of sample members. Welch's selection specification is premised on the view that labour force drop-out status is a purely voluntary phenomenon. Labour force drop-outs are viewed as choosing leisure and/or illegal income by Welch. But as Myers shows in his essay in *The Question of Discrimination* (Shulman and Darity, 1989), most of the black 'voluntary unemployed' are really involuntarily unemployed: they were seeking jobs but could not find them.

Because of the extreme sensitivity of selection correction to specification, Blau and Beller (1992) use an alternative approach to the drop-out issue. They ask what the earnings ratio would look like if LFPRs were sustained at earlier levels, and find labour force drop-out patterns do bias the ratios upwards significantly in the 1970s. William Rodgers (1994) uses a quartile approach to the labour force drop-out issue and finds that black–white earnings ratios were also biased upwards significantly in the 1970s.

CONCLUSIONS

In summary, the recent explanations for the widening gap between black and white earnings have focused on the alleged human capital roots of low black wages and salaries. Alternative explanations that focus on institutional and structural deficits of labour markets and employers have largely been ignored. While many analysts claim by deduction that the widening earnings gaps between whites and blacks must not be caused by discrimination, racism, or other institutionalized factors, we remain unconvinced. There is persuasive evidence that the US anti-discrimination effort was nearly dismantled precisely during the period when racial gaps earnings reopened in the 1980s. We also are dissuaded because the process of eliminating explanations by focusing on individual deficiencies of minorities themselves leaves much to be desired.

More reasonable as an explanation of how and why racial earnings gaps widened is that white males lost jobs. Put simply, the widening of the racial earnings gap is inextricably linked to the widening of overall inequality and the loss of white middle-class employment opportunities.

White males were squeezed out of the vanishing middle-class jobs, which had been their purview, especially well-paid blue-collar jobs. They were then crowded into a lower tier of occupations that they would not otherwise have held. They squeezed black males out of those jobs. In fact, they have begun to appropriate a set of jobs that were previously held by blacks and are making them 'white male' jobs. Black males and females in the most tenuous labour market positions have been pushed out, both by whites and by immigrants from South America and Southeast Asia.

Furthermore, those black males who had held blue-collar jobs and made the transition into white-collar employment actually went from operative positions to sales positions that paid less. In contrast, white males who made a similar transition went from blue-collar operative positions to sales positions that paid them more (Cotton, 1989).

In a sense, the argument here is that exclusion (discrimination) is endogenously linked to the employment needs of non-black males. As the occupational distribution eliminates jobs traditionally held by white males, they secure less attractive jobs at the expense of black males. The force of discrimination is then seen as instrumental. Its application intensifies when the dominant group's status is threatened, either because of improved productivity-linked characteristics of members of a potential rival group or because of a diminution in the job opportunities of members of the dominant group.

The endogenous model of discrimination also finds support in other contexts. For example, a study by Dhesi and Singh (1989) of economic inequality between religious caste groups in Delhi, India in 1970 revealed negligible evidence of discriminatory earnings differentials for the lowest Hindu caste members despite a wide gap in earnings between them and higher caste members. Their educational levels were so low that they would rarely be direct rivals with members of the higher castes for preferred occupations. In a sense, there was no 'need' for upper-caste Hindus to exercise direct discriminatory actions in the labour market toward the lowest-caste members because the latter could not even get in the game. In contrast, Dhesi and Singh found substantial evidence of discriminatory differentials in earnings between Sikhs and upper-caste Hindus. Sikhs, unlike lower-caste Hindus, on average possessed the education levels that would make them stronger and immediate rivals for the occupations typically held by upper-caste Hindus.

The endogenous model of discrimination suggests a rich and as yet unexplored research agenda with US data. One way to approach this is to estimate discriminatory earnings residuals over time and then see if the variation through time can be explained by changing labour market conditions for white males. Do the discriminatory residuals for blacks become larger when economic times are harder for whites (and white males in particular)? If so, there would be strong evidence to support the linkage we have hypothesized between widening racial inequality and widening general inequality.

ENDNOTES

1. Smith and Welch have continued to maintain the same position in more recent work for the same reasons. See, for example, Smith and Welch (1989) and Smith and Welch (1986).
2. This is much the same viewpoint as that adopted by Robert A. Margo (1990), who relies heavily on Smith and Welch's research.
3. Finis Welch, for one, has been a prominent expert witness in defence of businesses confronted with discrimination suits. For an example of the nature of the arguments he utilizes in his testimony see his essay 'Affirmative Action and Discrimination' in Shulman and Darity Jr (1989), pp. 153–89. It is of interest to note that Welch (p. 187) observes at the close of his essay that 'A number of recent studies have shown that the longer run gain in relative earnings of black men can be attributed to three primary sources: rising levels of school completion, emigration from the rural South, and increasing value of additional schooling' rather than affirmative action. The 'recent studies' that he refers to are his own work with Smith.
4. See Freeman, 'Changes' (1973), 'Decline' (1973) and (1981). A version of the last paper appeared as an NBER working paper in October 1978.
5. Papers representing the scope of the dissent include Darity and Myers 'Black Economic Progress' (1980); Darity, 'Illusions' (1980); Darity and Myers, 'Changes' (1980) and 'Vintage Effect' (1980).
6. On this point see Myers (1989). For a related analysis see Butler and Heckman (1977), pp. 235–81. Butler and Heckman also argued that the labour force drop-out effect artificially raised black–white earnings and income ratios, but they attributed the higher black labour force drop-out rate to the work disincentive effects of the American social welfare system. Why those effects – to the extent that they exist – would have a differential racial impact is not clear. We take up this issue in depth below.
7. Juhn, Murphy and Pierce (1991) is representative of this body of work.

4. Education and earnings inequality among family heads

Racial gaps in family incomes have widened. Compare Figures 4.1 and 4.2 showing the ratio of black–white incomes among families versus households. These figures compute the three-year averages of the ratios of black–white median incomes centred on the year displayed in the graph. The three-year average of the ratio of black–white median family incomes centred on the year 1970 was 0.6098; centred on 1973 it was 0.5895; centred on 1976 it was 0.5938; centred on 1979 it was 0.5790.

During the 1980s, however, the three-year averages were everywhere lower than the lowest three-year average before the 1980s. Centred on 1982, it was 0.5601; centred on 1985 it was 0.5682; centred on 1988 it was 0.5667. Thus the period of the 1980s was clearly one in which black families experienced lower incomes relative to white families when compared to the period of the 1970s and late 1960s. Even though the averages for the last years in the series –

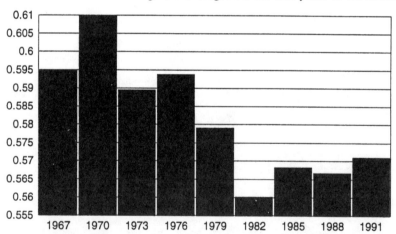

Source: US Bureau of the Census, Current Population Reports, Series P-60, No. 184, *Money Income of Households, Families, and Persons in the United States: 1992*, US Government Printing Office, Washington, DC, 1993.

Figure 4.1   Black–white family income ratios 1967–91 (medians, 3 year averages)

2+ persons related by blood, marriage, adoption. sharing some household

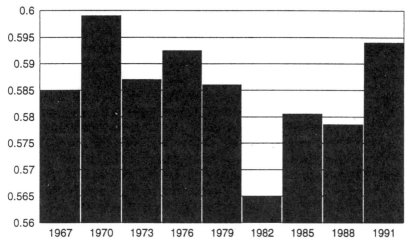

Source: As Fig. 4.1.

Figure 4.2   Black–white household income ratios, 1967–91 (medians, 3 year averages)

1990–92 – drifted up to 0.5710, the pattern is still the same: lower ratios in the 1980s than in any of the previous years. Thus, black families were relatively worse off in the 1980s than they were in the 1970s.

This conclusion holds for a very precise definition of 'family': two or more persons, related by blood, marriage or adoption, sharing the same household. Households can include either families or non-family members or both. Single persons, unmarried couples or unrelated room-mates can constitute a household in the *Current Population Survey (CPS)* definitions. When we compute the same income ratios for households the earlier conclusion of a persistent decline in relative black incomes is reversed. Figure 4.2 shows that the ratio of black–white median household incomes fell dramatically during the three-year interval centred on the recession year of 1982 but recovered thereafter. The ratio rose to approach the average of the 1970s by the beginning of the 1990s.

Thus, something peculiar was happening to black families between the 1970s and the 1980s. The result was a deterioration in black family incomes relative to white family incomes. In this chapter and the next we shall focus almost exclusively on families. When we explore the determinants of wage and salary earnings, we shall focus exclusively on family heads. However, in this chapter, when we compare wage and salary earnings of family heads, there is no artificial attempt to exclude some family units because the head had no earnings or worked less than full time. By including non-earners in the analysis we avoid the implication that they do not matter in our assessment of the overall economic status of black and white families.

[handwritten margin note: families + single persons unmarried couples unrelated room mates etc.]

In more detailed econometric analysis, however, formal account must be taken of the non-earners. In the next chapter, to capture the apparent shift in the fortunes of black families between the 1970s and the 1980s, we shall examine in some detail two representative years, 1976 and 1985. Much of the analysis in that chapter and some in this chapter relies on results of an econometric analysis discussed in detail in the appendix to Chapter 5. The summary results of these statistical computations all refer to family heads.

Why focus on family heads? Unlike other econometric analyses of labour market outcomes that generally look at individual male and female workers, our examination is designed to help us understand the widening income gap among families. At least part of the widening in total money incomes of black and white family heads must result from the changing earnings of family heads. Of course, some of the change also must rest with changing family structure, which we examine explicitly in the next chapter. First, however, we examine the relationship between a) skills and education and b) the earnings of young and older family heads.

SKILLS AND EDUCATION

Prominent in the debate among economists about the narrowing of earnings inequality after the 1960s was the role of improved education. It has typically been asserted that because of desegregation in Southern school systems, or because of direct increases in educational completion arising from migration to areas with superior schools or from anti-discrimination legislation, increased educational quantity and quality among blacks helped reduce racial earnings disparities. Nearly every econometric analysis of racial earnings gaps using post-1960s data shows the positive impact of at least schooling quantity on black educational progress or relative black economic status (Smith and Welch, 1989).

In more recent years, when it became apparent that black–white earnings gaps – particularly among young males – have widened, the focus of attention has shifted to deficiencies in the quality of education or the lack of acquisition of necessary skills among blacks. The focus has shifted to changing returns to skills and the reduction in the demand for less-skilled workers relative to more-skilled workers.

Unfortunately, 'skills' are unobserved. Thus, all skill shift arguments – even those based on analyses that use proxies for skills such as test scores – rest on weak empirical counterparts to the underlying human capital theory that motivated the debate about the original narrowing of earnings gaps. Since one cannot directly observe skills in data sets such as the *CPS* March Supplement Tapes, researchers have typically relied on measuring skills by years of education.

In the statistical analysis summarized in the appendix to this chapter a non-linear earnings education profile is estimated. We model the possibility of increasing or decreasing returns to skills as educational completion increases. A one-year increase in education does not have to yield the same increase in earnings for a tenth-grader as it would for a Ph.D.

Many researchers prefer a measure of 'experience', also not observed directly in the *CPS* data set. Experience is often measured by the difference between age and highest grade completed plus six years. Thus a person who is 40 years old, with 12 years of education, would have 40 – (12 + 6) or 22 years of experience. At best this is a crude measure of labour market experience. It values ten years of incarceration at the same rate as ten years of military experience; a year of work is the same as a year of unemployment. It equates the experience of a 30-year-old high school drop-out with that of a 39-year-old Ph.D.

Analyses such as that of Ronald Ferguson (1995), which first control for 'labour market experience' and then attempt to control for unobserved skills by accounting for test scores (such as AFQT scores), compound the confusion about experience. Two individuals with equal estimated labour market experience using the crude age-less-education measure may have very unequal abilities: a felon versus a decorated war veteran, a chronically unemployed drifter versus a steadily employed family head; a young high-school drop-out versus a tenured university professor. By introducing the proxy for unmeasured skills (such as AFQT scores) we introduce a variable highly correlated with unmeasured experience. The result is that the estimated impact of skills and education becomes suspect as unknown biases are introduced into the computations.

Our preferred strategy is to focus on years of education completed. While this gives but an implicit measure of skills, it nevertheless provides a useful benchmark for evaluation of the changing fortunes of young versus older black and white family heads.

THE DECLINING FAMILY INCOMES OF HIGH-SCHOOL GRADUATES

There may be some merit in the argument that there has been a secular shift downward in the rewards to less-skilled workers, despite the lack of evidence 'that the 1980s were characterized by *unusually large* shifts in labour demand away from low-skilled workers' (Howell and Wieler, 1995, p. 12, emphasis added). The shrinking middle class faces lower family incomes in part because the incomes of persons without college degrees have fallen in real dollars. This point can be made by reference to data on family incomes broken down by age and education of the head of the family. Computed from the *CPS* March

[handwritten margin notes: 1970-91 av. white family income ↑ but those graded h.s. grades for some blacks]

Supplement Tapes for various years, average family incomes, expressed in constant dollars, are detailed in Table 4A.1 (on p. 78) and are broken down by age and education level of the family heads. In 1970, the average white family income for a head with only a high-school degree was $31 238. The overall average for white families was $30 889. By 1991, the average white family income for a head with only a high-school degree was $30 252. Yet the overall average for white families was $34 589. Thus, among whites, families with heads who were only high school graduates fell behind the average.

Similarly, the family incomes of black families with high-school-educated family heads fell behind the average in recent years. In 1970, the average black family income for a head with only a high school degree was $22 876. The overall average for black families in that year was $19 822. By 1991, the average black family income for a head with only a high-school degree fell to $20 297, but the overall average for black families was $21 806. Thus black high-school-educated family heads received total family incomes that lagged behind the average black family income.

Since a decline in income is apparent for both blacks and whites it is tempting to conclude that there are no racial implications behind these changes. When one computes the ratio of black–white family incomes within age and educational cohorts, however, a clear distinction emerges between the relative position of black and white families.

Figure 4.3 shows the ratio of black–white family incomes among families with heads with high-school degrees but no further education. We graph the ratios for family heads aged 25 to 40 and for family heads aged 41 and above. Among the older heads of families there is little deterioration in the relative position of blacks. Indeed, there is some minor improvement. The black–white family income ratio among high school graduates aged 41 and above was 0.757 in 1970. It fell to 0.697 in 1976, recovered and fell again during the 1982 recession to 0.715 and rebounded in the 1980s to reach a level of 0.780 in 1991.

In real terms, the incomes of these black families with older heads were about the same in 1991 as they were in 1970 ($25 959 versus $25 793). The slight relative improvement is the result of a decline in the real incomes of similarly aged and educated white family heads, whose family incomes dropped from $34 065 in 1970 to $33 276 in 1991. Substantively, the black–white disparity was the same in the early 1990s as it was in the early 1970s.

This is not true for families with younger heads with no more than a high-school degree. The line with square markers in Figure 4.3 shows that by the 1980s there was a sharp drop in the ratio of black–white family incomes among 25- to 40-year-old heads of families with high-school degrees but no additional education. The ratio for this age–education group was 0.757 in 1970, 0.737 in 1973, 0.778 in 1976, 0.759 in 1979 and 0.731 in 1982.

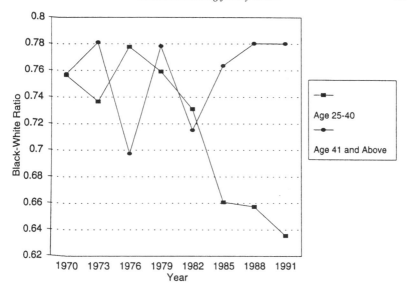

Sources: Authors' computations and *CPS* March Supplement Tapes

Figure 4.3 Black–white family income ratios, 1970–91, families headed by high-school graduates

Throughout the 1980s the ratio plunged downwards. It was 0.661 in 1985, 0.657 in 1988 and it fell further to 0.636 in 1991. In short, among somewhat younger families headed by persons with high-school degrees, the racial income gap widened. In this instance, the gap increased because of larger declines in the real incomes of black families compared with those of white families. Whereas white family incomes in this age–education group dropped about $2000 in real terms from 1970 to 1991 (from $29 531 to $27 594), black family incomes dropped almost $5000 (from $22 340 to $17 536).

[handwritten margin note: black white among young h.s. grads or less]

DECLINES IN FAMILY INCOMES OF YOUNG HIGH-SCHOOL DROP-OUTS VERSUS OLDER COLLEGE GRADUATES

A sharper distinction can be made between the incomes of young uneducated family heads and older well-educated family heads. When this distinction is made, one sees that blacks and whites are moving farther apart in terms of their prospects. The cause is a growing disparity between poorly educated blacks and whites. The skills mismatch hypothesis suggests the widening gulf between blacks and whites is occurring because of greater distance between the better educated and less well educated, with blacks over-represented among the latter group. We demonstrate below that there is yet another widening gulf that cannot be attributed to a race-neutral, skills mismatch explanation. There is a sharply widening gap between black and white less well-educated, young family heads.

Increasingly, the 'haves' of our society are better educated professionals with advanced degrees. They are often middle-aged and at the peak of their earnings profiles. The 'have nots' are, increasingly, young, uneducated family heads. Nevertheless, an important racial dimension exists regarding the status of these haves and have nots. In relative terms, young black heads of families with little education are worse off today than they were two decades ago, while black families with older, better-educated heads are not much worse off today than they were 20 years ago. Consequently, the racial income gap has expanded between families with young, uneducated heads and those with educated heads.

Figure 4.4 graphs the results of computing the ratio of black–white family incomes comparing heads aged 14 to 24 who have not completed high school with heads over age 41 who have college degrees. In this sense we are comparing the haves and have nots of our new era, the young and uneducated versus middle-aged professionals.

The results are clear: during the period from 1970 to 1991 the ratio of black–white family incomes among those with older, educated heads remained

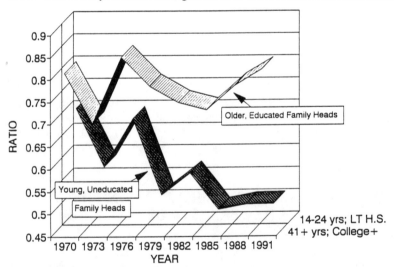

Source: Authors' computations from 1976, 1985 and 1993 IRP Family Extract Files (CPS March Supplements Tapes).

Figure 4.4   Black–white family income ratios, 1970–91, by age and education of family head

stable while the ratio fell sharply for families with younger, uneducated heads. At the start of the 1970s, the ratio of black–white income was 0.82 (family heads over the age of 41 who had completed college). At that same time the ratio was 0.71 for family heads aged 14 to 24 who had not completed high school. Thus there was a 15 per cent difference between the racial income ratio for families with young, uneducated heads and families with older, educated heads. Moreover, by 1991, the ratio had fallen to 0.50 for young, uneducated heads while it was still about 0.82 for older, educated heads. Thus, by 1991 there was a 66 per cent difference!

This quadrupling of the gap between the racial income inequality among young, uneducated families and older, educated families did not come about because of substantial improvements in the relative economic well-being of black families with older, educated heads. Rather, the widening of the gap came about as a result of the worsening position of black families with young, uneducated heads.

Figure 4.5 reveals that the percentage difference between the incomes of families with young, uneducated heads and older, educated heads grew from 1970 to 1991. Black family incomes for families with young, uneducated heads in 1970 averaged $12 179. For black families with older educated heads, the average was $42 520 in 1970. By 1991, for this better-educated group of blacks, family incomes rose to $46 120. They fell for the less well educated. The average black

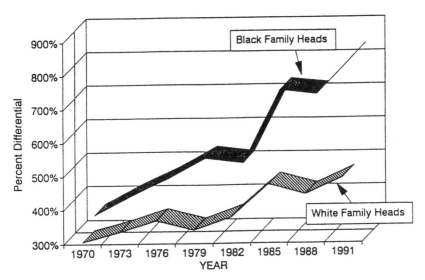

Source: As Fig. 4.4.

Figure 4.5 Differentials (%) in income, 1970–91, young uneducated vs older educated heads

family income for families with young uneducated heads was a mere $5612! Thus in 1970 the family incomes of blacks with older, better-educated heads was about *two and a half times* the total incomes of black families with younger uneducated heads. By 1991 it was more than *seven times* that of black families with younger, uneducated heads.

In short, the relative difference between the incomes of black families with older educated heads and the incomes of black families with younger uneducated heads went from 250 per cent in 1970 to 720 per cent in 1991. The relative difference rose among whites as well, but only from 200 per cent in 1970 to 390 per cent in 1991. The conclusion is clear: the income position of black families with young, uneducated heads deteriorated over the two decades. They were worse off relative to similarly situated whites and relative to better situated blacks.

EARNINGS OF FAMILY HEADS

Wage and salary income account for the largest share of family income. The wage and salary earnings of the head of the family contribute substantially to the determination of the overall family income position. Much of the foregoing discussion concerning the widening gaps in family incomes between blacks and whites and between young uneducated and older educated heads of families re-emerges in the following analysis of the earnings of family heads. Not surprisingly, the wedge driven between the incomes of black and white families with young, less-educated family heads is a wedge driven between the earnings of these families as well.

The deterioration in the relative position of black families with young, uneducated heads, when measured by the wage and salary earnings of the family head, is documented fully in Table 4A.2 (on p. 79). In 1970, young black heads of families who had not completed high school earned 61 cents for every dollar earned by similarly situated whites. By 1991, this was down to 35 cents. In contrast, older black heads of families who had college degrees earned 68 cents for every dollar earned by whites with similar credentials. This amount rose to nearly 86 cents by 1991.

As revealed in Table 4A.2, the decline in the relative position of young, uneducated black family heads could be demonstrated readily by the beginning of the 1980s, reaching a low in the range of 30 to 35 per cent. This was true despite the precipitous decline in the wage and salary earnings of young white family heads with little education. While black earnings for this group dropped from $3629 in 1979 to $1909 in 1991, white earnings plunged from $10 437 to $5401 during those years. Moreover, the wage and salary earnings of older, better-educated white family heads also declined!

In contrast, the gap in earnings between older, educated black family heads and young, uneducated black family heads widened from a low of 158 per cent

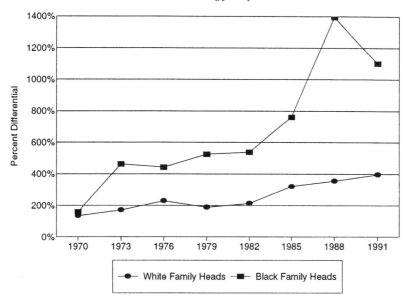

Source: As Fig. 4.4.

Figure 4.6   Differentials (%) in earnings, 1970–91, young uneducated vs older educated heads

to a high of 1390 per cent during the period 1970 to 1991. Figure 4.6, based on computations derived from Appendix Table 4A.2 also shows a considerably smaller growth in the gap between these two categories of whites, although the spread did grow.

These findings again call into question the strength of the returns to skills hypothesis. Recall that this hypothesis states that the relative rewards for highly skilled workers rose *vis-à-vis* less-skilled workers. Putatively, black earnings fell because of this shift toward those with higher levels of skill acquisition (Juhn, Murphy and Pierce, 1991). If the problem of declining incomes and earnings of black family heads – and thus the widening gap between black and white families – is to be attributed to the higher representation of blacks among the less skilled and the uneducated, then why is there a widening gap between black and white family heads with the *same* low degree of educational preparation? If the problem is that the price of skills has increased, why should race matter at all? Why is there a larger widening of the gap between the black haves and have nots than between the white haves and have nots? Like Card and Lemieux (1994) we find the evidence inadequate to support this explanation for the growing divergence between black and white earnings.

Our conclusion also runs counter to much of the existing literature on widening earnings gaps between black and white males, premised on a decline in the demand for low-skilled workers and/or an increase in the price of skills (Moss and Tilly, 1991). There are three differences between our computations and the empirical case for the 'conventional wisdom'. First, we focus here on family heads. Other analyses (for example Katz and Murphy, 1992, Bound and Freeman, 1992, and Juhn et al. 1991) generally examine individual workers or young workers only. Second, we focus on annual wage and salary incomes while others have looked at weekly or hourly wages. And third, we include both positive earners and non-earners in our calculations, while most other analysts restrict their samples to positive earners. The latter practice produces serious biases in the results if no attempts are made to account for the sample selection problem.

None the less, we do not discount the presence of a skill shift or changing premia for better educated workers. We just do not believe that this is the root cause of the widening gap in earnings between black and white family heads.

SKILLS PREMIA FROM PROFESSIONAL/MANAGERIAL OCCUPATIONS

By looking at occupations rewarding higher levels of skill acquisition, we can measure more directly the racial dimensions of the widening gulf between the haves and have nots. The shifts in the labour market towards higher-skilled, educated workers can be seen when one compares the wage and salary incomes of professional/managerial workers to the incomes of all other non-sales and clerical workers. A crude measure of the wage premium associated with such occupations is the excess of the earnings that these workers make over the remaining workers.

We compute the ratios of the earnings of family heads who are professional/managerial workers shown in Table 4A.4 (on p. 82) to the earnings of all other family heads, excluding sales and clerical workers. The bulk of the remaining occupations are in production and operative fields. These computations are performed within races and for male and female heads of families. We then derive a measure of relative wage premia by computing the ratio of the black–white wage premia. These results are displayed in Figure 4.7.

This figure reveals that initially there was a sizeable racial difference in the wage premium to professional/managerial occupations among male and female heads of families. With the exception of the downturn during the recession of 1982, that racial difference in the wage premium to professional/managerial male heads of families narrowed steadily. By the late 1980s, the ratio of professional/managerial wage and salary incomes to all other non-sales and

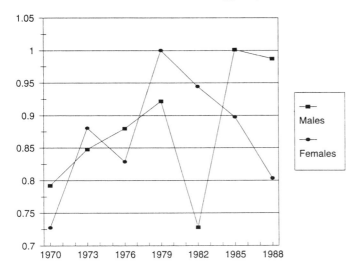

Note: Earnings premium is the ratio of wage and salary incomes of managerial/professional workers to earnings for all other workers, for family heads.

Source: As Fig. 4.4.

Figure 4.7 Black–white earnings premium to professional and managerial workers over other workers, 1970–88

clerical workers' wage and salary incomes was about the same among black and white male family heads. The same narrowing of the gap in wage premia did not persist among female heads of families. In the 1970s the ratios of professional/managerial wage and salary incomes to all other non-sales and clerical workers' wage and salary incomes for black and white female heads of families appeared to converge, but by the 1980s these ratios moved apart.

The downward shift came about not because of any decline in the wage advantage of black professional/managerial female heads of families over other black female heads of families. Rather, the downward shift took place because of the substantial increase in the wage premium among white female heads of families who are professional/managerial workers. Among family heads, black professional women now earn four to five times more than other black women. Among white female heads of families, in contrast, the advantage of professional/managerial workers over others is now an income five to six times higher.

These findings, using data on family heads, confirm the presence of changing returns to skills. But there are clear race and gender distinctions. There were larger increases in wage premia among white female heads than among black female heads – even though there is little evidence of any widening of the earnings gap between black and white female family heads. According to our calculations, displayed in Table 4A.3, the ratio of black–white wage and salary incomes among female family heads was an identical 0.78 in 1976 and 1985. If anything, there was a narrowing of the wage gap: the ratio was 0.71 in 1970; it rose to 0.76 in 1988. The differential wage premia could 'explain' the widening gap, if indeed that gap were widening among female family heads. It was not.

Among male heads of family, there was a widening of the earnings gaps after a period of narrowing during the 1970s. As Figure 4.7 reveals, the ratio of black–white wage and salary earnings of male heads of families rose from 0.68 to 0.77 between 1970 and 1979 and then fell from 0.72 in 1982 to 0.70 in 1985. Although there was a slight upturn in 1988 to 0.74, overall levels in the 1980s were below the heights reached in the 1970s. Among male-headed families, the rising price of skills *could* explain the widening gaps. Yet the wage premium among black male heads of family from professional/managerial occupations has remained relatively constant throughout the 1980s. The reason for the upsurge in the black–white relative premia is that the gap increased between the earnings of white professional/managerial workers and other non-sales/clerical workers.

RETURNS TO EDUCATION

Still another way to view the impact of changing rewards on better-educated family heads is to compute the returns to education directly. The analysis of the previous section does not control for other possible determinants of earnings. Factors such as changes in labour force participation rates and shifts in the age composition of the population are not accounted for in the previous computations of wage premia. Moreover, the conventional approach to estimating returns to education is first to estimate equations for earnings. Others who have done this (for example, Bound and Freeman, 1992) have generally found declining returns to education for black males. This, perhaps, is the crux of the continuing belief that the widening of black–white earnings gaps rests at least in part on increasing returns to highly skilled workers among whom blacks are apparently under-represented.

We already have acknowledged that our findings in this chapter are at odds with the conventional wisdom on the causes of the widening earnings gap between blacks and whites. The conventional wisdom was formulated by looking exclusively at individual black and white males with positive earnings. There are obvious limits in transferring the conventional wisdom to explain racial differences in earnings of family heads, among whom are non-trivial numbers of females and persons who did not work.

But there is another reason to be concerned about the 'increasing returns to skills' hypothesis. If we can measure skill acquisition by years of education completed, then there is no reason to believe that the *widening* of the racial earnings gap among family heads in recent years is caused by increasing differences in educational credentials. Educational completion among black family heads *increased* from the 1970s to the 1980s. It even increased among black non-family heads, aside from zero earners.

A quick comparison from 1976 and 1985 – two representative years from the 1970s and 1980s – makes this point apparent. Table 4.1 provides insights about the distribution of educational advances among blacks and whites. The table details two important breakdowns. The first differentiates positive earners and non-earners. The second is a breakdown of family heads versus non-family heads. Non-family heads largely consist of single individuals living alone.

Table 4.1   Educational attainment of earners and non-earners, 1976–85

	1976		1985		Change (%)	
	Black	White	Black	White	Black	White
Positive earners						
Family heads						
Male	10.48	12.37	12.02	12.94	14.69	4.61
Female	11.08	11.93	11.95	12.58	7.85	5.45
Non-family heads						
Male	10.47	13.29	11.83	13.58	12.99	2.18
Female	10.91	12.82	12.77	13.58	17.05	5.93
Non-earners						
Family heads						
Male	7.93	10.84	9.09	11.41	14.63	5.26
Female	9.28	9.85	9.74	10.64	4.96	8.02
Non-family heads						
Male	9.12	10.35	9.09	11.72	–0.33	13.24
Female	7.53	10.19	8.92	10.67	18.46	4.71

Source: Authors' computations from the *Current Population Survey*, March Supplement Tapes.

Among those with positive incomes, educational attainment increased for both family heads and non-family heads, despite gender. The percentage increase was larger for blacks than whites and was largest for black female non-family heads. This group, which experienced a 17 per cent increase in educational attainment, had completed 10.91 years of schooling in 1976 but 12.77 years by 1985. The figure of a mean of close to 13 years of schooling surpasses the educational attainment of black and white female family heads and black male family and non-family heads. It nearly equals the educational attainment of white male family heads.

This group, mostly comprising single black women, was slightly older than its white counterparts and older than female family heads in 1985. However, it was a younger group on average in 1985 than the corresponding group in 1976. The average age of black female non-family heads with positive earnings in 1976 was 45; in 1985 it was 40. This suggests impressive educational gains among younger black women without family responsibilities. This group certainly outdistanced all other groups of black women and was the only group of blacks, save for male family heads, that had an average level of education exceeding high school.

In sharp contrast to the educational gains of single black women is the deterioration of the educational prospects for black male non-family heads without earnings. These men, who had completed an average of 9.12 years of schooling in 1976, only completed an average of 9.09 years of schooling by 1985. This educational completion level was lower than that of whites in any category and even lower than black female family heads.

Yet these men were not as young as the single females with positive earnings. Their average age was 54 in 1985 and 56 in 1976. The youngest men had earnings but were not family heads. The average age of black male non-family heads with earnings was 39 in 1976 and 37 in 1985. Still, neither the black male non-earners nor the black male earners had managed to attain an average level of education equivalent to high-school graduation.

The implication is that, for single individuals, education completion diverged between black males and females – black males being 'burdened' disproportionately with educational levels below the high-school degree level and black females being 'blessed' with sharp increases in educational attainment, including high school degrees and some college education. Indeed, the recent pattern reverses a historic trend among blacks in which men receive more schooling than women. However, within families, black males saw educational growth substantially exceed that of black females or white family heads.

This is the backdrop against which we must examine the impact of educational attainment on earnings inequality among family heads. We shall show that educational attainment is improving and returns to education are increasing among family heads. Smith and Welch (1989) view this as evidence of the importance of human capital improvements in narrowing racial earnings gaps since 1940. But this same evidence also contradicts the 'increasing returns to skills' explanation for the widening of earnings gaps in recent years, at least among family heads.

To make the case that increasing returns to skills (measured here by years of schooling) could not cause the widening earnings inequality, we need to derive estimates of the effects of education on earnings, an econometric procedure that is described fully in the appendix to this chapter. Here we sketch heuristically how we obtain the results in Table 4.2.

Table 4.2   Returns to education, family heads, 1976–85

	Blacks 1976	Whites 1976	Blacks 1985	Whites 1985	Change in inequality
Single equation					
OLS	0.059606	0.074467	0.10114	0.087149	–0.02885
Heckman	0.025095	0.043016	0.06579	0.064929	–0.01878
BCG	0.049888	0.077849	0.07887	0.079400	–0.02743
Means, all families	10.056	11.901	11.095	12.414	–

Source: Darity and Myers 'Family Structure, Earnings Inequality and the Marginalization of Black Men.' A paper presented at the Western Economics Association Meetings, Lake Tahoe, July 1989.

First we computed the natural logarithm of annual wage and salary incomes for black and white family heads in 1976 and 1985. One advantage of using the natural log of earnings is that the estimated coefficients computed on the education terms are easily interpreted as 'the returns to education', or the percentage change in wage and salary income as a result of a one-year increase in educational completion. Another advantage is that the resulting distribution of earnings, when transformed, yields a shape that more closely parallels actual distributions of earnings – not quite bell-shaped but skewed to the left and truncated below zero. Of course, it is not possible to compute the log of zero. Therefore the zero earners are excluded from the regressions.

Until recently, such exclusion has been virtually universal within the labour economics literature. It is quite unsatisfactory for our purposes because of the stark differences observed in Table 4.1 between the educational levels of earners and non-earners among family heads. Since we wish to measure the returns to education we need somehow to account for the selective exclusion of family heads with no earnings. Several methods for accomplishing this goal are discussed in the appendix.

After controlling for age, work effort (or the percentage of the year spent working or looking for work), region and central city residence we obtain estimates of the coefficients of education and education squared. These coefficients are then used to compute the returns to education presented in Table 4.2.

By estimating the returns to education for blacks and whites separately for 1976 and 1985, a convenient interpretation of the results emerges. As we detail in the appendix, the racial difference in the returns to education in 1976 minus the racial difference in the returns to education in 1985 reveals the impact on the change in earnings inequality of returns to education. If the result is positive, the effect is to increase racial earnings inequality; if the result is negative, the effect is to reduce racial earnings inequality. If returns to education are identical for blacks and whites in each year but the returns to education increase uniformly between 1976 and 1985, then there can still be an increase in earnings inequality if blacks are disproportionately less well educated – the thrust of the 'increasing returns to skills' argument.

There are three different estimates of the returns to education presented. The ordinary least squares (OLS) estimates do not account for selection bias or the endogeneity of work effort. The Heckman estimates correct for selection bias via exclusion of zero earners and account directly for the endogeneity of work effort. The Barnow, Cain and Goldberger (BCG) equation estimates correct for selection bias via labour force participation; labour force participation *is* considered endogenous.

Table 4.2 reveals that educational completion rose for black and white family heads from 1976 to 1985, but the increase was sharper for blacks than whites. Returns to education also rose considerably for blacks from 1976 to 1985. While the OLS estimates of the returns to education among black family heads show an increase from 5.96 per cent in 1976 to 10 per cent in 1985, when selection bias is taken into account, using the Heckman correction method, the estimates for blacks are 2.7 and 6.8 per cent.

Using the BCG method, the returns to education among black family heads amount to nearly 5 and 8 per cent. In all estimates white returns exceeded the black returns in 1976; by 1985 black and white returns to education converged. In short, returns to education rose sharply enough for blacks that they approximated those for whites by 1985. Of course, there are slight variations in the exact value of these returns, depending on the equation structure used and the estimation procedures. When no statistical account for the omission of zero earners is taken in the single-equation model, returns to education are inflated, reaching an obviously upward-biased value of 10 per cent for black family heads. Still, the broad finding holds. Black returns to education improved in the 1980s.

One can compute the impact of these increasing educational returns on earnings inequality.[1] The ratio of black–white earnings in year t to black–white earnings in year $t + 1$ is one measure of inequality. As this ratio rises, racial inequality increases, or the racial earnings gap widens. Table 4.2 shows that a uniform increase in one year of education reduces inequality in each of the equation specifications.

Put simply, these results, along with those concerning the managerial/ professional workers' wage premia, all cast doubt on the argument that increasing returns to skills are at the heart of the declining ratio of black–white earnings among family heads.

Despite an established wage premium associated with professional/managerial workers, a widening gap between young, uneducated family heads and older, college-educated family heads, and an increase in the returns to education, none of these factors fully explains the rise in earnings inequality between black and white family heads. The evidence points in just the opposite direction. Of course, the culprit might be changing family structures. We address this possibility in the next chapter.

ENDNOTE

1. To assess the impact on earnings inequality of changing patterns of educational achievement between blacks and whites and earners and non-earners, we compute the derivative of $\ln(I)$ and evaluate it for two differences. The first difference is the change in educational attainment from 1976 to 1985 within racial groups. The second is the racial difference in educational attainment for each year. These two assessments can be written as:

$$\partial \ln(I)/\partial X_i \times \Delta X_i = \left[\partial \ln\left(Y_{76}^B\right)\big/\partial X_i - \partial \ln\left(Y_{85}^B\right)\big/\partial X_i\right]\left(X_{i76}^B - X_{i85}^B\right)$$
$$- \left[\partial \ln\left(Y_{76}^W\right)\big/\partial X_i - \partial \ln\left(Y_{85}^W\right)\big/\partial X_i\right]\left(X_{i76}^W - X_{i85}^W\right)$$

$$\partial \ln(I)/\partial X_i \times \Delta X_i = \left[\partial \ln\left(Y_{76}^B\right)\big/\partial X_i - \partial \ln\left(Y_{76}^W\right)\big/\partial X_i\right]\left(X_{i76}^B - X_{i76}^W\right)$$
$$- \left[\partial \ln\left(Y_{85}^B\right)\big/\partial X_i - \partial \ln\left(Y_{85}^W\right)\big/\partial X_i\right]\left(X_{i85}^B - X_{i85}^W\right)$$

The first can be interpreted as the change in earnings inequality that can be attributed to the actual changes in educational achievement by blacks and whites from 1976 to 1985. The second is the change in inequality due to actual differences in educational completion between blacks and whites in each year. Neither distinguishes between that component of change that is strictly the result of improvements in endowments or characteristics and that component attributable to reduced differentials in how those endowments translate into earnings, that is, differentials in returns to education. Intuitively, if racial differences in returns to education diminish, or if for each black returns to education rise faster than white returns, then inequality ought to decline. Ignoring the secondary impacts of education on earnings via labour force participation, the change in the log of the ratio of black to white earnings in 1976 to black to white earnings in 1985 is:

$$\partial \ln(I)/\partial Ed = \left(\pi_{76}^B - \pi_{76}^W\right) - \left(\pi_{85}^B - \pi_{76}^W\right)$$
$$= \left(\pi_{76}^B - \pi_{85}^W\right) - \left(\pi_{76}^W - \pi_{85}^W\right)$$

where π is the return to education or the derivative of $\ln(Y)$ with respect to education in the single-equation model. However, this derivative is computed for equivalent increments in education. That is why we weight the changes by the actual values of ΔX. And, simply knowing that black and white education increased is insufficient to assure that improved returns to education guarantee reduced earnings disparities.

APPENDIX

Table 4A.1   Black–white family income by age and education, 1970–91

	1970	1973	1976	1979	1982	1985	1988	1991
Whites, total	$30 889	$32 235	$30 822	$32 797	$30 574	$32 422	$34 389	$34 589
Elementary								
– high school	$23 923	$24 468	$21 978	$23 227	$20 796	$21 019	$21 630	$20 227
14–24	$17 144	$15 970	$14 055	$15 968	$13 412	$11 861	$12 691	$11 334
25–40	$24 133	$24 042	$20 688	$22 307	$19 090	$18 299	$19 098	$17 784
41 +	$24 207	$25 085	$22 752	$23 956	$21 782	$22 452	$22 980	$21 702
High-school								
graduate	$31 238	$32 281	$29 865	$31 794	$28 619	$29 552	$30 577	$30 252
14–24	$21 693	$21 712	$19 116	$22 448	$19 110	$19 054	$18 447	$17 692
25–40	$29 531	$30 126	$27 269	$29 455	$25 982	$26 995	$27 987	$27 594
41 +	$34 065	$35 680	$33 447	$34 944	$32 003	$32 633	$33 638	$33 276
Some college	$35 609	$36 209	$33 500	$35 347	$33 513	$34 211	$36 616	$36 632
14–24	$20 298	$22 037	$21 749	$24 802	$22 760	$19 711	$21 189	$20 913
25–40	$33 388	$33 560	$31 211	$32 715	$30 348	$31 823	$33 433	$33 447
41 +	$40 390	$41 734	$38 191	$39 698	$37 981	$38 029	$40 976	$40 300
College graduate								
and above	$46 728	$47 891	$45 414	$47 642	$45 169	$49 298	$51 947	$52 077
14–24	$23 829	$24 776	$23 407	$25 787	$26 786	$25 782	$27 964	$27 228
25–40	$41 929	$43 618	$40 689	$41 965	$39 690	$42 211	$47 360	$46 851
41 +	$52 177	$53 416	$51 796	$54 226	$50 696	$56 147	$56 229	$55 963
Blacks, total	$19 822	$20 762	$20 193	$21 490	$19 083	$19 778	$21 255	$21 806
Elementary								
– high school	$16 863	$17 481	$16 877	$17 100	$14 836	$14 883	$14 949	$15 240
14–24	$12 179	$9 245	$9 655	$8 232	$7 570	$5 727	$6 269	$5 612
25–40	$17 094	$16 883	$14 754	$15 291	$13 643	$10 821	$10 620	$11 429
41 +	$17 213	$18 520	$18 280	$18 616	$15 942	$17 102	$17 273	$17 536
High-school								
graduate	$22 876	$23 016	$20 646	$22 904	$19 698	$19 525	$20 849	$20 297
14–24	$18 129	$16 619	$12 991	$14 592	$12 576	$9 689	$12 296	$10 305
25–40	$22 340	$22 195	$21 208	$22 359	$18 995	$17 837	$18 395	$17 536
41 +	$25 793	$27 870	$23 324	$27 194	$22 890	$24 918	$26 244	$25 959
Some college	$26 589	$26 505	$25 452	$25 404	$23 190	$23 240	$26 302	$26 328
14–24	$22 504	$23 141	$15 387	$16 006	$17 181	$10 752	$13 835	$14 471
25–40	$26 251	$26 416	$24 838	$23 775	$21 731	$21 912	$24 785	$24 126
41 +	$28 376	$28 407	$32 055	$31 274	$28 075	$27 970	$32 956	$30 846
College graduate								
and above	$40 485	$37 261	$37 645	$39 993	$33 408	$36 607	$38 749	$41 921
14–24	$24 014	$21 798	$14 983	$29 314	$14 187	$22 145	$28 843	$23 145
25–40	$39 367	$38 766	$35 516	$38 570	$31 250	$33 531	$34 665	$37 750
41 +	$42 520	$37 529	$44 062	$42 603	$37 956	$41 102	$44 249	$46 120

continued

Table 4A.1 *continued*

	1970	1973	1976	1979	1982	1985	1988	1991
Black–white ratio	0.6417	0.6441	0.6551	0.6552	0.6242	0.6100	0.6181	0.6304
Elementary								
– high school	0.7049	0.7144	0.7679	0.7362	0.7134	0.7081	0.6912	0.7534
14–24	0.7104	0.5789	0.6869	0.5155	0.5644	0.4828	0.4940	0.4951
25–40	0.7083	0.7022	0.7132	0.6855	0.7147	0.5913	0.5561	0.6427
41 +	0.7111	0.7383	0.8034	0.7771	0.7319	0.7617	0.7516	0.8080
High-school								
graduate	0.7323	0.7130	0.6913	0.7204	0.6883	0.6607	0.6818	0.6709
14–24	0.8357	0.7654	0.6796	0.6500	0.6581	0.5085	0.6665	0.5825
25–40	0.7565	0.7367	0.7777	0.7591	0.7311	0.6608	0.6573	0.6355
41 +	0.7572	0.7811	0.6973	0.7782	0.7152	0.7636	0.7802	0.7801
Some college	0.7467	0.7320	0.7598	0.7187	0.6920	0.6793	0.7183	0.7187
14–24	1.1087	1.0501	0.7075	0.6454	0.7549	0.5455	0.6530	0.6920
25–40	0.7862	0.7871	0.7958	0.7267	0.7161	0.6886	0.7413	0.7213
41 +	0.7026	0.6807	0.8393	0.7878	0.7392	0.7355	0.8043	0.7654
College graduate								
and above	0.8664	0.7780	0.8289	0.8394	0.7396	0.7426	0.7459	0.8050
14–24	1.0078	0.8798	0.6401	1.1368	0.5296	0.8589	1.0314	0.8500
25–40	0.9389	0.8888	0.8729	0.9191	0.7874	0.7944	0.7319	0.8507
41 +	0.8149	0.7026	0.8507	0.7857	0.7487	0.7320	0.7869	0.8241

Table 4A.2 *Black–white family heads, wage and salary earnings by age and education, 1970–91*

	1970	1973	1976	1979	1982	1985	1988	1991
Whites, total	$18 843	$19 237	$17 634	$18 386	$16 239	$16 599	$17 251	$16 565
Elementary								
– high school	$12 600	$12 270	$9 730	$10 246	$8 327	$7 601	$7 841	$6 773
14–24	$13 008	$11 544	$8 877	$10 437	$8 615	$6 901	$6 181	$5 401
25–40	$17 338	$16 767	$13 518	$14 554	$11 935	$11 031	$11 030	$9 724
41 +	$11 272	$11 099	$8 840	$9 126	$7 310	$6 705	$6 964	$5 846
High-school								
graduate	$20 426	$20 341	$17 782	$18 285	$15 689	$15 423	$15 280	$14 134
14–24	$15 745	$15 316	$13 376	$15 612	$12 637	$11 407	$10 942	$9 636
25–40	$22 512	$22 197	$19 515	$20 596	$17 485	$17 376	$17 447	$16 384
41 +	$19 618	$19 916	$17 339	$17 099	$14 863	$14 457	$14 151	$12 908
Some college	$23 134	$23 135	$20 605	$21 148	$18 582	$18 197	$19 131	$18 447
14–24	$12 908	$14 159	$13 653	$15 316	$12 377	$10 628	$11 063	$10 657
25–40	$25 331	$24 356	$22 183	$22 693	$19 982	$19 842	$20 547	$20 250
41 +	$23 430	$24 171	$20 518	$20 501	$17 850	$17 234	$18 483	$17 523
College graduate								
and above	$29 944	$30 589	$28 299	$29 106	$26 187	$27 870	$28 607	$27 279
14–24	$13 367	$13 365	$12 891	$14 954	$12 095	$13 082	$13 973	$13 002
25–40	$30 797	$31 746	$28 797	$28 843	$25 926	$27 028	$29 759	$28 579
41 +	$30 351	$31 104	$29 111	$30 096	$26 944	$29 003	$28 121	$26 736

continued

Table 4A.2   continued

	1970	1973	1976	1979	1982	1985	1988	1991
Blacks, total	$11 125	$11 313	$10 637	$11 364	$9 404	$9 510	$10 427	$10 594
Elementary								
– high school	$8 858	$8 444	$7 337	$7 078	$5 696	$4 929	$4 829	$4 965
14–24	$7 992	$4 138	$4 531	$3 629	$2 717	$2 482	$1 723	$1 909
25–40	$10 906	$9 465	$8 131	$8 481	$7 310	$5 268	$5 250	$5 380
41 +	$7 992	$8 425	$7 282	$6 896	$5 347	$5 018	$4 953	$5 096
High-school								
graduate	$14 095	$13 804	$12 468	$13 822	$10 852	$10 266	$10 828	$10 520
14–24	$12 971	$10 751	$8 500	$8 704	$6 695	$6 006	$6 849	$5 246
25–40	$14 549	$14 425	$13 820	$14 828	$11 481	$10 618	$10 923	$10 612
41 +	$13 880	$14 501	$12 124	$14 247	$11 074	$10 937	$11 588	$11 556
Some college	$16 805	$15 655	$15 028	$15 900	$13 053	$13 304	$14 915	$14 441
14–24	$13 193	$13 988	$9 461	$10 779	$8 000	$5 565	$7 061	$7 886
25–40	$18 195	$16 942	$16 012	$16 420	$13 725	$13 979	$15 158	$14 266
41 +	$16 704	$14 446	$16 363	$16 521	$13 826	$13 543	$16 614	$15 340
College graduate								
and above	$22 276	$23 968	$22 158	$22 992	$17 586	$20 592	$23 047	$22 968
14–24	$10 705	$14 122	$8 163	$19 178	$5 343	$11 032	$14 090	$12 108
25–40	$24 908	$25 960	$22 097	$23 364	$18 316	$20 303	$21 213	$23 372
41 +	$20 599	$23 322	$24 531	$22 682	$17 332	$21 354	$25 763	$22 913
Black–white								
ratio	0.590405	0.588085	0.603210	0.618079	0.579100	0.572926	0.604410	0.639541
Elementary –								
high school	0.703016	0.688183	0.754060	0.690806	0.684040	0.648467	0.615852	0.733058
14–24	0.614391	0.358455	0.510420	0.347705	0.315380	0.359658	0.278822	0.353453
25–40	0.629023	0.564502	0.601494	0.582726	0.612484	0.477563	0.475998	0.553270
41 +	0.709013	0.759077	0.823756	0.755643	0.731464	0.748397	0.711219	0.871707
High-school								
graduate	0.690052	0.678629	0.701158	0.755920	0.691695	0.665629	0.708643	0.744305
14–24	0.823817	0.701946	0.635467	0.557520	0.529793	0.526519	0.625962	0.544417
25–40	0.646278	0.649863	0.708173	0.719946	0.656620	0.611073	0.626079	0.647705
41 +	0.707514	0.728108	0.699233	0.833207	0.745072	0.756519	0.818897	0.895259
Some								
college	0.726420	0.676680	0.729338	0.751844	0.702454	0.731110	0.779626	0.782837
14–24	1.022079	0.987923	0.692961	0.703774	0.646360	0.523617	0.638243	0.739983
25–40	0.718290	0.695599	0.721814	0.723571	0.686868	0.704516	0.737722	0.704494
41 +	0.712932	0.597658	0.797495	0.805863	0.774566	0.785830	0.898896	0.875421
College graduate								
and above	0.743922	0.783550	0.782996	0.789940	0.671555	0.738859	0.805639	0.841966
14–24	0.800853	1.056640	0.633232	1.282466	0.441753	0.843296	1.008410	0.931241
25–40	0.808780	0.817741	0.767337	0.810041	0.706472	0.751184	0.712810	0.817803
41 +	0.678693	0.749807	0.842671	0.753655	0.643260	0.736269	0.916145	0.857009

Table 4A.3 Black–white wage and salary earnings ratio of family heads by sex, age and education, 1970–88*

	1970		1973		1976		1979		1982		1985		1988	
	Males	Females	Males	Females	Males	Females	Males	Females	Males	Females	Males	Females	Males	Females
Less than 25 years	0.91	0.64	0.93	0.78	0.82	0.76	0.77	0.74	0.85	0.46	0.73	0.63	0.81	0.57
Elementary through high school	0.83	0.50	0.64	0.83	0.70	1.11	0.60	0.52	0.57	0.66	0.68	0.53	0.51	0.44
High-school graduate	0.97	0.96	0.96	0.81	0.92	0.69	0.75	0.78	0.88	0.46	0.76	0.69	0.99	0.51
Some college	1.12	0.59	1.11	1.19	0.81	0.58	1.04	0.84	0.96	0.44	0.52	0.88	0.65	0.83
College graduate and more	0.93	0.73	1.18	0.16	0.54	1.28	1.38	2.43	0.84	0.00	1.02	0.04	0.88	1.83
25–40 years	0.69	0.73	0.72	0.69	0.74	0.78	0.82	0.72	0.77	0.75	0.74	0.74	0.74	0.72
Elementary through high school	0.79	0.86	0.77	0.74	0.86	0.67	0.84	0.87	0.91	0.96	0.75	0.61	0.87	0.75
High-school graduate	0.74	0.81	0.78	0.87	0.83	0.93	0.87	0.88	0.84	0.78	0.76	0.80	0.77	0.78
Some college	0.75	1.45	0.83	0.70	0.79	1.09	0.93	0.77	0.82	0.81	0.83	0.90	0.83	0.86
College graduate and more	0.80	1.45	0.86	0.95	0.78	1.09	0.83	1.00	0.72	0.39	0.83	0.95	0.75	0.98
Over 40 years	0.64	0.63	0.68	0.79	0.68	0.74	0.71	0.69	0.66	0.71	0.66	0.83	0.71	0.82
Elementary through high school	0.81	0.80	0.89	0.95	0.95	1.11	0.93	0.85	0.89	0.97	0.90	1.00	0.84	1.05
High-school graduate	0.76	0.84	0.80	0.88	0.81	0.84	0.95	0.83	0.86	0.91	0.84	1.08	0.89	1.13
Some college	0.74	1.26	0.61	1.50	0.87	0.82	0.86	1.12	0.86	1.00	0.89	1.00	0.98	1.03
College graduate and more	0.67	1.29	0.77	1.37	0.83	1.80	0.81	1.22	0.69	0.95	0.78	1.18	1.04	1.03
Total	0.68	0.71	0.71	0.75	0.72	0.78	0.77	0.73	0.72	0.73	0.70	0.78	0.74	0.76

* Small number of cases available

Table 4A.4 Wage and salary income, family heads, 1970–88 (professional/managerial to all others, excluding sales and clerical)

	1970		1973		1976		1979	
	Black	White	Black	White	Black	White	Black	White
Males								
Professional/managerial	$18 602.79	$28 590.86	$22 009.00	$30 553.86	$21 823.03	$28 655.84	$24 693.34	$29 577.27
Others	$12 771.64	$15 556.16	$13 259.80	$15 607.03	$11 942.26	$13 793.27	$13 169.38	$14 540.93
Total	$13 756.45	$20 106.01	$14 674.40	$20 584.97	$13 593.51	$18 928.09	$15 182.66	$19 753.46
Females								
Professional/managerial	$14 272.08	$16 919.88	$16 794.40	$18 164.50	$16 597.09	$17 448.92	$17 219.72	$17 207.79
Others	$3 429.44	$2 958.47	$3 365.81	$3 205.40	$3 210.10	$2 797.16	$3 481.74	$3 479.90
Total	$4 485.67	$6 312.15	$5 039.39	$6 714.87	$5 248.66	$6 730.04	$5 621.29	$7 678.74

	1982		1985		1988	
	Black	White	Black	White	Black	White
Males						
Professional/managerial	$19 371.45	$29 090.30	$25 356.80	$30 846.54	$27 803.25	$31 694.93
Others	$11 328.84	$12 388.50	$9 985.94	$12 163.61	$11 014.08	$12 392.19
Total	$12 965.95	$17 901.03	$12 896.35	$18 383.83	$14 016.14	$18 995.851
Females						
Professional/managerial	$15 310.44	$15 736.23	$16 299.13	$16 614.90	$17 944.84	$20 086.17
Others	$3 146.20	$3 053.90	$3 366.35	$3 080.29	$3 720.83	$3 346.65
Total	$5 279.35	$7 235.83	$6 058.50	$7 759.61	$6 771.16	$8 922.65

5. Family structure, labour force participation and earnings inequality

The most obvious, but largely untested, explanation for this increased racial earnings inequality among family heads is the fact that black families are increasingly headed by females. This chapter presents results showing that this explanation, taken alone, also is far from satisfactory.

The percentage of African American families headed by females climbed from 20 to 25 per cent in the 1950s to more than 40 per cent in the 1980s (Darity and Myers, 1984, pp. 765–80). By the 1990s, slightly less than half of all black families were headed by females. The period from the 1970s to 1980s, during which racial earnings gaps among family heads widened, was a period of unprecedented increase in the proportion of black families headed by females. From the mid-1970s until the mid-1980s, the proportion of black families headed by females soared (see Ellwood and Crane, 1990, pp. 65–84). In 1976, 36 per cent of black families were headed by females. By 1985, 45 per cent were headed by females. It is tempting to blame deterioration in the earnings of black family heads on this trend, since females have lower labour force participation rates than males and lower labour force participation yields lower earnings.

But how much of the drop in blacks' relative earnings can be attributed to the dramatic shift in family structure? What other policy-relevant factors might explain this loss in earnings, even accounting for the devastating decrease in two-parent families among African Americans? To answer these questions, we first must recognize that earnings are generally lower for persons who work less – either because of working fewer hours or because of working only part of the year. Female family heads generally work less than male family heads. Thus we must disentangle the work effort and the family structure effects on earnings in order to assess the relative importance of increasing female headship on the widening of racial earnings gaps.

How is the shift in family structure related to changes in earnings inequality? Superficially, the answer is that female-headed families have lower incomes on average than male-headed families.[1] Females earn lower wages and salaries, on average, than males. Thus one potential explanation for the decline in the relative incomes of black families is the phenomenal increase in recent decades in the percentage of black families headed by females.

This rise is also evident among whites, but not as marked an increase. In 1970, nine per cent of white families were headed by females with no spouse present. By 1991, the figure was 13 per cent. Among black families in 1970, 28 per cent were headed by females, and in 1991 it was 46 per cent.

This superficial explanation ignores the fact that there were wide variations in the changes in family structure within various cohorts. The increase in female-headed families over time, as well as the numbers of these families in a given year, varies with respect to the educational level of the family head, the age of the family head, and the earnings history of the family head. In most cases within age, education and earnings histories the percentage of families headed by females differs markedly by race. Even within specific age and educational categories, black families are substantially more likely to be headed by females than are white families.

EVIDENCE ON CHANGING FAMILY STRUCTURES

Tables 5.1 and 5.2 detail the percentages of black and white families headed by females at four levels of educational completion: elementary school through some high school, high-school graduation, some college, college graduation or above. Within each educational grouping, the tables break down the percentage of families headed by females by three age groups: aged 14–24, aged 25–40, and aged 41 and above. Finally, within each age grouping the tables present the fraction of families headed by females by their earnings histories for the previous year. There are the positive earners – those with some wage and salary incomes during the previous 12 months; and there are the non-earners – those without positive wage and salary incomes in the previous year.

Within races, three main patterns are found:

1. Differences in family structures narrowed between the highly educated and less well educated between 1970 and 1991.
2. Although families with young, less well educated heads were more likely to be female-headed, there was a noticeable growth between 1970 and 1991 in female headship, even among the young but better educated.
3. Families with earners as heads were less likely to be headed by females than were families with non-earners as heads. Yet these differences narrowed between 1970 and 1991.

These within-race changes suggest that increasing female family headship might be a weak candidate for explaining the decline in relative earnings of black family heads. This is due to a pattern of changing family structure which was occurring among *both* blacks and whites and even among better-educated blacks and whites.

Table 5.1 White families headed by females by age, race and education (%), 1970–91

	1970	1973	1976	1979	1982	1985	1988	1991
Total	9	10	11	11	12	13	13	13
Elementary – high school	11	12	13	14	15	16	16	18
14–24	14	17	21	24	25	27	37	40
Non-earner	72	72	70	77	70	61	66	72
Positive earner	8	8	10	15	14	14	25	26
25–40	10	13	18	18	20	21	20	23
Non-earner	34	43	47	42	47	48	46	48
Positive earner	6	8	11	13	13	14	12	15
41 +	11	11	12	12	13	14	14	14
Non-earner	18	16	16	15	16	16	16	16
Positive earner	7	7	7	9	10	11	11	12
High school graduate	10	11	12	13	14	14	14	15
14–24	9	9	12	11	13	16	19	23
Non-earner	42	42	62	38	29	47	50	59
Positive earner	7	8	9	10	11	12	15	18
25–40	7	10	13	13	16	15	16	16
Non-earner	19	23	29	24	27	23	27	27
Positive earner	6	9	11	12	14	14	15	15
41 +	11	11	11	12	13	13	13	13
Non-earner	17	17	14	13	13	13	13	12
Positive earner	10	9	10	12	13	13	12	13
Some college	7	8	9	11	12	12	13	13
14–24	6	4	8	7	15	13	18	20
Non-earner	21	15	12	23	30	42	37	50
Positive earner	5	4	8	6	13	10	16	17
25–40	5	7	9	11	13	13	15	14
Non-earner	17	12	14	21	16	17	25	22
Positive earner	5	7	9	10	13	12	13	13
41 +	8	9	9	10	11	12	12	11
Non-earner	16	14	12	11	11	12	9	10
Positive earner	6	7	8	10	10	13	13	12
College graduate and above	4	4	5	5	6	7	7	7
14–24	3	1	3	6	6	8	10	7
Non-earner	8	6	5	0	13	0	13	0
Positive earner	2	1	3	6	5	8	10	7
25–40	2	3	4	4	6	6	6	7
Non-earner	6	4	7	5	9	7	8	7
Positive earner	2	3	4	4	6	6	6	7
41 +	6	6	6	6	7	7	7	7
Non-earner	8	8	8	8	7	7	6	7
Positive earner	5	5	5	5	6	7	7	7

Source: Authors' computations from *Current Population Survey*, March Supplement Tapes, 1970–91.

Persistent disparity

*Table 5.2   Black families headed by females by age, race and
education (%), 1970–91*

	1970	1973	1976	1979	1982	1985	1988	1991
Total	28	35	35	40	41	44	43	46
Elementary – high school	30	36	36	43	43	46	48	50
14–24	39	63	54	67	72	69	74	86
Non-earner	88	98	92	90	84	95	83	96
Positive earner	24	39	26	47	58	39	57	71
24–40	35	44	48	56	54	59	67	67
Non-earner	86	83	88	90	83	83	90	88
Positive earner	26	29	31	42	37	41	48	54
41 +	27	30	30	36	36	39	39	40
Non-earner	41	45	39	46	42	45	43	43
Positive earner	20	21	21	26	29	31	33	35
High school graduate	28	35	40	39	42	46	43	48
14–24	32	43	53	52	49	62	57	65
Non-earner	100	98	91	91	86	88	91	91
Positive earner	26	30	41	44	33	52	42	57
25–40	29	38	39	41	45	50	46	52
Non-earner	71	75	77	81	77	74	73	83
Positive earner	24	30	33	34	37	44	39	44
41 +	24	26	34	31	35	36	36	39
Non-earner	40	45	48	47	40	41	41	46
Positive earner	21	21	28	26	33	34	33	36
Some college	22	33	30	41	37	43	37	44
14–24	17	24	30	51	47	69	46	74
Non-earner	100	100	39	100	87	80	63	100
Positive earner	11	20	29	45	32	68	42	71
25–40	26	33	35	44	39	43	39	45
Non-earner	36	59	57	94	61	72	55	69
Positive earner	26	30	33	38	35	38	37	42
41 +	19	37	22	32	31	38	32	41
Non-earner	41	30	38	39	36	48	30	43
Positive earner	14	39	18	30	29	35	32	40
College graduate and above	8	20	20	20	26	25	31	28
14–24	31	12	58	31	36	4	0	23
Non-earner	0	0	61	0	71	0	0	0
positive earner	31	12	57	31	0	5	0	23
25–40	3	17	17	13	28	24	30	27
Non-earner	0	0	14	29	31	44	38	27
Positive earner	3	18	18	11	28	22	29	26
41 +	12	24	17	30	22	28	34	30
Non-earner	8	24	10	30	21	29	38	44
Positive earner	13	24	18	29	23	28	33	27

Source: Authors' computations from *Current Population Survey*, March Supplement Tapes,
1970–91.

The between-race changes in percentages of female-headed families show that changing family structure is not even a weak candidate for explaining the decline in relative earnings of blacks and the widening earnings gap between black and white families. The following conclusions emerge:

1. There was only a slight increase in the ratio of the percentage of black families headed by females to the percentage of white families headed by females from 1970 to 1991.
2. The gaps in family structure were largest among the better educated.
3. There was a narrowing of the gap in family structure between young less well educated blacks and whites.
4. Much of the widening of the gap in family structure occurred among non-earners who were older college graduates. The percentage of black families headed by females relative to the percentage of white families headed by females among persons over 41 years without wage and salary earnings rose from 1:1 in 1970 to 6:1 in 1991.

Therefore, if an increase in black female-headed families is to 'explain' the widening gaps in earnings, the explanation must lie in a selection bias argument. The highest potential earners must have withdrawn from the labour market, leading to reductions in the earnings of remaining family heads.

Below we summarize the findings that cast doubt on the family structure explanation for the widening of racial earnings gaps.

Widening Gaps Among Better Educated Family Heads

Within each racial group female-headed families were more prevalent among the less educated. Among white families whose family heads had not completed high school, between 11 per cent and 18 per cent were female-headed over the 20-year period. Among black families whose family heads had not completed high school, 30 to 50 per cent were female-headed. White families with better educated family heads were less likely to be female-headed. In 1970 only 4 per cent of white families with family heads who were college graduates were headed by females. By 1991, this rose to 7 per cent, still well below that of high-school drop-outs.

The fraction of black families headed by better-educated females was also lower than that headed by black high-school drop-outs. But by 1991 the percentage gap between the black better educated and black less well educated was conspicuously narrower than the gap between the white better educated and the white less well educated. In 1970, among black families whose family heads were college graduates, only 8 per cent were headed by females. This was 27 per cent of the rate of black family heads who had not completed high school. Compare this with the smaller gap among whites that year: 4 per cent of families headed by females among better-educated whites was 36 per cent of the white families headed by females among less well-educated whites in 1970.

By 1991 this relative advantage of black better-educated family heads had disappeared. Among those black families whose family heads had college degrees, 28 per cent were headed by females. This was 56 per cent of the proportion of families headed by females among less well-educated black family heads. The increase in the ratio of the percentage of black families headed by females among the better educated and the less well educated signals the narrowing in the gap between the two. By 1991, the differential had narrowed between white better-educated and less well-educated families as well. The proportion of white families headed by females among those with college degrees rose to only 39 per cent of the proportion of white families headed by females among those who had not finished high school. This was not much different from the ratio in 1970.

Figures 5.1 and 5.2 reveal these trends. While white and black female headship is more prevalent among young high-school drop-outs than young college graduates, at least among whites the trend towards greater female-headed families among younger family heads is evident at every education level. Across all age groups and for blacks and whites, moreover, there was a narrowing in the disparity in female headship between college-educated heads and those with less than high-school degrees.

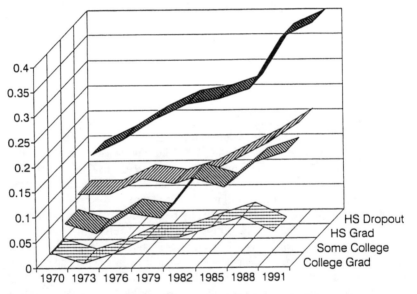

Source: Authors' computations from *Current Population Survey*, March Supplement Tapes. (Same source for Figs 5.2–5.9)

Figure 5.1   Female family headship, 1970–91, white families with heads aged 14–24

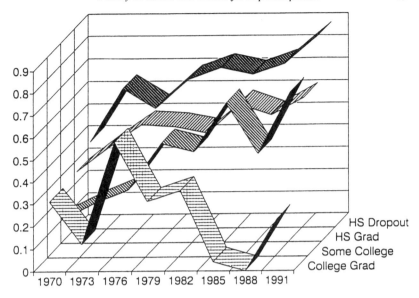

Figure 5.2   Female family headship, 1970–91 black families with heads aged 14–24

Figure 5.3 computes the ratio of the percentage of families headed by females among college graduates and high-school drop-outs separately for blacks and whites. While it is clear that families headed by high-school drop-outs are more likely to have female heads than are families headed by college graduates, it is also clear that the differences between these groups narrowed between 1970 and 1991. The convergence was most pronounced among blacks.

Changing Gaps Between Earners and Non-earners

Part of the reason why changing family structure may not be a transparent explanation for the widening of ratios is that earners within different age–education cohorts experienced widely varying changes in family structure between blacks and whites. Figure 5.4 shows that among 25- to 40-year-old white family heads, the female headship rate among college-educated earners converged with that of non-earners, while it remained flat among high-school drop-outs. That is to say, among the best-educated white family heads, female headship increased more rapidly for those with earnings than it did for those without earnings, while among the less educated the growth of female headship for earners was about the same as for the non-earners.

However, Figure 5.5 shows that among 25- to 40-year-old black family heads, the female headship rate among college-educated earners dropped

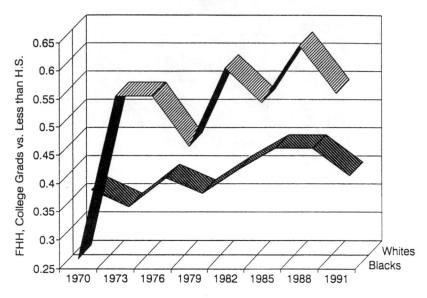

Figure 5.3   Female family headship, 1970–91, college graduates vs high-school drop-outs

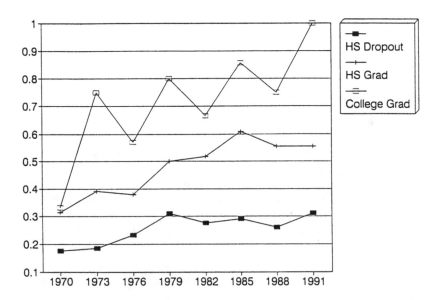

Figure 5.4   White female family headship, 1970–91, earners vs non-earners, aged 25–40, by education

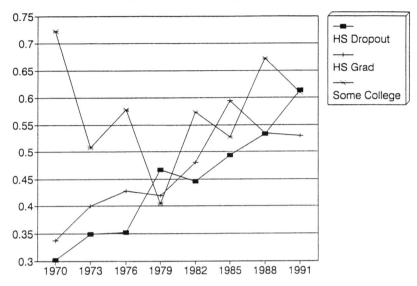

Figure 5.5   Black female family headship, 1970–91, earners vs non-earners, aged 25–40, by education

relative to that of non-earners in the 1970s and rose again in the 1980s, while it rose steadily throughout the entire 20-year period among high-school drop-outs. Therefore it is apparent that there are racial differences in the evolving patterns of family headship between earners and non-earners in different education groups. The net impact among educated whites, 25 to 40 years of age, is that the earner–non-earner disparity vanishes by the 1990s; among less educated whites, the disparity is nearly as large in the 1990s as it was in the 1970s. In contrast, among blacks the net effect in this age group is that, since the 1970s, whatever convergence was taking place between the family structures of those with earnings and those without earnings, it has become uniform across education groups.

On balance, the effect of these changes across different age groups, education levels and different earnings statuses is to leave the ratio of female family headship rates between blacks and whites not much larger in 1991 than it was in 1970. Figure 5.6 shows that the increases during the 1970s largely plateaued in the 1980s. Of course, the fraction of black families headed by females is about four times that of white families, but the changes over the years do not seem sufficient to explain the deterioration in the relative earnings position of black families.

As Figures 5.7 and 5.8 reveal, the relative differences in family structures between blacks and whites are more pronounced among better educated than

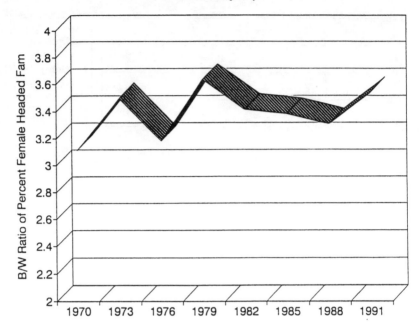

Figure 5.6   Black–white ratio of percentage of female-headed families, 1970–91

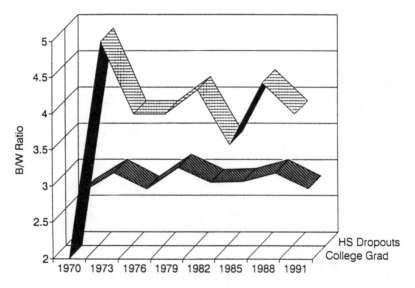

*Figure 5.7   Black–white ratio of percentage of female-headed families,
1970–91, high-school drop-outs vs college graduates*

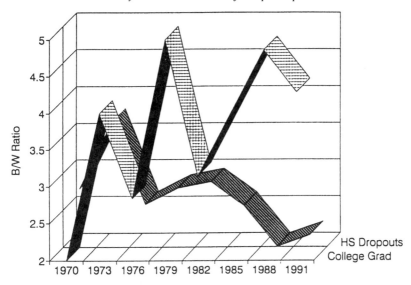

Figure 5.8   Black–white ratio of percentage of female-headed families, 1970–91, young high-school drop-outs vs older college graduates

less-educated heads. Figure 5.7 plots the ratio of black–white female headship rates for college graduates and high-school drop-outs. That ratio is nearly constant for high-school drop-outs, while it declines in the late 1970s and early 1980s among college graduates.

Figure 5.8 focuses on young (14- to-24 year-old) high-school drop-outs versus older (41 years and older) college graduates. It shows, again, that the surge in black female headship relative to white female headship occurred among *better-educated* and older heads. Moreover, even among older non-earners there was a much more pronounced increase in female headship among blacks than among whites who had college degrees in comparison to those who were high-school drop-outs, as Figure 5.9 reveals. These startling findings cast doubt on the contention that the cause of the widening gap in family earnings was the increase in female headship among blacks.

Young, Uneducated Family Heads

The persistent pattern of relatively lower rates of female headship among families whose heads had positive earnings is evident among both whites and blacks, even those aged 14 to 24 who had not completed high school. In 1970, 8 per cent of white family heads among earners were women, while 72 per cent of non-earners were women. In 1979, 15 per cent of white earners were women

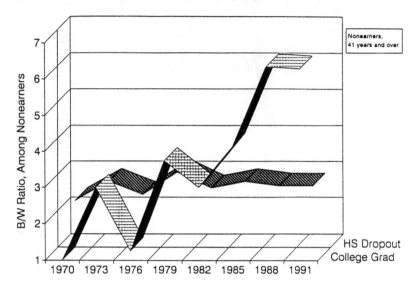

*Figure 5.9   Black–white ratio of percentage of female-headed families,
1970–91, older high-school drop-outs vs college graduates*

while 77 per cent of non-earners were women. In 1988, 25 per cent of white
earners were women; among non-earners, the proportion was 66 per cent. And
by 1991, 26 per cent of young, white uneducated family heads who were
earners were female; 72 per cent of young, white, uneducated non-earner
family heads were female. Thus, among white families with young, uneducated
family heads, the gap between female heads with earnings and female heads
without earnings narrowed principally because of the growth in female-headed
families among the earners.

A still more dramatic example of such growth is evident among black
families. In 1970, 24 per cent of black family heads 14 to 24 years of age with
positive earnings, who had not finished high school, were females. In that
same category of race, education and age, but without positive wage and salary
earnings, 88 per cent of the families were headed by women. In 1979, the
respective percentages were 47 and 90. By 1988, the respective percentages were
57 and 83, and by 1991, they were 71 and 96. In short, by the start of the 1990s,
the vast majority of black families with young, uneducated family heads were
headed by women, with little difference in the incidence of female headship
whether the family head worked outside the house or not.

Although most young, uneducated family heads – whether white or black –
who had no wage and family earnings were females, these facts alone do not
point to an obvious cause. If, for example, declining labour force participation

rates or the incentives of welfare were at the root of the growth of the percentage of female-headed families among young uneducated families, then one would expect to observe a continuing gap in female family headship between those families with heads who worked outside the house and those with heads that did not. At least among young, uneducated black family heads such evidence is not extant. And, even among whites, there was a phenomenal growth in the rate of female headship in this age–education group of wage earners.

In summary, the evidence on rising female headship among blacks versus whites does not provide the simple and straightforward explanation for the widening racial gaps in earnings. Although less well-educated black family heads are more likely to be female, this is also the case among white families. Moreover, there has been considerable narrowing of the differences in family structure between black better-educated and less-educated families. These patterns may arise because of a selection process – albeit an unusual one – where the better-educated black female family heads are withdrawing from the market. If that selection process is what is driving the wedge between black and white family earnings, then the causal link becomes labour force withdrawal and not family structure *per se*. We need, then, to look more carefully at the labour force behaviour of black and white family heads.

DECLINING LABOUR FORCE PARTICIPATION RATES

Examining the two-decade span of years from 1970 to 1991 requires consideration of the pattern of declining labour force participation rates (LFPR) from the mid-1970s to the mid-1980s in its proper context. Among all family heads these rates dropped and reached a low, but since then LFPRs either have levelled off or risen slightly. Still, the overall trend for the 20-year period is one of decline, although the worst of the reductions seems to be over.

In particular, the labour force participation rates of black family heads have rebounded during the post-Reagan years. From a low of 62 per cent in 1985, the rates rose to 65 per cent by 1991. Still, even the 1991 rate falls far below the highs of the early 1970s. White labour force participation rates among family heads were stable throughout most of the 1980s, hovering around 74 and 75 per cent.

This aggregate pattern of seemingly improved labour force participation rates among black family heads after the mid-1980s obscures the more ominous trend alluded to above: a wider spread between haves and have nots, the young and the old, and the educated and the uneducated. The labour force participation rates of black and white young family heads without high-school degrees declined steadily from 1970 to 1991. Among blacks this rate dropped sharply from 63 per cent in 1970 to 49 per cent in 1982 to 42 per cent in 1991. Among whites the rate also dropped sharply from 70 per cent in 1970 to 56 per cent in 1982 to 52 per cent in 1991. Thus, among both black and white young family heads with little education, labour force participation underwent a precipitous decline over the past two decades.

In contrast, the labour force participation rates of better educated, mature family heads while already high for both blacks and whites, declined slightly and, at least for blacks, rebounded in the last years of the 1980s. Thus for black family heads aged 41 and above, with college degrees, labour force participation rates of 85 per cent in 1970 were only slightly lower at 83 per cent in 1991. Among comparably aged and educated whites, the labour force participation rate of 85 per cent in 1970 fell non-trivially to 79 per cent in 1991.

Tables 5.3 and 5.4 detail these results for all age and education cohorts. The tables also break down labour force participation rates by male and female heads of families within age education cohorts for those who had positive wage and salary incomes.[2] What is clear from these numbers is that black female heads of families who worked, whether uneducated and young or older with college degrees, had substantially higher labour force participation rates in 1991 than they had in 1970.

Young, uneducated black female heads of families with positive wage and salary incomes had labour force participation rates of 42 per cent in 1970. By 1991 their labour force participation rate was 62 per cent. Older, educated black female heads of families with positive wage and salary incomes had a labour force participation rate of 82 per cent in 1970 and a rate of 97 per cent in 1991. White females with positive earnings concluded 1991 with LFPRs of about 92 per cent – little different from that for young uneducated and older educated female family heads. In 1970, the rate was at a low of 57 per cent for young, uneducated white female family heads and at a stable 90 per cent among educated, older female heads of families. Among white female heads of families with earnings, labour force participation rates converged.

Patterns of labour force participation changed in substantially different ways for blacks and whites. Moreover, at least for blacks, there were substantive alterations in labour force attachment between the haves and the have nots. As Figure 5.10 reveals, the ratio of the labour force participation rates of young uneducated family heads to those of older educated heads declined sharply among blacks. This ratio, equal to about 0.70 in 1970, plummeted below 0.30 in 1991. Among whites, the ratio dipped from 0.95 in 1970 to 0.76 in 1991.

Although the labour force participation rate of young, uneducated family heads relative to older, educated family heads fell for both whites and blacks, the decline was most dramatic among blacks. By 1991, older, educated black family heads had labour force participation rates more than three times that of young, uneducated black family heads. Plainly the gap widened between black haves and have nots.

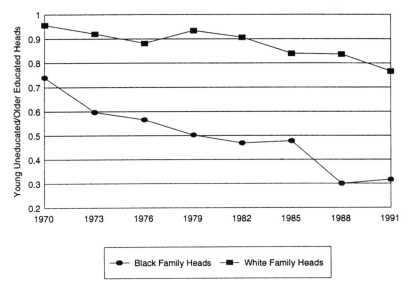

Source: Authors' computations from *Current Population Survey*, March Supplement Tapes, 1971–91.

Figure 5.10   Young educated/older educated labour force participation, 1970–91, blacks vs whites

Not surprisingly, then, the labour force participation rates of young, uneducated black heads of families declined relative to those of young, uneducated white heads of families, while the labour force participation rates of older, educated black heads of families rose relative to those of older, educated white heads of families. Figure 5.11 reveals this pattern. The black–white ratio of labour force participation rates among heads of families, 14 to 24 years of age and without high-school degrees, plunged from 0.77 in 1970 to 0.44 in 1991. Among those over 41 years of age with college degrees it inched up from 0.99 in 1970 to 1.06 in 1991.

These findings about the widening gap in labour force participation between the black have nots and haves as well as between the black have nots and the white have nots point up two forceful conclusions. The first is that race alone is not sufficient to determine the changing labour force status of family heads over the years. Both age and education play prominent roles. The second, however, is that race cannot be ignored. Blacks at the bottom and whites at the bottom are far from identical in their labour force experiences. Moreover, a much greater proportion of blacks than whites are at the bottom.

Table 5.3 Labour force participation of family heads, 1970–91*

	1970		1973		1976		1979		1982		1985		1988		1991	
	Blacks	Whites	Blacks	Whites	Blacks	Whites	Blacks	Whites	Blacks	Whites	Blacks	Whites	Blacks	Whites	Blacks	Whites
Entire population	0.7290	0.8035	0.8774	0.7917	0.8578	0.7701	0.8519	0.7671	0.6303	0.7492	0.6195	0.7374	0.6215	0.7355	0.6522	0.7451
Elementary–high	0.6743	0.7003	0.6061	0.6685	0.5584	0.6056	0.5258	0.5920	0.4941	0.5617	0.4365	0.5240	0.4222	0.5254	0.4207	0.5179
14–24	0.6266	0.8155	0.4753	0.7933	0.4929	0.7240	0.4000	0.7787	0.3692	0.7284	0.3681	0.6750	0.2418	0.6532	0.2631	0.6011
Male	0.9473	0.9103	0.9281	0.9169	0.8736	0.8866	0.9355	0.9209	1.0000	0.9331	0.9209	0.9499	0.9631	0.9357	0.9474	0.9559
Female	0.4191	0.5695	0.5726	0.5841	0.7308	0.6400	0.6273	0.7093	0.7425	0.6586	0.6133	0.6864	0.6323	0.7493	0.6238	0.9176
25–40	0.7678	0.8903	0.6683	0.8584	0.6470	0.8271	0.6454	0.8348	0.6048	0.8008	0.5025	0.7887	0.4863	0.7785	2.5367	0.7717
Male	0.9383	0.9510	0.9496	0.9477	0.9857	0.9692	0.9598	0.9578	0.9798	0.9652	0.9325	0.9663	0.9580	0.9847	0.9316	0.9702
Female	0.7513	0.7331	0.7451	0.1555	0.7862	0.7999	0.8161	0.7958	0.8716	0.8483	0.8003	0.8457	0.7875	0.8292	0.8072	0.8485
															0.6931	0.7821
41 +	0.6357	0.6422	0.5933	0.6071	0.5312	0.5439	0.4942	0.5170	0.4631	0.4841	0.4186	0.4396	0.4152	0.4392	0.3931	0.4240
Male	0.9040	0.9103	0.9217	0.9041	0.9288	0.9228	0.9115	0.9185	0.9314	0.9186	0.9430	0.9178	0.9122	0.9116	0.9495	0.9233
Female	0.7837	0.8189	0.8472	0.8383	0.8583	0.8781	0.8663	0.8866	0.8914	0.8815	0.8888	0.8994	0.9009	0.8528	0.8862	0.9158
High-school graduate	0.8227	0.8761	0.7570	0.8612	0.7335	0.8246	0.7596	0.8176	0.7032	0.7933	0.7087	0.7755	0.8946	0.7599	0.7203	0.7659
14–24	0.8125	0.8418	0.6826	0.8643	0.5720	0.8110	0.6658	0.8430	0.5714	0.8673	0.5657	0.8055	0.4978	0.7733	0.6141	0.8410
Male	0.9129	0.8679	0.9335	0.9043	0.7185	0.8526	0.7896	0.8814	0.8335	0.9112	0.7174	0.8782	0.5761	0.8413	0.9836	0.9793
Female	0.8072	0.7474	0.8795	0.8758	0.8065	0.7783	0.8305	0.7855	0.7952	0.8461	0.8089	0.8391	0.7902	0.8102	0.8961	0.7821
25–40	0.8392	0.9378	0.7820	0.9295	0.7932	0.9043	0.7929	0.9090	0.7465	0.9000	0.7458	0.8967	0.7340	0.8981	0.7603	0.9106
Male	0.9359	0.9647	0.9412	0.9667	0.9160	0.9437	0.9300	0.9461	0.9359	0.9494	0.9157	0.9558	0.9145	0.9573	0.9746	0.9780
Female	0.8533	0.8177	0.8155	0.8438	0.8820	0.8917	0.8861	0.8965	0.9210	0.8994	0.9241	0.9160	0.8883	0.9027	0.8993	0.9043
41 +	0.8014	0.8352	0.7582	0.8123	0.7119	0.7725	0.7430	0.7494	0.6734	0.7045	0.6927	0.9820	0.6830	0.6593	0.8931	0.8551
Male	0.9320	0.9524	0.9232	0.9455	0.9515	0.9519	0.9729	0.9580	0.9579	0.9522	0.9378	0.9528	0.9612	0.9437	0.9668	0.9505
Female	0.8800	0.8796	0.9218	0.8946	0.9780	0.9094	0.8997	0.9117	0.9176	0.9216	0.9520	0.9132	0.9420	0.9332	0.9186	0.9251

Some college	0.8564	0.8650	0.8229	0.8593	0.8000	0.8544	0.7830	0.8443	0.7682	0.8242	0.7800	0.8132	0.7798	0.8080	0.8130	0.8158
14–24	0.8214	0.7794	0.8327	0.8320	0.8981	0.8596	0.7884	0.8747	0.5559	0.8277	0.7214	0.8115	0.6410	0.8042	0.7274	0.8474
Male	0.8890	0.8131	0.8858	0.8592	0.8159	0.8832	0.9377	0.9106	0.8058	0.9009	0.6031	0.8834	0.7372	0.8516	0.8823	0.9497
Female	0.9324	0.7318	0.8389	0.7378	0.7390	0.8583	0.8101	0.7736	0.7059	0.8327	0.9011	0.7703	0.8120	0.8576	0.7993	0.8090
25–40	0.9235	0.9345	0.8456	0.9173	0.8395	0.9204	0.7945	0.9187	0.8258	0.9101	0.8089	0.9101	0.8063	0.8964	0.8534	0.9239
Male	0.9687	0.9587	0.9563	0.9462	0.9271	0.9429	0.8960	0.9499	0.9380	0.9462	0.9196	0.9543	0.8720	0.9402	0.9773	0.9834
Female	0.9269	0.8029	0.8534	0.8328	0.9472	0.9045	0.8904	0.8770	0.9113	0.9075	0.9645	0.9259	0.9112	0.9207	0.9185	0.8994
41 +	0.8069	0.8273	0.7810	0.8163	0.7868	0.7890	0.7604	0.7659	0.7490	0.7355	0.7391	0.7145	0.7597	0.7242	0.7592	0.7260
Male	0.9557	0.9528	0.9479	0.9432	0.9545	0.9582	0.9638	0.9639	0.9703	0.9593	0.9487	0.9498	0.9645	0.9522	0.9392	0.9587
Female	0.9608	0.8447	0.8902	0.9073	0.9741	0.9464	0.9704	0.9197	0.9736	0.9171	0.9263	0.9230	0.9590	0.9259	0.9449	0.9174
College graduate and more	0.8744	0.8835	0.8396	0.8849	0.8868	0.8765	0.8295	0.8841	0.8320	0.8655	0.8250	0.8603	0.8500	0.8508	0.8695	0.8507
14–24	0.6185	0.6982	0.7833	0.7729	0.6059	0.7930	0.7490	0.8257	0.4514	0.7483	0.3655	0.7550	0.9180	0.8178	0.9819	0.8823
Male	0.7536	0.8089			0.7435	0.8453		0.8284	0.9141	0.7706	0.5659	0.7726	0.8856	0.8718	0.9764	0.9276
Female	0.5796		0.9381	0.9808	1.0000	0.6530		0.7564		0.3077	0.7599	0.8527	1.0000	0.7968	1.0000	0.8582
25–40	0.9219	0.9366	0.9007	0.7870	0.8976	0.9408	0.8545	0.9398	0.8794	0.9399	0.8830	0.9285	0.8810	0.9410	0.9099	0.9514
Male	0.9349	0.9471	0.9437	0.9022	0.9507	0.9523	0.9443	0.9477	0.9805	0.9599	0.9310	0.9536	0.9160	0.9802	0.9890	0.9845
Female	0.9572	0.8240	0.7536	0.8504	0.9614	0.9398	0.9832	0.9028	0.9332	0.9375	0.9387	0.8976	0.9529	0.9293	0.9436	0.9205
41 +	0.8472	0.8524	0.7966	0.8621	0.8706	0.8217	0.7966	0.8339	0.7872	0.8040	0.7705	0.8032	0.8067	0.7807	0.8308	0.7850
Male	0.9487	0.9521	0.9251	0.9052	0.9582	0.9556	0.9481	0.9620	0.9833	0.9575	0.9318	0.9626	0.9540	0.9503	0.9537	0.9579
Female	0.8195	0.9020	0.8894	0.9003	0.9627	0.9003	0.9041	0.9260	0.9484	0.9215	0.8892	0.9292	0.9686	0.9361	0.9734	0.9180

Source: Authors' computations from *Current Population Survey*, March Supplement Tapes, 1971–91.

* Positive earners only.

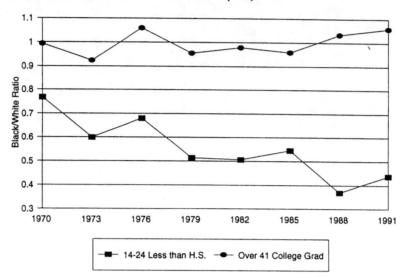

Figure 5.11 Black/white ratio of labour force participation, 1970–91, young uneducated vs older educated heads

A MODEL OF RACIAL EARNINGS INEQUALITY AND FAMILY STRUCTURE

In order to gauge the effects of family structure and labour force participation on earnings inequality, we have developed and estimated a formal model of the linkages, using data for two years: 1976 and 1985. By comparing the mid-1970s' experience to the mid-1980s' experience, we are able to answer many of the questions concerning the causes of the widening racial gap in earnings of family heads.

The details of the specification and estimation of this model are presented in the appendix to this chapter. The main contours of the model, however, are sketched in Figure 5.12. There we see that earnings of family heads depend on a) the work effort (labour force participation during the year) of the family head, b) family structure (the percentage of families headed by females), and c) individual 'endowments', including 'human capital'. Family structure and work effort depend on the attractiveness of alternative income sources, measured here by expected welfare benefits. Family structure also depends on the availability of marriageable males, measured here by the expected ratio of unmarried males in the labour force or in school to unmarried females.

The model permits the assessment of the relative impact of family structure and labour force participation on widening earnings gaps.

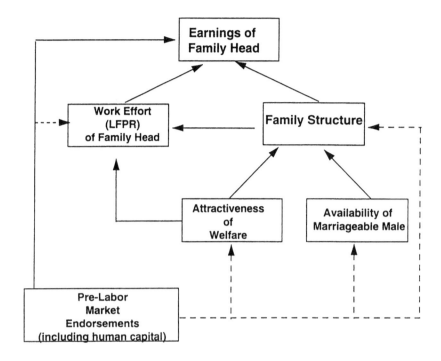

Figure 5.12   Model of racial earnings and family structure

THE EFFECTS OF FAMILY STRUCTURE AND LABOUR FORCE PARTICIPATION ON EARNINGS INEQUALITY

Figure 5.13 shows the results of computing the impact on black and white labour force participation of welfare and family structure in 1976 and 1985. The impact is measured as an elasticity or the percentage change in labour force participation as a result of a 1 per cent change in welfare or female-headed families. When this measure is greater than one, the impact is termed elastic; when it is less than one, the impact is inelastic.

The attractiveness of welfare is measured by the expected annual income from public assistance, estimated by finding the product of the probability of welfare receipt and the average amount received for those who obtained public assistance income. The underlying equations for these estimates are reported elsewhere (Darity and Myers, 1995). Family structure is measured by whether or not the head is female. A formal model linking family structure to a host of factors, including the attractiveness of welfare and the availability of marriage partners,

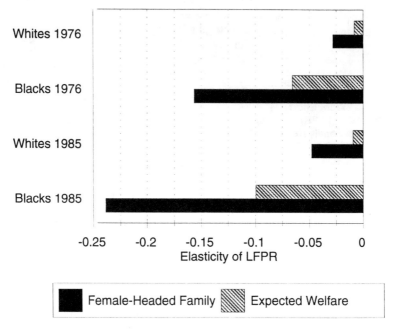

Source: Authors' computations from Table 5A.4. Elasticity of labour force participation rates with respect to a) expected welfare benefits and b) percent families headed by females. Y-axis demonstrates the percent change in LFPR due to a 1% increase in expected welfare/fhh.

Figure 5.13 Effects of family structure and welfare on labour force participation, 1976–85

was estimated in earlier work. The key point to remember here is that welfare can influence labour force participation through two routes: directly via possible work disincentives, and indirectly via possible marriage disincentives.

Figure 5.13 reports the net effects of welfare on labour force participation and the direct effects of increasing percentages of families headed by females. For blacks and whites, in 1976 and 1985, increased attractiveness of welfare was found to lower labour force participation. Also in 1976 and 1985, increased female family headship was found to lower labour force participation for both groups.

Moreover, welfare and female family headship lower labour force participation more for blacks than for whites in both 1985 and in 1976. Therefore the evidence suggests that family structure and the attractiveness of welfare have bigger negative impacts on blacks than on whites, pointing to a possible explanation for the widening earnings gap.

However, a closer look at Figure 5.13 reveals that the net impact on labour force participation is exceptionally small. A 1 per cent increase in female-headed families reduces labour force participation of black family heads by about 0.16 of 1 per cent in 1976 and about 0.24 of 1 per cent in 1985. Among whites the elasticities are –0.03 and –0.05. Thus, even though the effects are greater for blacks than whites, and the effect grew (in absolute value) between 1976 and 1985, the effects none the less are extraordinarily small.

Whether the small impact of changing family structure on labour force participation results in a widening of earnings inequality depends, of course, on whether changing labour force participation contributes to a widening or a narrowing of earnings inequality. In the appendix we show that uniform increases in labour force participation had the effect of reducing black–white earnings inequality between 1976 and 1985. Since labour force participation declined for both blacks and whites between 1976 and 1985, this suggests that these changes indeed contributed to increased racial disparity in earnings of family heads.

Thus, working its way through the effects of labour force participation on earnings, the family structure impact certainly could be a contributing factor in increased earnings inequality. The size of the actual impact is an empirical matter. Before examining this effect, it is useful to display in Figure 5.14 the percentage impact on earnings of a uniform increase in female-headed families. The startling finding is that this effect is larger for whites than for blacks, and the effect declined for both blacks and whites between 1976 and 1985.

In Figure 5.15 we have computed the net effects of changes in family structure on earnings inequality and evaluated these effects under a variety of scenarios.

Uniform Changes in Female-Headed Families

The first scenario is one where there is a uniform increase in female-headed families. The results in the appendix show that a) increased female headship lowers labour force participation and b) lower labour force participation lowers earnings. However, the negative impact of increasing female headship on earnings is larger in each year among whites than among blacks. A uniform increase in female-headed families lowers white income more than it lowers black income. Therefore Figure 5.15 reveals that a uniform increase in the proportion of black and white families that are headed by females would have reduced racial earnings gaps. This reduction represents about 20 per cent of the total change in earnings inequality.

Actual Differences in Female-headed Families

The previous measure fails, however, to reveal how much of the actual change in earnings inequality is due to observed changes in family structure. To know

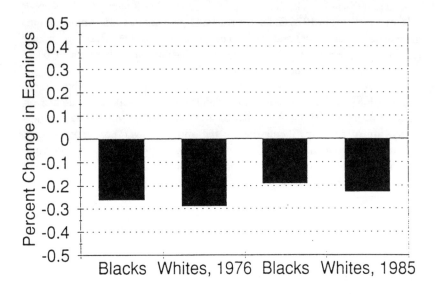

Source: As Table 5A.5.

Figure 5.14   Effects of family structure on earnings, 1976–85

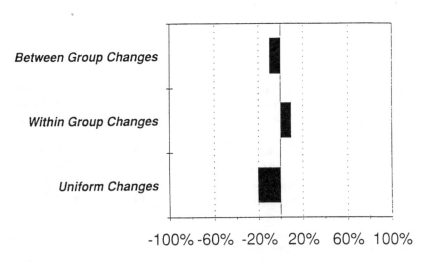

Source: As Table 5A.5, rows 6–8.

Figure 5.15   Earnings inequality growth due to family structure changes (%)

this, we must decide how to weigh the actual changes. We consider two differences. The first difference is the change in family structure from 1976 to 1985 within racial groups. The second is the racial difference in family structure for each year. We term these respectively 'within-group' differences and 'between-group' differences. The first can be interpreted as the change in earnings inequality attributable to the actual changes in family structure among blacks and whites over the period from 1976 to 1985. The second is the change in inequality due to actual differences in family structure between blacks and whites in each year.

Within-group differences

Evaluated by the within-group changes in family structure – where the percentage increase in the proportion of white families headed by females, which rose from 10.8 to 13.3 per cent, is less than the percentage increase in the proportion of black families headed by females, which soared from 36.1 to 44.8 per cent – *the effect is to increase earnings inequality.* Greater weight is given to the larger actual percentage changes in female-headed families among blacks than whites in evaluating the derivation of the earnings changes.

Between-group differences

Between-group differences in black and white proportions of families headed by females reduce earnings inequality. The between-group difference widened from 0.253 in 1976 to 0.316 in 1985. This means that greater weight in the evaluation of the effects of female-headed families on earnings is given to recent years than earlier years. But in recent years the negative impact of female-headed families on earnings is smaller than it was in earlier years. The *net effect of this effect is to reduce earnings inequality.*[3]

Nevertheless, whether the change in family structure is weighed by within-group changes or between-group differences, the effect is minuscule. At most, less than 10 per cent of the increase in racial earnings inequality among family heads can be attributed to changes in the proportions of families headed by females.

In summary, the evidence does not demonstrate a substantial impact of changing family structures on increasing earnings inequality among family heads. The most important point to remember is that although black families are far more likely to be headed by females than are white families, the deleterious impact of female-headed families on earnings is far larger for whites than for blacks. Moreover, the deleterious impact diminished between 1976 and 1985. Even if there had been uniform changes in family structures between blacks and whites, at most one-fifth of the growth in earnings gaps could have been explained by increasing female-headedness. In a nutshell, family structure alone cannot be the central cause of the widening earnings gaps between blacks and whites.

THE ROLE OF DISCRIMINATION

If the cause of the widening earnings gaps is not the rise in female-headed families, what is? We perform a statistical decomposition of the changes in black and white earnings between 1976 and 1985 using estimates of the model described in Figure 5.12. The decompositions ask:

- What would racial earnings gaps have been had blacks received the same 'treatment' as whites? That is, what if black and white earnings equations had the same coefficients?
- What would racial earnings gaps have been had blacks been endowed with the same characteristics as whites?
- What would racial earnings gaps have been had black and white characteristics remained unchanged from 1976 to 1985?
- What would racial earnings gaps have been had blacks and whites received the same treatment in 1985 as they received in 1976?

The first of these questions involves current discrimination; the second involves current differences in endowments; and the last two involve intertemporal changes in both endowments and discrimination.

Again, in the appendix, the full details of the procedure are discussed. Here, however, we summarize the main results. The actual growth in racial earnings inequality between 1976 and 1985 was 5 per cent. Figure 5.16 shows this as the bar labelled 'actual'. Using the full model as the base, we can compute four components of the change in inequality and identify what the growth would have been under alternative scenarios. 'Equal characteristics' in Figure 5.16 refers to the conceptual equating of black and white characteristics in both 1976 and 1985. This computation asks: Suppose blacks were just like whites in both years, what would have happened to the racial earnings gaps? Equality of endowments would lower the incidence of black female-headed families and raise black labour force participation, thereby increasing black earnings in 1976 and 1985. However, equality of endowments is not enough to reverse the widening earnings gaps. When endowments are equalized, black incomes increase while white incomes remain unchanged. Still, there is an increase in inequality of 2.68 per cent. In other words, much of the inequality remains even after conceptually making black family heads white.

'Intertemporal equality' refers to changing characteristics of blacks and whites. If blacks and whites retained their 1976 endowments of education, family backgrounds, age structure and the like in 1985, then what would earnings

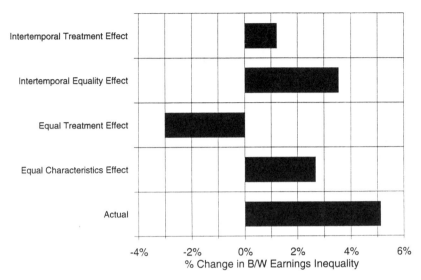

Source: As Table 5A.6.

Figure 5.16   Change (%) in black–white earnings inequalities among family heads under alternative decomposition

inequality be? At the outset, it is clear that the answer is ambiguous because indicators of black and white characteristics show mixed changes between 1976 and 1985. Although blacks and whites saw improvements in education, work effort fell, and the incidence of female-headed families rose. The growth in the earnings gap would have been only slightly smaller had blacks and whites retained their 1976 characteristics. It would have been 3.5 per cent instead of 5 per cent. At this point, then, little can be said about the merits of a) making blacks like whites, or b) preventing the putative deterioration of black traits.

In sharp contrast to the uneven results obtained by equalizing endowments of blacks and whites are the findings from equalizing treatment. These results are denoted by 'Equal treatment' and 'Intertemporal treatment'. The first refers to the conceptual experiment when we equalize the treatment of blacks and whites in both 1976 and 1985. In each year, discrimination in current and pre-labour market activities is eliminated. The result is that blacks have a drastically reduced incidence of female-headed families, lower expected welfare income, and thus higher work effort and higher earnings. Equality of treatment at each step along the causal path we have modelled would have generated a *growth in relative black family earnings* from 1976 to 1985, rather than the actually observed declines. This occurs even when black and white endowments remained unchanged.

Equating 1985 treatment with 1976 treatment yields impressive increases in black log earnings. It appears blacks would have earned more in 1985 if they had retained their 1985 characteristics but had 1976 treatment. White incomes, however, would also have increased for this intraracial equalization. The result: a small increase in the earnings gap.

In summary, we decomposed racial earnings inequality into components attributable to a) differences in characteristics of blacks and whites, and b) differences in how these characteristics affect outcomes. If we call those differences which are due to how characteristics affect outcomes 'discriminatory treatment' or 'discrimination', we must conclude that racially disparate treatment plays a continuing role in explaining earnings inequality in America.

CONCLUSIONS

How is the shift in family structure related to changes in earnings inequality? Superficially, the answer is that female-headed families have lower incomes on average than male-headed families. Females earn lower wages and salaries, on average, than males. Thus one potential explanation for the decline in the relative incomes of black families is the phenomenal increase in recent decades in the percentage of black families headed by females. This rise is also evident among whites, although not as marked.

This explanation, however, ignores the fact that even better-educated and higher-earning black family heads were significantly more likely to be females than heads among comparably situated white families. Moreover, the rate of growth in female-headed families among the young and uneducated was greater among whites than among blacks. The percentage of families with female heads among white family heads aged 14 to 24 without a high-school degree almost tripled between 1970 and 1991, rising from 14 per cent to 40 per cent. The percentage of families with female heads among black families with family heads aged 14 to 24 without a high-school degree only doubled, rising from about 40 per cent to a little more than 80 per cent. So it is not clear that rising female headship among black families unambiguously increases the earnings gaps between black and white families.

The evidence on changes in labour force participation rates suggests another possible explanation for widening racial earnings gaps. The overall trend for the 21-year period from 1970 though 1991 is one of decline in the labour force participation rates of black family heads. In 1970 about 73 per cent of black family heads were in the labour force; by 1991, only 65 per cent were working or looking for work. Labour force participation rates also declined for white family heads although the ratio of black–white labour force participation rates dropped, particularly for female-headed families. For example, in 1976 the ratio was 0.94

for male-headed families, 0.93 for female-headed families and 0.85 for all families. In 1985 the ratio dropped to 0.93 for male-headed families, 0.85 for female-headed families and 0.82 overall.

Thus a plausible explanation for the deterioration in the earnings position of black families is the relative decline in labour force participation rates among black female family heads. However, this explanation, along with the female headship explanation, must be examined within the context of a structural model that admits the possibility that there are differing impacts of family structure and labour force participation rates on black and white family earnings.

We first sketched the barest of such models: an earnings equation that includes gender and work behaviour as independent variables. We then specified a more elaborate model that incorporates a structural relationship between family structure and work. Our central finding is that the drop in relative earnings of black family heads cannot be blamed solely on the increase in the share of African American families headed by females. More important is the deteriorating economic position of young, uneducated family heads, who happen to be disproportionately female. Among blacks, the percentage of young, uneducated family heads who are female doubled from 1970 to 1991, while it nearly tripled among whites. This increase occurred among both those with earnings and those outside the labour force. The racial earnings gap does not arise simply because blacks are more likely than whites to be heads of single-parent families, but because the deleterious effects of being a young, uneducated head of family differ between blacks and whites.

But even more important is the role of continuing economic discrimination. We find that much of the racial gap in earnings can be attributed to unequal treatment of similarly situated family heads. Had black and white family heads experienced exactly the same market evaluation of their endowments, black–white earnings gaps would have narrowed rather than widened between the 1970s and the 1980s. Had black and white endowments remained unchanged from the 1970s until the 1980s, the racial earnings gaps would not have been as great in the 1980s as they actually were, but those gaps would still have increased. Thus the increase in the share of families headed by females among African Americans alone, while important for understanding the reduction in labour force participation rates of black family heads, are not the central cause of the low relative income of black families.

ENDNOTES

1. Analysis of data on female-headed families (or 'lone mothers') in the United Kingdom shows lower employment probabilities associated with presence of young children, child-care expenditures – which are correlated with number of young children – and welfare. See Jenkins (1992) and Ermisch and Wright (1991).

2. To simplify the table's presentation, the labour force participation rates of those with zero earnings in the previous year – usually zero – are not included for these gender-based breakdowns. Of course, in the larger cohorts, both the positive earners and the zero-earners are included in the calculation of the labour force participation rates. Thus, for example, among white educated family heads aged 41 and over, the labour force participation rate in 1991 was 79 per cent. Among male positive earners in this age–education group among whites, the labour force participation rate was 96 per cent and among females it was 92 per cent. In other words, there were large numbers of non-earners among older educated white family heads – who, with their low labour force participation rates, helped to drive the average down for the group. Notable is the fact that among blacks there are smaller differences between the rate for the cohort and the rate for the positive earners, suggesting that there are proportionately fewer non-earners among these educated black family heads.
3. A technical discussion of the derivation of these results is presented in the appendix.

APPENDIX

The Model

Consider the following conventional specification of the earnings equation:

$$\ln(Y) = \psi_0 + \Sigma\psi_i X_i + \psi_{n+1}LFPR + \psi_{n+2}Sex \tag{1}$$

where $\mathbf{X}$ is a vector of independent variables,[1] and *LFPR* denotes work effort, measured by the percentage of the year spent working or looking for work. *LFPR* is not a dichotomous variable such as is usually employed to measure labour force participation, principally because the value will always be 1 for persons with positive wage and salary incomes. The 'work effort' measure, instead, is continuous and varies among those with earnings. It is the sum of weeks working and weeks unemployed divided by 52.[2] Still, results from this specification are likely to be biased, since those with earnings are likely to have higher than average labour force participation rates. This is our naive model.

An alternative specification considers the selection process as being determined by 'reservation' wages. Persons with offer wages below their lowest acceptable wage decline to work, although they may continue to look for work, and thus have non-zero work effort. Heckman's method for correcting this type of selection bias is to estimate:

$$\ln(Y) = X_0 + \Sigma\psi_i X_i + X_{n+1}LFPR + \lambda \tag{2}$$

where λ is the inverse Mills ratio estimated from the probit equation for $\Pr(Y>0)$. Since the errors in the work effort equation and the earnings equation need not be uncorrelated, this yields a variant of the Heckman earnings equation. Here, in a three-step estimation, we first obtain instrumented estimates of

LFPR, then we perform the first stage of the Heckman estimation and obtain estimates of the inverse Mills ratio. Thus, we estimate the log earnings equation:

$$\ln(Y) = \xi_0 + \Sigma\xi_i X_i + \xi_{n+1} LFPR' + \lambda \qquad (3)$$

The earnings equation we consider here is regarded by Willis as second-generation earnings equations.[3]

In Willis's view, first-generation earnings equations principally consider schooling and experience variables. Labour force participation is ignored. The focus is usually on the individual, without any particular consideration given to family status.[4] Willis points out that second-generation models attempt to take into account the inherent self-selectivity or sampling bias associated with estimating earnings simply by restricting the sample to those with positive earnings.[5]

Our approach is to expand upon second-generation earnings equations to show that there may be *two* relevant aspects of selection: one by which some withdraw from the labour market, another by which some work less than the full year.[6] Family structure enters by way of the structural equation determining work effort. Female family heads are less likely to have positive earnings, and when they work they have lower earnings because they work less than male heads of families.

The selection process is captured in a single equation: instruments are obtained for the continuous variable *LFPR*, while the standard Heckman procedures are employed to account for zero earners. This is the method embodied in Equation (3).[7]

The independent variables in the earnings equation are: geographic location (North Central, Northeast, South), age, age squared, education and education squared. The first-stage estimates in the probit equation for Heckman's lambda include as independent variables: age, age squared, grade, grade squared and state unemployment rate. The first-stage estimates of the fraction of the year in the labour force include as independent variables: age, age squared, grade, grade squared, state unemployment rate, population density, number of children less than age 6, number of children aged 6–18 years and ratio of guarantee to needs.

Our analysis will focus ultimately on the factors contributing to changing earnings inequality. It is useful at this point to make explicit how this change is measured. Denote wage and salary income in year k for race j by Y_k^j. Earnings inequality, Y^B/Y^W, between blacks (B) and whites (W) increases from year t to $t + 1$ if:

$$I = \ln(Y^B)_t - \ln(Y^W)_t - \ln(Y^B)_{t+1} + \ln(Y^W)_{t+1} > 0$$

Moreover, a factor x contributes to an increase in racial inequality if:

$$\partial I/\partial x = \partial \ln(Y^B)_t/\partial x - \partial \ln(Y^W)_t/\partial x - \partial \ln(Y^B)_{t+1}/\partial x + \partial \ln(Y^W)_{t+1}/\partial x > 0$$

for uniform increases in x for blacks and whites in both years. One naive experiment is to compute the effects of sex on earnings inequality by estimating the ψ_{n+2}s. Of course, if *LFPR* also depends on sex, then the computation must involve the ψ_{n+1}s as well.

Results

Earnings of family heads: a naive model
Consider Equation (1), which posits a direct relationship between sex, work force effort and log earnings. What effect does female headship have on the racial earnings gap? From Table 5A.1 we note that there are negative and significant impacts of being a female on the earnings of family heads. The negative effects are larger, however, for white family heads than black family heads in each year. Moreover, the effects diminish between 1976 and 1985 for both blacks and whites. Just looking at the coefficients on the female variable reveals that the gross effect of sex on inequality ($\partial I/\partial$female) is positive ($-0.76574 - (-0.90777)$ $- (-0.66524) + (0.78362) = 0.023649 > 0$). The net effect, however, must account for the impacts of sex on labour force participation. In the simplest of specifications – with labour force participation a function of age, education, region, number of young children and several interactions between gender and education, and young children – we find a negative effect of being female on labour force participation. Since at least for black family heads reduced labour force participation lowers earnings, the net effect of being female turns out to be to *reduce* earnings inequality.[11] In this simple estimate, then, female headship cannot be the explanation for the rise in racial earnings inequality.

Earnings of family heads: a detailed model

Of course, 'being female' is not just a matter of adding a sex variable to the earnings equation. In our specification in Equation (3), the focus is on labour force participation which is functionally related to family structure. Table 5A.2 displays the results of estimating the log earnings equation (3) for blacks and whites in 1976 and 1985. The estimates use the Heckman method to correct for the sample selection bias resulting from exclusion of zero earners and adjusts for the endogeneity of work. The algorithm used presents the corrected standard errors. Here, the selection term is insignificant in 1976 and barely significant in 1985. The coefficients on work effort (*LFPR*) are all statistically significant. Other statistically significant variables are: the regional dummy variable for South in 1976 but not in 1985; central city residence for whites in 1976; and age of the family head. Education is not statistically significant in 1976, although the squared term is significant for whites and blacks in 1985.

Table 5A.1   Earnings and work of family heads, 1976 and 1985 (t statistics in parentheses)

Variables	Log($LFRP/1-LFRP$) 1976 Black	White	1985 Black	White	ln(Y) 1976 Black	White	1985 Black	White
Intercept	-0.8368	-1.6771	-2.2220	-0.0494	1.8586	6.6924	1.7285	7.2539
	(-0.0733)	(-4.348)	(-1.630)	(-0.135)	(-4.665)	(8.882)	(0.547)	(14.069)
Age	0.3522	0.4110	0.4762	0.3729	0.0952	0.1483	0.1441	0.1504
	(7.735)	(30.932)	(10.121)	(31.347)	(8.825)	(55.220)	(12.966)	(49.941)
Age squared	-0.0036	-0.0046	-0.0053	-0.0043	-0.0011	-0.0017	-0.0016	-0.0017
	(-6.985)	(-30.693)	(-9.846)	(-32.644)	(-8.700)	(-54.488)	(-12.644)	(-50.028)
Grade	0.0527	0.1520	0.0213	0.0980	0.0654	0.1086	0.0071	0.0925
	(0.425)	(3.491)	(0.139)	(2.387)	(2.297)	(12.031)	(0.206)	(8.700)
Grade squared	-0.0005	-0.0044	-0.0020	-0.0033	0.0006	-0.0012	0.0036	-0.0004
	(-0.077)	(-2.501)	(-0.311)	(-2.074)	(0.419)	(-3.213)	(2.474)	(-0.952)
Number of children under 6 years old	0.0267	0.0787	0.1292	0.0204				
	(1.406)	(1.902)	(0.839)	(0.568)				
Number of children between 6 and 18	-0.0829	-0.1114	-0.2259	-0.0830				
	(-1.298)	(-4.922)	(-2.845)	(-3.547)				
Female	-4.5169	-1.8140	-1.8905	-1.0235	-0.7657	-0.9078	-0.6652	-0.7836
	(-5.363)	(-4.242)	(-2.263)	(-2.957)	(-15.511)	(-48.065)	(-16.822)	(-44.186)
Female X grade	0.3651	0.0836	0.1547	0.0335				
	(4.928)	(2.417)	(2.281)	(1.246)				
Female X no. of Children under 6	-0.6414	-1.1527	-0.6145	-1.1081				
	(-2.281)	(-6.736)	(-2.330)	(-8.612)				
Nonh Central					-0.0717	-0.0430	-0.0149	-0.0284
					(-1.170)	(-2.900)	(-0.194)	(-1.732)
North Eastern					-0.1404	-0.0273	0.1162	0.0337
					(-2.176)	(-1.842)	(1.524)	(1.950)
South					-0.0771	-0.0224	-0.0564	-0.0292
					(-1.337)	(-1.699)	(-0.842)	(-1.854)
Central City					0.0645	0.0394	0.0220	0.0059
					(1,571)	(3.292)	(0.554)	(0.429)
Fitted work					4.9379	-1.5891	4.2170	-1.5939
					(5.468)	(-2.060)	(1.292)	(-3.020)
Adjusted R^2	0.0530	0.0549	0.0501	0.0543	0.2694	0.2664	0.2502	0.2194
F-value	14.443	151.040	15.475	169.384	74.493	845.053	83.365	742.767
(significance)	(0.0001)	(0.0001)	(0.0001)	(0.0001)	(0.0001)	(0.0001)	(0.0001)	(0.0001)
No. of observations	2160	23241	2468	26398	1993	23241	2468	26398

Source: Current Population Survey, March Supplement Tapes, 1976 and 1985; IRP Family Extract Tapes, 1976 and 1985.

Effect of work effort on earnings inequality   Increases in work effort ought to raise family heads' earnings and reduce the earnings gaps between blacks and whites. Following this reasoning, as work effort *declined* for black and white family heads, an increase in earnings inequality should be seen. However, the effect of uniform increases in labour force participation among black and white family heads is computed to reduce the racial earnings gaps.

Persistent disparity

Table 5A.2   Log earnings equation, Heckman correction for selection, 1976 and 1985 (t-statistics in parentheses)

	1976		1985	
	Blacks	Whites	Blacks	Whites
Constant	7.03535	6.22569	7.64379	7.62339
	(7.106)	(3.931)	(6.945)	(7.554)
North Central	−0.02156	0.01742	0.08971	−0.03762
	(−0.205)	(0.288)	(0.706)	(−0.701)
North East	−0.06345	0.03166	0.09478	−0.00263
	(−0.610)	(0.558)	(0.736)	(−0.052)
South	−0.33248	−0.09648	−0.08388	−0.01934
	(−3.226)	(−1.634)	(−0.715)	(−0.392)
Central City	−0.01843	−0.08754	−0.05631	−0.00882
	(−0.354)	(−1.983)	(−0.949)	(−0.206)
Age	0.07339	0.08693	0.06273	0.0583
	(2.105)	(2.949)	(1.723)	(2.080)
Age squared	−0.00075	−0.00095	−0.00055	−0.00047
	(−1.691)	(−1.993)	(−1.229)	(−1.278)
Grade	−0.01724	0.03886	−0.06642	−0.03649
	(−0.398)	(0.487)	(−1.073)	(−0.763)
Grade squared	0.00296	0.00151	0.0045	0.00402
	(1.019)	(0.568)	(1.884)	(2.299)
LFPR-Fitted	0.79261	1.10869	0.70259	0.74374
	(2.644)	(2.067)	(2.248)	(1.987)
Lambda	−0.07558	0.05569	−0.8396	0.74728
	(−0.114)	(0.051)	(−1.833)	(−1.633)
R^2	0.12073	0.17009	0.18383	0.16688
Breusch–Pagan X^2	55.5651	429.11	126.197	344.2
Number of observations	1993	2324	2468	2639

Note: This run uses proportion of weeks worked or unemployed instead of the dichotomous variable of labour force participation; *LFPR* is derived from the equation $\ln((LFPR)/1 - (LFPR))$ which is a function of Age, Age squared Grade, Grade squared, State unemployment, State population density, Children aged less than 6, Children aged 6–18 and, for 1985, the ratio of state needs to AFDC payment for families of 3 children or more. Selection based on Probit equation for positive wage, a function of Age, Age squared, Grade, Grade squared, and State unemployment.

Source: IRP Family Extract Tapes, 1976 and 1985.

To see this, recall that the inequality increases when:

$$\partial \ln(Y^B)_t/\partial x - \partial \ln(Y^W)_t/\partial x - \partial \ln(Y^B)_{t+1}/\partial x + \partial \ln(Y^W)_{t+1}/\partial x > 0$$

for uniform increases in x. The effect of increased work effort, then, equals $0.79261 - 1.10869 - 0.70259 + 0.74374 = -0.2749$.

In other words, had black work effort increased at a magnitude equal to the white increase, and selection and endogeneity of work accounted for, racial earnings gaps would have diminished. Since, in fact, work effort declined for both blacks and whites, the implication is that these declines contributed to the widening of the racial gap in earnings of family heads.

Effect of family structure on earnings inequality   The effects of family structure on earnings inequality work their way through a labour force participation equation. Recall that the principal explanation for using a continuous variable to denote work effort in the log earnings equation was to avoid the tautological relationship between those who had earnings and those who worked: whenever a person had positive earnings, that person also necessarily worked. By using the fraction of the year that a person worked, we were able to create a continuous analogue to the labour force participation rate. Work effort lies between zero and one; whenever the labour force participation rate is equal to one, there is a positive value of work effort.

Now, in order to estimate the effects of family structure on earnings, we first estimated a logistic model of labour force participation rates, which depends on expected welfare benefits, female family headship and other factors. Table 5A.3 reports these results.

Whether the family head was white or black in years 1976 or 1985, female family heads were less likely to be looking for work or to be working than were male family heads. While the coefficients are nearly identical for blacks and whites in 1976, the marginal effects, that is, the derivatives, are greater for blacks than whites. The same is true for 1985, even though the differential is smaller. In other words, being a female reduces labour force participation more for black family heads than it does for white family heads.

Similarly, increases in welfare income reduce labour force participation of family heads, with the marginal impacts again greater for black family heads than for white family heads. Indeed, a $1000 increase in real Aid to Families with Dependent Children (AFDC) annual benefits would have reduced black and white labour force participation by only about six percentage points in 1976. By 1985, a $1000 increase in AFDC benefits would change labour force participation rates by only 11 percentage points for blacks and about seven percentage points for whites.

Table 5A.3   Maximum likelihood estimates of labour force participation rates, 1976 and 1985 (t-statistics in parentheses)

	1976		1985	
	Black family heads	White family heads	Black family heads	White family heads
Constant	−0.4566	−2.5141	−3.1984	−4.5552
	(−0.642)	(−3.031)	(−4.018)	(−5.372)
Female-headed	−1.4737	−1.4769	−1.1541	−1.5871
	(−12.193)	(−9.532)	(−9.486)	(−11.398)
State unemployment	−0.1518	−0.0808	−0.0220	0.0404
	(−2.152)	(−1.211)	(−0.476)	(1.232)
Guarantee/needs	–	–	−0.0975	0.6086
			(−0.384)	(2.648)
Children under 6	0.0113	−0.1494	0.0632	−0.1345
	(0.131)	(−1.334)	(0.688)	(−1.159)
Children 6–18	0.0132	−0.0908	0.1280	0.1361
	(0.282)	(−1.283)	(1.849)	(1.750)
Age	0.1884	0.2626	0.2586	0.2620
	(7.620)	(9.867)	(9.344)	(10.040)
Age squared	−0.0025	−0.0034	−0.0033	−0.0035
	(−9.400)	(−12.615)	(−10.846)	(−13.310)
Grade	−0.0870	0.1135	−0.0273	0.1974
	(−1.138)	(1.369)	(−0.325)	(2.388)
Grade squared	0.0093	−0.0009	0.0067	−0.0025
	(2.218)	(−0.230)	(1.613)	(−0.704)
Expected welfare	−0.0003	−0.0004	−0.0005	−0.0004
	(−4.682)	(−1.849)	(−4.845)	(−2.356)
X^2	539.8500	955.7400	604.9400	1499.50
Number of observations	2160	2324	2468	2629

Source: Current Population Survey, March Supplement Tapes, 1976 and 1985.

In the ten intervening years, the gap in the effects of welfare on labour force participation widened between black and white family heads, but average expected welfare income was considerably below $1000 in both years for both black and white family heads. In other words, a major expenditure on welfare would not have reduced labour force participation even in the most recent years by more than 11 percentage points. Translated in terms of a work week, the result of more than doubling expected annual welfare income would have amounted to a reduction of less than *five* hours per week in time spent looking for work or working. Thus, the work disincentive effects of welfare are of questionable magnitude.

Even more important than family structure or welfare in affecting labour force participation is the age of the head of the family. Table 5A.4 displays the computed elasticities of labour force participation with respect to these three statistically significant factors: age of family head, gender (female) of family head, and expected welfare income. Welfare income exhibits distinctly inelastic impacts on labour force participation of black and white family heads, confirming the small marginal impacts found before. The impacts grew between 1976 and 1985 and they are considerably larger for blacks than whites. Yet they are so small that they pale in comparison with the impacts of the other significant variables.

Table 5A.4   Labour force participation elasticities, 1976 and 1985

	Blacks 1976	Whites 1976	Blacks 1985	Whites 1985
Age	2.316176	2.130714	3.847392	2.727529
Female-headed household	–0.15686	–0.02842	–0.23861	–0.04800
Expected Welfare	–0.06579	–0.00815	–0.09943	–0.00959

Source: Authors' computations from Table 5A.3.

Female headship has a considerably more pronounced effect for blacks than whites. A 1 per cent increase in the probability that a family is female-headed lowers labour force participation rates five to five and a half times more for blacks than whites. But then, it only lowers the black labour force participation rate by less than one quarter of 1 per cent. The inelastic impact of family structure on work behaviour is simply much larger for black family heads.

Age of family head, however, has a very elastic impact. Quite clearly, increases in the age of the head of family have larger percentage impacts on labour force participation than either welfare income or the family head's being female. A 1 per cent decrease in the age of the family head, computed at the average age, reduces labour force participation rates by more than 2 per cent to nearly 4 per cent. The impacts are larger for blacks than whites, with the gap widening from 1976 to 1985.

We employ these results from Table 5A.3 in order to compute the effects of family structure on earnings inequality.

Note that the ratio of black–white earnings in year t to black–white earnings in year $t + 1$, given by I, is our measure of inequality. As this ratio rises, inequality increases; that is, the racial earnings gap widens. The natural logarithm of this ratio, $\ln(I)$, measures the percentage change in inequality. When it is positive, inequality is increasing; when it is negative, inequality is decreasing. Thus, the impact of a variable, X, on earnings inequality can be measured by whether it increases the log ratio or reduces it.

We compute in Table 5A.5 that a uniform increase in the proportion of black and white families that are headed by females would reduce racial earnings gaps by about 1 per cent. The net effect is computed to be –0.01054. Since earnings gaps actually increased by 5 per cent, this reduction represents about 20 per cent of the total change in earnings inequality.

Table 5A.5   Effects of family structure on earnings inequality, 1976 and 1985

	Blacks 1976	Whites 1976	Blacks 1985	Whites 1985	Net effect	% of total gap
Mean LFPR	0.6576	0.7701	0.6195	0.7374	–	–
Mean FHH	0.3605	0.1079	0.4483	0.1323	–	–
Coef. of FHH on LFPR	–1.4737	–1.4769	–1.1541	–1.5871	–	–
Coef. of LFPR on $\ln(Y)$	0.79261	1.10869	0.70259	0.74374	–	–
Derivative of $\ln(Y)$	–0.26301	–0.2899	–0.19114	–0.22857		
Evaluated at uniform changes in FHH	–	–	–	–	–0.01054	–20.62
Evaluated at actual within-group changes in FHH	–	–	–	–	0.004814	9.42
Evaluated at actual between-group differences in FHH	–	–	–	–	–0.00504	–9.85

Source: Authors' computations from Tables 5A.2 and 5A.3.

Note: FHH = female-headed household

This measure, however, fails to tell how much of the actual change in earnings inequality is due to observed changes in family structure. Yet, to know this, we must decide how to weigh the actual changes. To assess the impact on earnings inequality of changing family structure between blacks and whites, we compute the derivative of $\ln(I)$ and evaluate it for two differences. The first difference equals the change in family structure from 1976 to 1985 within racial groups. The second equals the racial difference in family structure for each year. These two assessments can be written as:

Within-group difference

$$\partial \ln(I)/\partial X_i \times \Delta X_i = \left[\partial \ln\left(Y_{76}^B\right)\!/\partial X_i - \partial \ln\left(Y_{85}^B\right)\!/\partial X_i \right]\!\left(X_{i76}^B - X_{i85}^B\right)$$
$$- \left[\partial \ln\left(Y_{76}^W\right)\!/\partial X_i - \partial \ln\left(Y_{85}^W\right)\!/\partial X_i \right]\!\left(X_{i76}^W - X_{i85}^W\right)$$

Between-group difference

$$\partial \ln(I)/\partial X_i \times \Delta X_i = \left[\partial \ln\left(Y_{76}^B\right)\!/\partial X_i - \partial \ln\left(Y_{76}^W\right)\!/\partial X_i \right]\!\left(X_{i76}^B - X_{i76}^W\right)$$
$$- \left[\partial \ln\left(Y_{85}^B\right)\!/\partial X_i - \partial \ln\left(Y_{85}^W\right)\!/\partial X_i \right]\!\left(X_{i85}^B - X_{i85}^W\right)$$

The first can be interpreted as the change in earnings inequality attributable to the actual changes in family structure among blacks and whites over the period from 1976 to 1985. The second is the change in inequality due to actual differences in family structure between blacks and whites in each year. Neither distinguishes between that component of change resulting directly from improvements in endowments or group characteristics and that component attributable to reduced differentials in how those endowments translate into earnings.[9]

While a simpler way to measure the effects of family structure on earnings inequality would be to compute the derivatives of log earnings for each year with respect to work effort and of work effort with respect to the probability of female family headship, as is done in our naive model, these derivatives assume equivalent increments or uniform changes in family structure. For this reason we weight the changes by the actual values of ΔX. Simply knowing that black and white probabilities of female headed families increased is insufficient to assume that family structure changes increased earnings disparities.

Between-group differences in black and white proportions of families headed by females reduce earnings inequality. Yet the parallel rise in both black and white incidence of female-headed families – the within-group change – translates into increases in racial earnings gaps. The impact of changing family structures, then, depends on how these changes are weighted.

Evaluated at the actual gaps between blacks and whites, where percentage differences narrowed between 1976 and 1985, the impact is clearly one of reduced earnings inequality. As the relative gap between black and white proportions of families headed by females narrowed, the earnings gap diminished.

Evaluated at the within-group changes in family structure – where the percentage increase in the proportion of white families headed by females, which rose from 0.1079 to 0.1323, is less than the percentage increase in the proportion of black families headed by females, which soared from 0.3605 to 0.4483 – the impact is to increase earnings inequality. In other words, since the percentage changes in female-headed families were larger for blacks than for whites, the earnings gaps widened.

Neither of these changes, however, is very large. Whether the change in family structure is weighed by within-group changes or between-group differences, the impacts are minuscule. At most, less than 10 per cent of the percentage increase in racial earnings inequality among family heads can be attributed to changes in the proportions of families headed by females.

Decomposition of earnings inequality Table 5A.6 presents values of the percentage change in racial earnings gaps between 1976 and 1985.[10] The first row of the table refers to the percentage change in earnings gaps using earnings Equation (3). This value is computed as:

$$\ln(Y^B)_{76} - \ln(Y^W)_{76} - \ln(Y^B)_{85} + \ln(Y^W)_{85}$$

and is about 5 per cent.

Table 5A.6 Decomposition of earnings inequalities

Single equation (actual gap)	0.051115
Full-model equation	0.055864
Equal characteristics effect	0.026823
Equal treatment effect	−0.03012
Intertemporal equality effect	0.035312
Intertemporal treatment effect	0.012039

Source: As Fig. 5.13.

Solving the full model, where the effects of labour force participation, family structure and expected welfare are permitted to work their way through the underlying equations, also yields a gap of 5 per cent.[11] The full model results confirm the qualitative conclusion that racial earnings gaps widened among family heads over the period 1976 to 1985.

Using the full model as the base, we can compute four components of the change in equality. Row three refers to the conceptual equating of black and white characteristics in both 1976 and 1985. This computation asks: Suppose blacks were just like whites in both years, what would have happened to the racial earnings gaps? The equality of endowments would lower the incidence of black female-headed families and raise black labour force participation, thereby increasing black earnings in 1976 and 1985. However, the equality of endowments is not enough to reverse the widening of the earnings gaps. The log earnings for blacks and whites in 1976 and 1985 are 9.184852, 9.719227, 9.138942 and 9.729181, yielding a change in inequality of 5.5864 per cent using the full model. When endowments are equalized, black incomes increase while white incomes remain unchanged. The values are 9.458631, 9.719227, 9.441761 and 9.729181, yielding a change in inequality of 2.6823 per cent. In other words, much of the inequality remains even after conceptually making black family heads white.

The fifth row relates to changing characteristics of blacks and whites. If blacks and whites retained their 1976 endowments of education, family background, age structure and the like in 1985, then what would earnings inequality be? At the outset, it is clear that the answer is ambiguous because indicators of black and white characteristics show mixed changes between 1976 and 1985. Although blacks and whites saw improvements in education, work effort fell, and the incidence of female-headed families rose. The growth in the earnings gap would have been only slightly smaller had blacks and whites retained their 1976 characteristics. At this point, then, little can be said about the merits of a) making blacks like whites; or b) preventing the putative deterioration of black traits.

Analysts focusing on the flight of the middle class from inner-city areas frequently point to diminished capacities of blacks to compete in the labour market when not armed with values and work habits found in stable neighbourhoods. While the results of rows three and five cannot be substitutes for a rigorous assessment of the impacts of values and motivations on work behaviour, they do speak to the issue of equalization of observable characteristics. Black female family headship grew in this period. Labour force participation fell. These are some of the most obvious correlates of 'underclass' behaviours discussed in the literature. Yet providing equality of backgrounds at best only slightly reduces inequality in earnings.

In sharp contrast with the uneven results obtained by equalizing endowments of blacks and whites are the findings from equalizing treatment. These results are presented in the fourth and sixth rows. Row four equalizes the treatment of blacks and whites in 1976 and 1985. In each year, black coefficients are replaced with white coefficients. The result is that blacks have drastically reduced incidence of female-headed families, lower expected welfare income, and thus higher work effort and higher earnings. Equality of treatment at each step along the way of the causal path we have modelled would have generated a growth in relative black family earnings from 1976 to 1985. This occurs even when black and white endowments remained unchanged.

Equating 1985 treatment with 1976 yields impressive increases in black log earnings. It appears blacks would have earned more in 1985 if they had retained their 1985 characteristics but had 1976 treatment. White incomes, however, would also have increased in this intraracial equalization. The white income increase would have been so much that the racial earnings gaps would have widened. To see this, recall that the log earnings for blacks and whites in 1976 and 1985 are 9.184852, 9.719227, 9.138942 and 9.729181, yielding a change in inequality of 5.5864 per cent. When black and white treatment is equalized across years, the log earnings are 9.184852, 9.719227, 9.212285 and 9.758699. In other words, both black and white incomes increased measurably in 1985 and reduced the earnings gap. Yet the result is not enough to eradicate the earnings gap completely.

ENDNOTES

1. Generally, the independent variables in 'human capital' earnings equations include skill and experience variables, taking in, but not limited to, age and education. Increasingly analysts have augmented the vector of skill-related characteristics to include measures of occupation, veteran status and union membership. See, for example, Montgomery and Wascher (1987).
2. For ease of exposition we shall refer throughout to this work effort variable as *LFPR*.
3. Willis (1986).
4. In Killingsworth and Heckman (1986). The authors note the dangers in this omission, particularly with respect to female earnings.
5. While most researchers now recognize the importance of accounting for selection bias, particularly in studies of racial earnings inequality, unresolved is the issue of specifically what technique is most robust in accounting for sample selection. Blau and Beller (1992) note that the Heckman method commonly used to correct for selection bias may lack robustness and thus they employ an alternative method that simulates labour force participation rates across years and computes estimated earnings for non-labour force participants following a procedure adopted by Smith and Welch (1986). See also Manski (1989).
6. Still another form of selection, considered by Ihlanfeldt (1988), is that of location of work. Perhaps workers possessing greater amounts of positive earnings characteristics are more likely to search out jobs in areas where there are higher earnings, such as in the suburbs. Since blacks are disproportionately found in the central city, racial earnings gaps may understate the degree of discrimination. Nevertheless, Ihlanfeldt finds in 10 out of 12 regressions that the locational selection factor is insignificant.
7. Since the continuous variable, *LFPR*, is estimated as a reduced form equation, omitting such determinants of labour force participation as family structure, we have also estimated the following structural equation:

$$P\{LFPR > 0\} = 1/(1 + \exp - [\phi_0 + \Sigma\phi_i Z_i + \phi_{n+1}FHH + \phi_{n+2}Ex(welfare)])$$

where *LFPR* denotes labour force participation rate, *FHH* indicates female-headed family, Ex(welfare) is expected welfare income and Z denotes exogenous variables.

More specifically, the probability that the family head was in the labour force in the previous year is a function of female headship, the state unemployment rate (by race), the ratio of state guarantee to needs, number of children younger than age six, number of children aged 6–18 years, age, age squared, grade, grade squared, and expected welfare income.

We have also estimated a structural form for the female-headed family variable and these structural estimates are used in the derivation of some of our policy estimates in the results section. The equation is given by:

$$P\{FHH = 1\} = 1/(1 + \exp - [[\theta_0 + \Sigma\theta_i W_i + \theta_{n+1}MF + \theta_{n+2}Ex(welfare)])$$

where *MF* is the ratio of unmarried males in the labour force or in school to unmarried females.

Welfare reciplency and public assistance earnings are not strictly exogenous to the labour force participation decisions. It is necessary, then, to replace actual AFDC income with an instrument that is a function only of currently exogenous variables. One important set of variables determining both AFDC recipiency and welfare income includes a vector of state AFDC parameters. We construct a variable, expected welfare, which is the product of the probability of receipt of welfare and welfare income for those receiving public assistance or AFDC, both equations appropriately estimated from a set of exogenous variables.

$$Ex(welfare) = P\{AFDC > 0\} \cdot \exp(\ln AFDC), \text{ for } AFDC > 0$$
$$P\{AFDC > 0\} = 1/(1 + \exp - [\alpha_0 + \Sigma\alpha_i X_i + \Sigma\rho_i P_i])$$
$$\ln(welfare) = \beta_0 + \Sigma\beta_i X_i + \Sigma\gamma_i P_i + \Sigma\zeta_i Z_i$$

The probability of receipt of welfare and log-AFDC income are functions of age, age squared, grade, grade squared, number of children younger than age six, number of children aged 6–18 years, a dummy variable for state AFDC work requirement, a dummy variable for state unemployed parent programme, Northeast, Northcentral, South, percentage of state population that is black, percentage of population in the state on welfare, the mean AFDC income in the state in the previous year, the ratio of the state guarantee to state needs for family of three. The recipiency equation also includes the variable for population density; the AFDC income equation includes the variable for central city residency.

These estimates, along with the underlying equations used to estimate the *MF* (sex ratios), are found in Darity and Myers (1991).

8. This is computed by finding:

$$\partial \ln(Y_t^j)/\partial LFPR \cdot \partial LFPR/\partial Female + \partial \ln(Y_t^j)/\partial Female$$

for each race and each year yielding a net effect on *I* of being female equal to –0.24764.

We have also estimated Equation [1] with a version of *LFPR*-fit which does not include female as an argument. The estimate of the net effect of being female on *I* is –0.08221.

9. The choice of weighing scheme for producing these decompositions is far from a settled matter. That is why we choose both weighing procedures. For a variant of the between group difference, see Juhn, Murphy and Pierce (1991).

10. The table reproduces the final column of appendix tables A.10 to A.15, in Darity and Myers (1991) that provide the detailed decomposition results.

11. The full model includes equations for sex ratios, welfare and family structure, the details of which are presented in Darity and Myers (forthcoming). There, we specify individual-specific measures of the ratio of unmarried males in the labour force to unmarried females from a reduced form logistic model for the probability that a sample respondent was an unmarried male in the labour force (Pr{*UMLF*}) and for the probability that a sample respondent was an unmarried female (Pr{*UF*}). These predictive equations, dependent on mortality ratios and institutionalization rates, are used to compute in the sample of family heads the following sex-ratio:

$$(UMLF/UF) = \Pr\{UMLF\}/\Pr\{UF\}$$

where

$$\Pr\{*\} = 1/(1 + \exp(-X\beta))$$

Exogenous variables include the following: the head of family's age, age squared and education; the number of children in the household under 6 years of age and the number between 6 and 18 years of age; the type of residence (apartment or house); the abortion ratio in the state in the previous census year; the fraction of abortions received by unmarried women in the state in the previous census year; the percentage of the population by race that is institutionalized in the state in the previous census year; the ratio of male–female mortality; the AFDC monthly guarantee for three children in 1975 and 1984; the ratio of the AFDC monthly guarantee to the state need-level; the percentage of the state's population on welfare in the previous census year; the percentage of the population that was black in the previous census year; population density in the previous census year; percentage change in welfare population in the previous censuses; the average AFDC monthly benefit per recipient in the previous census; the presence of work requirements, and of an unemployed parent programme in the state's welfare system during the previous year. See previous notes for the specification of the FHH and Expected welfare equations.

6. Forecasts and prospects

PER CAPITA INCOMES

One pattern that departs from the negative trend in relative family incomes is
the change of per capita incomes. Individual blacks appear to becoming better
off, despite the evidence that black families are falling behind. None the less,
the upward trend in the ratio of black–white per capita money incomes is one
that moves from a very low number. In 1967 black per capita income (expressed
in current dollars) was $1402. White per capita income in the same year was
$2604, almost twice that of blacks. Thus for every dollar of income that whites
received blacks received only about 54 cents.

   In 1978, black per capita income was $4034, while white per capita income
rose to $6797. Blacks received more than 59 cents for every dollar that whites

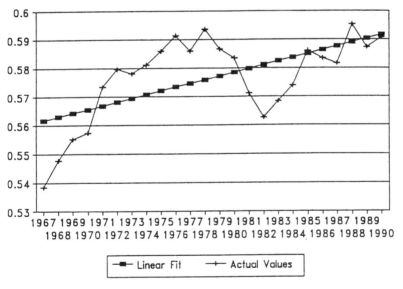

Source: Authors' computations, US Bureau of the Census, Current Population Reports, Series
P-60, No. 184, *Money Income of Households, Families and Persons in the United States: 1992*,
US Government Printing Office, Washington, DC, 1993.

Figure 6.1   Black–white per capita money income, 1967–90

received. By 1982, when black per capita income equalled $5360, white per capita income totalled $9527. The black–white ratio had declined to about 56 per cent. The ratio rose again to around 59 per cent by 1990 with blacks earning a per capita income of $9017 while whites earned $15 265. Thus, relative to whites, blacks received the same relative income in 1990 that they received in 1978.

The positive movements in per capita incomes are neither dramatic nor particularly reassuring. The estimated slope of the fitted line connecting the ratio of black–white per capita incomes each year is only 0.0013. That means each ten-year interval brings on average only an increase in the black–white ratio of about ¹⁄₁₀ of 1 percent. If we were to extrapolate these numbers and to ask how long it would take before equality in per capita incomes were reached, the answer would be 313 years. That is, given the existing trend, blacks and whites would not have equal incomes until the year 2303! In other words, racial parity in per capita income would be reached in 12 generations, given the trends displayed in Figure 6.1.

Furthermore, from a century-long view there is no evidence of an upward movement in relative black per capita income anyway. Vedder, Gallaway and Klingaman (1990, p. 130) have estimated that the black–white ratio of per capita income was 0.59 in 1880, identical to our 1990 estimate!

FAMILY INCOMES

Earnings inequality, particularly among family heads, is not likely to diminish in the years ahead. There are several factors at work. First, as the fraction of black families headed by females continues to grow, the share of lower-earning family heads among blacks increases. Even if the next generation of female-headed families were disproportionately drawn from the professional and managerial ranks – unlikely as that may be – the effect would not necessarily reduce racial inequality. If present trends continue, whereby even professional black women who head families are losing ground relative to professional white women, and are losing their relative advantage over other black female-headed families, racial inequality among family heads will continue to worsen.

A second factor at work is the continued decline in the relative earnings and the educational prospects of young black males. These individuals – should they become family heads – are not likely to be in a position to experience significant earnings growth over the years. More likely, they will either be non-earners or non-family heads, further contributing to the growth in female-headed families.

Perhaps more intriguing is the education factor. Education gains of the past decades were unevenly shared among family heads, earners and non-earners. Among black males, educational gains were limited to those with jobs and those who headed families. Some of these employed family heads held well-paid managerial and professional positions. Yet those non-family heads without jobs – including the increasing numbers of black males incarcerated or deeply scarred by arrest records and criminal involvement – saw no educational gains. And black female heads of families – whether they received wage and salary income or not – only realized modest educational gains.

It was those black females who did not head families, and who often had good jobs in professional and managerial occupations, whose educational levels rose substantially. Yet, since their educational levels lagged slightly behind those of comparably situated whites, there was little additional advantage conveyed to them. Thus, although uniform increases in educational completion ought to reduce racial inequality, the unevenness of educational gains within the black community resulted in muted progress.

Blacks suffer a major disadvantage with respect to advanced education, masked by the convergence in mean years of schooling. Among persons 25 years and older in 1990, 46 per cent of whites had some college education while only 37 per cent of blacks did (U.S. Deptartment of Commerce, 1991). Blacks will lack access to professional–managerial positions in the future as a result of this continuing gap in advanced education.

For example, there remains a large racial gap in the receipt of scientific degrees (Johnson, 1991b, pp. 13–18). Whereas whites comprised 75 per cent of the population in 1990, they received 88 per cent of science and engineering doctorates in 1987. Blacks comprised 12 per cent of the population in 1990 but received only 1.5 per cent of science and engineering doctorates in 1987. Blacks will necessarily be excluded from the managerial age – the age of science and technology – with this significant under-representation in advanced degrees.

The net effect of continuing inequality in more advanced education – even in the face of apparent convergence in average education completion – is to leave the black community underdeveloped. The United Nations has designed a Human Development Index as a measure of the quality of life across countries as an alternative to pure per capita income rankings. Computation of a separate Human Development Index score for African Americans indicates that the quality of life for the average black in the United States is similar to that of persons living in Portugal, Singapore and Korea. It is below that of persons living in Argentina, Poland, Hungary, Costa Rica and Hong Kong (Darity, 1991).

Recall Figure 6.1, which describes the trends of per capita incomes over the past decades. Part of the long-term decline in the ratio of black–white family incomes is due to the reduction in the relative wage and salary earnings of black family heads. But since there are mixed effects involved in the determination of black family heads' earnings – some positive and some negative –it is useful to extrapolate to year 2000 using entire family income information on past and current trends.

Estimating a straight line from 1967 to the year 2000 shows a predicted drop in the ratio of black–white family income to 0.60. That is, black families in the

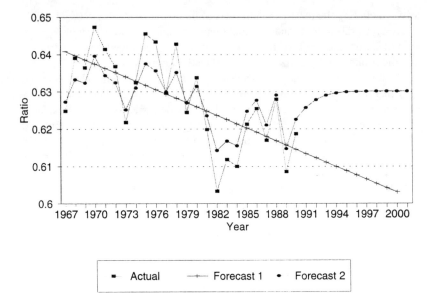

Source: As Fig. 6.1.

Figure 6.2   Black–white family income, 1967–90 and forecasts to year 2000

year 2000 can expect to earn 60 cents for every dollar white families earn if the quarter-century trend continues. Figure 6.2, with the results plotted as Forecast 1, reveals this outcome.

The past trend, however, shows several periods of slight improvement in the ratio of black–white family income. For example, family income rose from 0.625 in 1967 to almost 0.65 in 1970. After dropping to nearly 0.62 in the early 1970s, it rose again above 0.64 by the mid-1970s. There was a prolonged skid during the late 1970s until the recession of 1982, when the ratio fell to just above 0.60. The overall assessment, then, of the period between the end of the Great Society and the beginning of the Reagan Revolution was a deterioration of relative black family incomes.

However, the 1980s recovery from the recession and the rebound of the ratio of black–white family incomes, albeit only up to the level of the late 1960s, suggests that there may be a separate positive trend. This upward swing, led in part by the gains of male-headed families in managerial and professional occupations, may be short-lived if the recession years of the early 1990s pull down the relative earnings of these male managers and professionals along with those of females.

Nevertheless, it is possible to obtain estimates and forecasts based on a more sophisticated rendering of the ups and downs of relative incomes.[1] The results are displayed in Figure 6.2 as Forecast 2. The recent trend dominates the forecast, suggesting a growth in the ratio of black–white family income, but a growth which tapers off by the end of the century. The upshot is that even in this more optimistic scenario – no recessionary effects, no offsetting effects via the growth of female-headed families and the deteriorating plight of young black males – the ratio of black–white family earnings will be only 0.63.

This process can be averted if the growth of poor, female-headed families is curbed. As long as young men continue to be marginalized, however, the prospects for increasing the share of black families with male heads seems remote. Strengthening female-headed families, while obviously beneficial in the short run, offers little hope for reducing the earnings gap further. Since the culprit in this link remains the deteriorating position of young black males with little training or education beyond high school, the solution must lie in salvaging what otherwise could be a lost generation of men.

FAMILY STRUCTURE TO THE YEAR 2000

In a separate analysis we have computed forecasts of the fraction of black families headed by females using a model similar to the one presented here (see Darity and Myers, 1995). We concluded that the dramatic changes in black family structures in the past generation may foreshadow even more alarming transformations in the future. We identified two scenarios with vastly different implications for the black two-parent family over the next decades. One possible scenario is that the current pattern of reduced supplies of marriageable males will result in future generations of even greater numbers of black families headed by females and eventually virtually all black children will be raised in single-parent families.

The other scenario is one in which welfare continues to erode, families will become older, and the sex ratio impacts will be less severe. In the latter case, the current crisis of female-headed families must be viewed as an anomaly and the aging of the black family as a catalyst for the return to more normal patterns of two-parent family structures. In the former case, one speculates that the children of this generation's female-headed families will be struck as hard by the male shortage in the years to come as were their mothers. The effect will be the formation of even younger female-headed families than we now observe.

The conclusions hinged on what assumptions are made about the changing age structure of black family heads. The obvious implication is that if black families drift towards younger heads, wherein the available males are poorly educated and facing declining labour market prospects, the result will be fewer male-headed families.

Another way to look at the prospects for the future, however, is to project the recent time trends into subsequent years and to assume that the underlying factors affecting the trends of black and white families either have distinct impacts or identical impacts on blacks and whites. We can simply question what the future of black families will be if they follow the same patterns as whites in recent years as opposed to the trends they have experienced themselves. While it is not obvious how blacks are to follow these patterns – or even whether it is realistic or feasible for them to follow such patterns – it is at least worth asking what the difference would be if blacks somehow moved off the course they now are pursuing and were instead on the path that whites in America have faced over the years.

This is a deceptively simple exercise that yields disturbing results. Even if blacks managed to follow the trends of whites, nearly half of all black families would still be female-headed by the year 2000. On the course blacks are now following, clearly more than 50 per cent of black families will be female headed by the year 2000. But the difference is not great in the short run between the course they are now on and that of mimicking the white trends.

Figure 6.3 shows that the slope of the timeline for the growth of black female-headed families is significantly steeper than that for whites. This slope is estimated from exponentially smoothed data for the years 1970 to 1991, data plotted in the graph and labelled 'fitted'. The forecasts from these fitted data would project a rate of black female headship in the year 2000 of 55 per cent

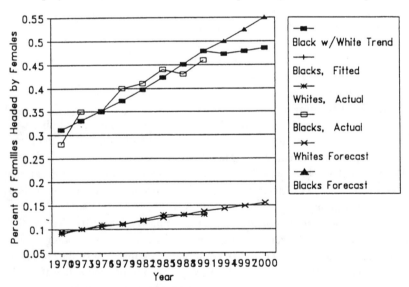

Source: Authors' computations, CPS March Supplement Tapes, 1991.

Figure 6.3　The year 2000: forecasts of female headship

and of white female headship of 16 per cent. If blacks faced the same trends as whites, slightly fewer black families would be female-headed in year 2000, but not by a wide margin. By that year 49 per cent of black families would be female-headed, under the assumption that racial differences in the trends disappeared.

In part, the problem is that both black and white families are travelling along a steeply sloped trajectory whereby the male-headed family is likely to become less and less prevalent in the years ahead. Among blacks deterioration of the two-parent family is clearly heavily concentrated among less well educated, younger family heads. But, unfortunately, even better educated young family heads are finding it difficult to form and sustain the traditional two-parent union.

Indeed, the growth in female headship among better educated young blacks is outpacing that of less well educated black family heads, who admittedly already have very high rates of female headship. Figure 6.4 shows that among positive earners aged 25 to 40, with some college education or with college degrees, the rate of female-headed families in 1991 nearly equalled that of families with young, uneducated heads in the 1970s and 1980s. The steepest rise in female headship has been among the most educated, employed black family heads in this age group. Thus policies that focus on welfare reform and problems of the underclass are not likely to be effective in curbing the growth in female headship among black families, if only because the problem has now gone far beyond the boundaries of the inner city and the poorest, least educated in our communities.

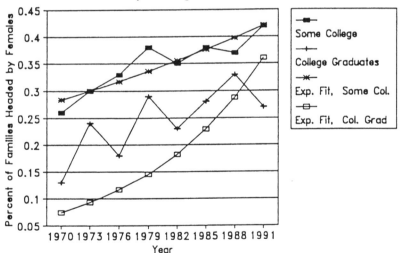

Source: As Fig. 6.3.

Figure 6.4   Female headship among better educated black families with positive earners, 1970–91

The role of the declining availability of young black males cannot be neglected here. The size of the pool of marriageable males is not increasing in the black community. While we find a relatively inelastic impact of sex ratios on the formation of female-headed families among blacks, we do find a statistically significant relationship between the two. The marginalization of young black males translates not just into fewer marriage partners for inner-city, poor mothers, but also for upwardly mobile middle-class women. The reach of the marginalization of young black males goes beyond the central cities and ultimately affects family structure across the economic spectrum of black communities.

ENDNOTE

1.   Specifically, we estimate a polynomial distributed lag model.

7. Remedies for racial economic inequality

At the outset of this monograph we identified the problem of widening income and earnings gaps between black and white families. Our empirical assessments demonstrate that although there is a plausible relationship between the widening gaps and the growing proportion of black families headed by females, changing family structures among blacks cannot be blamed for the deterioration in the relative economic position of blacks. Surely, the destabilization of the African-American family is of great concern and indeed may loom in the background of the widening gap between blacks at the top and at the bottom of the income distribution.

But the substantial effect of declining two-parent families among blacks is to widen intraracial inequality rather than interracial inequality. The latter is the result of persistent racially unequal evaluations of personal endowments in the determination of earnings. These disparities are the source of our discussion in this chapter. The question we pose is: What can be done?

RACIAL INEQUALITY: WHAT IS TO BE REMEDIED?

The problem of how to reduce intraracial inequalities evokes few of the emotions produced by the problem of interracial inequality. Less concern is given to blacks killing blacks than killing whites. Less concern is given to blacks stealing from other blacks than blacks stealing from whites. Less concern is given to blacks who rise economically at the expense of other blacks than blacks who rise at the expense of whites.

The attempt to reduce racial economic inequality in the 1990s comes during an era when there is increasingly hostile opposition to the adoption of redistributive measures that ostensibly make one group better off while making another group worse off. There is virtually uniform opposition among whites in the United States to the adoption of quotas or other racial preferences in hiring or employment that favour blacks and other racial minority group members.[1] The majority may argue in favour of equal opportunity, but when it comes to taking away from them to benefit others, they insist that a line must be drawn.

To be precise, the opposition comes not only from staunch opponents of expansion of economic opportunities for minorities, overt racists, or conservatives and neoconservatives of many stripes – including a growing and vocal group of minority conservatives. The opposition is now very evident in the inner circles of the new Democratic Party leadership, a centrist leadership that gained its legitimacy from an appeal to core democratic principles espousing fairness and equity in a society where every voice counts.

The centrist opposition believes race based strategies offend the basic populist sentiment that special interests skew the distribution of outcomes in an unfair manner. This applies even if the special interests are those of a group that has previously experienced discrimination under the very model of democratic fairness of equal protection of the law and basic protection against discrimination and unfair treatment that has failed to protect these groups.

Process matters a great deal in the centrist ideology. If the rules are not fair, then the outcomes of the process are suspect. If the rules of the game are fair, then remedies designed to correct the unequal outcomes become suspect. And particularly when the remedies appear to be unfair to the non-aggrieved party, the centrists are offended.

Many political pragmatists argue that since the centrist perspective dominates both the traditional liberal and conservative perspectives – after all a new president has been elected based on this perspective –the best hope for reducing racial inequality is to find remedies that are fair to the majority while offering hope of improving the well being of the minority. These are thought to be non-race-based remedies because they can improve the well-being of the minority without consciously making the minority better off at the expense of making the majority worse off.

Some will call these non-race-based strategies 'race-neutral', but this is a misnomer. The policy would only be race-neutral if it left the underlying racial distribution unaffected – such as a policy that increases overall income or output but leaves black and white shares of income or output unaffected. Arguably, blacks would be better off in an absolute sense from such expansion of economic prospects, but they would be no better off in a relative sense. A non-race-based remedy is one that has no race criterion in its application, although it may still result in an increase in the well-being of the minority relative to the majority.

Thus it is important to make the distinction between policies that are race-neutral and known to have or expected to have no impact on the relative distribution of rewards, and policies that are non-race-based and can in fact have a positive or negative effect on the relative distribution of rewards, but not at the expense of providing specific entitlements to racial minorities in preference to racial majorities. This distinction helps to demarcate the pragmatic centrists and the traditional conservatives.

Many traditional conservatives and most neoconservatives question the basic desirability of further reducing the gap between blacks and whites. After all, in their view, much of the savings behaviour from high earners that must be relied upon to spur economic growth and financial investment will come about because of the wide inequalities between the top and the bottom. Pragmatic centrists, such as Clinton adviser and Nobel Laureate, Robert M. Solow, argue in contrast that racially unequal outcomes are neither necessary nor desirable for economic growth.[2]

But they also argue that the real task òf the policy maker is to improve the economic performance of the economy so as to make the size of the pie larger, even if the price we pay is to leave the distribution of the pie unchanged. Such policies as improved investment in human capital inevitably will generate larger benefits to the young and disadvantaged, many of whom are members of racial minority groups. Yet such a result is neither assured nor intended by the non-race-based strategy of improved investment in human capital. The strategy works because it assures improved absolute positions of minorities, even if the direction of change in their relative position is uncertain.

Certain race-based strategies known generically within the labour econometrics literature as 'federal antidiscrimination legislation' include not just equal opportunity laws but the regulatory and enforcement efforts designed to achieve equality through affirmative action, racial preferences and even quotas and set-asides. Some of the opposition to these strategies, even within the pragmatic centrist position, comes from the belief that these race-based remedies have not achieved the desired result of reducing racial inequality. The problem is not just that the race-based strategies are perceived as unfair, but that they are also perceived as inefficient.

The most prominent perspective on the inefficiency of race-based strategies comes from a school of thought that might be called the 'minority conservative' school. Adherents include Shelby Steele and Glenn Loury, as well as more confirmed traditional black conservatives such as Walter Williams and Thomas Sowell (see Shelby Steele, 1990 and Sowell, 1984). The important and apparently valid empirical point is that the beneficiaries of race-based strategies have largely been middle-class or better-educated blacks.[3] The strategy of making the highest earners among blacks better off arguably has the short-term effect of reducing the observed earnings gaps between blacks and white. But, if the low earners are in fact made worse off – because the strategy reduces their incentive to self-invest or creates some other perverse incentives – then the impact could well contribute to a widening of the overall gap in income between the races.

So, which types of inequality are race-based remedies – to which there seems to be so much opposition – supposed to remedy? Interracial or intraracial inequality? The gap between blacks and whites or the gap between blacks at the top and those at the bottom? And, which interracial and intraracial inequalities are we attempting to remedy? The most obvious are those related to earnings. Adding to wage and salary earnings incomes from self-employment, farming, interest, rents, dividends, royalties, and government transfers yields a similar but slightly larger gap between blacks and whites.

Even larger gaps between blacks and whites are found in asset holding and wealth. While black families may receive about 60 cents for every dollar of income whites receive, they hold seven cents of wealth for every dollar of wealth held by whites. That is why the earnings gaps and the income gaps severely underestimate the broader gap in social and economic well-being between blacks and whites.

But blacks also are less likely to hold elected office or control shares in major corporations, and more likely to be in jail or unemployed or outside the labour force than whites. The racial disproportionality of imprisonment, unemployment and labour force participation, along with under-representation in public office and corporate America, are all indicators of another type of inequality: unequal access to power. The lack of political power arises from the problem of minority voting; how can a minority exert influence in a democracy when the minority group is racially dispersed? If blacks congregate in identical geographical areas, they may gain political control over some isolated areas, but they will not necessarily have influence on other spheres of life which directly affect them. If blacks disperse randomly across space, they can expect at most minority status everywhere, with only the power to stop things but not the power to make things change.[4]

Just as problematic is the absence of control over productive resources that comes via participation on corporate boards, university governing bodies and other public and private decision-making institutions. Here again, black–white inequality is an inequality of power.

The biggest gap of all, however, could be access to power over intergenerational transmission of status. An example is control of what becomes a criminal violation and what sanctions are adopted to punish those violations. Although blacks are seriously over-represented in America's prisons, and although that over-representation in recent years is directly a result of the national war on drugs, the absence of concrete control over, and thus power over, national drug policies, national sentencing reforms and penal revisions has meant that blacks lack power and control over an important aspect of intergenerational transmission of status. Why status? Because imprisonment means loss of voting rights, the right to perform certain jobs, or the right to be employed in certain industries. It means loss of moral authority. And it means loss of freedom.

In summary then, what is to be remedied? The problems are both interracial and intraracial in origin. The inequalities range from earnings to power.

SUMMARY OF REMEDIES

In a convenient and simplistic way, it is useful to conceptualize two broad categories of remedies for racial inequality: race-based and non-race-based. Figure 7.1 sketches some examples of these two broad categories of remedies. The vast majority of Americans are opposed to race-based remedies. On the race-based side are affirmative action, set-asides, quotas and various forms of preferential scoring. On the non-race-based side are various forms of assistance, generally means-tested programmes for low-income persons, but also assistance to businesses or other institutions if their activities are designed to aid those at the bottom and may have the effect of disproportionately benefiting blacks. These include educational vouchers, income transfers and grants for entrepreneurship development.

What should be clear from this simple distinction between race-based and non-race-based remedies is that they implicitly attack the problem both of intraracial and interracial inequalities in different ways. The race-based remedy focuses ostensibly on results. It hopes to achieve some degree of reduction in inequality by using the observed racial gap as the direct yardstick for assessing the degree of movement toward equality. Thus, if blacks only have 1.3 per cent of all the state's contracts for providing janitorial services, a minority business set-aside programme that sets as a goal a black share of 10 per cent of all contracts seeks to narrow the gap explicitly and directly by providing more contracts to blacks. The non-race-based remedy, however, hopes to create equality of opportunity among a class of persons, without regard to race, who are willing and able to contract with the state. This class may include small white as well as small black

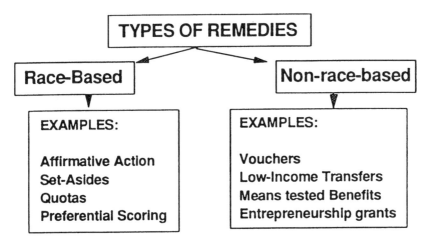

Figure 7.1   Types of remedies

businesses. An entrepreneurship training programme might disproportionately benefit blacks but would not be reserved for them.

There are many real-world policies that fall somewhere between these categories: targeting recruitment of minority scholars by dedicated visits to historically black colleges and universities, hiring goals, timetables and linkages of managers' performance to success in meeting 'diversity' goals. Are these or are these not race-based strategies? For simplicity we shall describe these grey areas as being race-based when they seem to fall closer to reliance on race alone than completely rejecting race as a determining criterion for selection.

The only way fully to appreciate the degree of disagreement over the choice of race-based as opposed to non-race-based remedies to racial inequality is to acknowledge the two extremes of justifications for remedies in the first place. The first is the retrospective inequity justification, which argues in effect that the remedy is a payment for a past wrong. The notion of reparations for the enslavement of Africans and Jim Crowism rests on a clear retrospective inequity justification. The other extreme is to justify remedies based on the contention that future inequities will make us all worse off. That is to say, we need to right the wrongs if we want to have a bigger pie tomorrow. This is the heart of liberal arguments in favour of diversity: there are efficiency gains by creating equality of opportunity for the next generation.

At first glance, these distinctions displayed in Figure 7.2 seem to parallel the distinctions in Figure 7.1. Race-based remedies can and indeed often do find

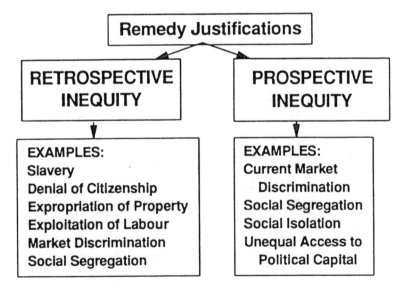

Figure 7.2   Remedy justifications

their justification in retrospective inequities. And those who justify remedies for racial inequality based at all on prospective inequities frequently point only to non-race-based remedies as the desired choice.

But not all race-based remedies rest solely on retrospective inequity justifications. Take, for example, the issue of divestiture of monopolies to minorities or the award of television or radio stations to minority groups. This is an example of a race-based remedy using a prospective inequity justification. Richard America argues that antitrust laws should be amended to make 'social over-concentration' akin to other forms of monopoly power now regulated by the Sherman Antitrust Act. The form of remedy would include divestiture of such monopolies to minority share owners. His argument is that under-representation, just like monopoly control, is socially inefficient. Thus the state should rectify the inefficiency through regulatory actions.

This idea does not fully anticipate the likely dynamics of such a regulatory regime. Firms threatened with possible divestiture because of 'social over concentration' would presumably make visible though non-structural changes in ownership to ward off possible litigation. They would certainly agree to negotiated settlements of increased minority ownership if such settlements prevented complete divestiture. The race-based strategy may improve minority ownership prospects, but it is unclear that it would bring about increased efficiency – the initial justification for the remedy.

Reparations, in contrast, are rarely justified by anything resembling prospective inequities. They usually explicitly acknowledge retrospective inequities. In making his economic case for reparations, Robert S. Browne (1974), founding editor of the *Review of Black Political Economy*, has detailed some of the key elements of a reparations formula and an implementation plan necessary for the scheme to be successful. He argues correctly, quoting Myrdal, that the absence of land reform as a component of the emancipation of black slaves contributed to the subsequent persistent inequality of wealth. While this point is made to buttress his case for reparations, it is also a point worth examining as a source for alternative strategies for reducing racial economic inequality.

In essence, what land reform would have achieved is the break-up of the ongoing proto-feudal plantation system and the creation of small owner-operated agricultural enterprises among former slaves. What happened instead was the displacement of the slaves from the former plantations and the creation of three classes of agricultural workers among blacks: tenant farmers, convict lease workers, and marginal owners frequently attached to unproductive land.

Ultimately, the effect was to drive many blacks with the slightest amount of education and/or entrepreneurial acumen out of agriculture and into provision of services to other largely segregated blacks. This contributed in part to the rise of a small black rural aristocracy in the South. Browne sees the absence of land reform as a failure to redistribute wealth. An alternative interpretation is that the lack of land reform meant that wealth inequality grew within the black community.

In discussing two familiar strategies that justify affirmative action programmes, Thomas Hill (1991, p. 110) claims that '"forward looking" appeals exclusively to the good results expected from such programmes; the other, "backward-looking," focuses on past injustice and demands reparations'.[5]

This distinction is really a distinction between equity considerations and efficiency. Forward-looking strategy, or expectation of good results, usually means that the good result is a larger pie that in principle can result in increased consumption by both the minority and the majority. The policy is Pareto-efficient because it results in an increase in the consumption of one party without a corresponding reduction in the consumption of another.

The policy may fail the Pareto test if the increased pie necessarily comes about by changing the shares of the pie consumed by the respective parties. But even here some would adopt a Hicks–Kaldor criterion that asks whether the gains to the winners exceed the casualties of the losers so that, at least in principle, redistribution can occur to relieve the distress of the losers and still leave the gainers better off.

The backward-looking strategy, on the other hand, is explicitly a redistributive one with no pretence of leaving the losers better off or no worse off than before reparations. Rather, reparations are by design intended to rectify past wrongs and are expected to make the losers relatively worse off. The question of fairness of this backward looking strategy comes from the recognition that the current beneficiaries of the reparations may not be the victims of the prior distress, and the current victims of the reparations may have been innocent beneficiaries of the previous discrimination or they may not have benefited at all.

The core of the reparations arguments thus rests on demonstrating the benefits that current generations of whites have accumulated as a result of prior discrimination against blacks. Otherwise, the reparations argument is flawed by the absence of guilty beneficiaries from previous discrimination and the presence of innocent victims should the reparations be extracted. It is adequate to show how much blacks lost from the slave trade; reparations theorists also must show that whites gained and continue to benefit from the economic development that was supported directly by the slave trade.

An example of a non-race-based remedy that has significant impacts on ownership prospects is worker ownership of firms. One such strategy discussed in the literature involves Employee Stock Ownership Plans (ESOP). The advantage is that they provide workers in poor and inner-city areas with added incentives to increase productivity and thus to increase profitability of local businesses.

Spillover effects can generate positive impacts on the minority community. It is not clear whether these plans address the issue of intraracial inequality. Will gaps widen between workers and non-workers? It is not obvious that such plans will reduce interracial inequality either. Squires (1992) finds wide variations in black–white wage gaps across a variety of ESOP firms: the mean black–white gap among ESOP firms is similar to the mean in industries generally.

Now, there are race-based strategies that are clearly prospective. The justification is clearly one of efficiency. The intention is to make blacks better off without making whites worse off. These strategies typically involve linkages between African Americans and Africa, wherein African Americans gain ownership of property in the motherland.

Two specific proposals evolved from the second African/African American Summit in Libreville, Gabon. Both aim to achieve Pareto-efficient gains for black Americans through race-based remedies. They are both intimately linked to the idea of improving ownership and earnings prospects for African Americans via partnerships with Africans.

The first involves the use of dual citizenship in order to permit blacks in the United States to own and manage businesses and agricultural enterprises as residents of African states without having to renounce their United States citizenship. The key to operationalizing these special benefits to African Americans, who will be able to acquire valuable physical capital and fertile and highly rich agricultural land at below-market rates, is that they must be willing to offer some of their expertise and skills to help improve industry and technology in African countries. A skills bank would link talented African Americans with African countries in need of technical and managerial support (see Reed, 1993).

The second and more controversial of the proposals was the idea of repatriation of African American prisoners. One version of the proposed idea was advanced by Nation of Islam Minister Louis Farrakhan, who 'proposed that African countries be willing to take some of America's black prisoners and allow them to develop areas in their countries, much like what was done with British prisoners in the development of America and Australia' (Reed, 1993).

One of the central aspects of dual citizenship proposals is that it creates privileges by providing rights that the majority only secures within a single state. Such rights include the right to vote, the right to protection by the state and economic security, and the right to inherit or to hold real property (see Hammar, 1985, pp. 438–50). When a person holds dual citizenship in different democracies, that person gains new privileges above and beyond those held by citizens in each state.

In the United States, for example, the right to vote in a local election is restricted to persons who reside – usually for some minimal period – in the location. Providing the right to vote in multiple jurisdictions, even when the person resides in both, in effect awards the person additional power beyond the one vote to which he or she has a right. The dual citizenship creates a new privilege (Miller, 1989, pp. 945–50). Much of the literature on problems of dual citizenship pertains to guest workers, such as Turks in Germany or Sudanese in Saudi Arabia. In the case of African Americans in Africa, it is not clear that whites will view the new privilege as a loss that they bear.

Can race-based remedies be Pareto-efficient? In other words, is it possible to make blacks better off without making whites worse off by using remedies that target blacks for improvement? In the previous example, the answer is yes only if whites do not believe that the dual citizenship bestowed on blacks deprives whites of some privilege.

It is easier to talk about Pareto-efficient race-based remedies in the abstract than to conceive of concrete examples. Nevertheless, such abstraction has prevailed for years, particularly in university circles.

The argument runs as follows. Society is changing. Our ability to compete depends on our ability to produce a highly productive workforce that mirrors the social and demographic distribution of the more highly diverse populations of the world than the racially homogeneous populations of many advanced industrialized nations. To achieve diversity in the workforce, however, we must disproportionately allocate resources to the young and growing portions of the population, which for a variety of reasons happen to be disproportionately minority. According to this view, diversity enhances both the quality of the workforce and the productive capacity of the overall economy.[6]

To some, this 'excellence through diversity' perspective is a smokescreen for permitting the extension of affirmative action programmes in the face of continued court and public opposition. That this perspective is frequently promoted within university settings may further implicate universities in charges of attempting to promote 'politically correct' strategies.[7]

But to others it is a sincere attempt to justify redistributive policies on Pareto-efficient grounds: 'We need to reduce the racial gap if we are to improve our ability to increase the size of the pie.' Or, equivalently, 'Whites benefit when blacks are made relatively better off.'[8]

One of the main objections to race-based policies is that they do not work. Another objection is that they do not ensure long-term reductions in racial inequality through wealth accumulation and capital transfers from one generation to a next. Roy Brooks (1992) makes both points in his book, *Rethinking the American Race Problem*. Brooks contends that existing civil rights laws and policies are the primary contributors to obstacles found by middle-class and working-class blacks. He argues that basic civil rights policy or 'formal equal opportunity', which should be an instrument of promoting racial inclusion and equality, has in fact 'given little or no priority to specific civil rights interests of middle class and working class African Americans and ... [has] reduced the opportunities available through law to effectively remedy the uneven distribution of societal hardships between races and classes'. He (Brooks, 1992, pp. 4–5) contends, 'As they are currently interpreted and applied, then, civil rights laws and practices accommodate, prolong and intensify intraclass racial disparity.'

This conclusion is not supported by available evidence in schooling, housing, employment or military enlistment, all of which demonstrate the substantial narrowing of the racial gap since the passage of the civil rights laws of the 1960s. But that does not deter Brooks from asserting the ineffectiveness of civil rights laws. He argues, moreover, that there are smaller negative impacts of civil rights laws on the poverty class. But, like Wilson, Brooks believes that the policy of racial integration contributes to the rise of underclass subcultures. Thus civil rights cannot be relied upon to return to intraclass racial disparities. Brook's strategy is to promote self-help:

> No amount of government intervention, with either economic or legal resources, will solve America's race problem unless it is combined with a strong private initiative on the part of African Americans – namely, self-help. African Americans must package an intensive, long-term program to prepare primarily the working class and poverty class, especially members of the underclass, to take advantage of government-created opportunities in employment, housing, and education. Once these vital socioeconomic resources become more accessible, African Americans must be mentally and behaviorally ready to compete aggressively for such resources. This book outlines a program of self-help that can respond to these needs.

His justification for a black self-help strategy is that government will not act in the interests of blacks. The government cannot be counted on to reduce racial inequality. Thus racial relations are not likely to improve and therefore blacks must fend for themselves.

Why do civil rights laws work against the interests of the black middle class? Brooks says that 'strict scrutiny' tests discourage affirmative action in public sector employment to remedy past discrimination in this sector. This curious conclusion emerges despite overwhelming evidence of substantial growth of black employment in the public sector following the enactment of the 1964 Civil Rights Act.

And how will self-help solve the problem of racial inequality? Brooks (1992, p. 14) will rely on the generosity of the black middle class:

> I envision a program of household support in which middle class African Americans work one-on-one, long-term, with poorer families and underclass to impart and to coach the behaviors, values, and attitudes of mainstream society, as well as the survival techniques that African Americans have found essential in a racist society.

CHOOSING REMEDIES

The deterioration in the position of black families may be the result of retrenchment in public support for policies aimed at improving the lot of racial minority group members. These policies include equal opportunity in education and in employment, vigorous enforcement of antidiscrimination laws and affirmative action strategies. But it may be impossible to continue to implement race-based remedies in an era when white households are losing ground.

At the precise moment when we observe a renewed deterioration in the economic position of a historically important segment of our population, the nation has moved away from support for direct policies designed to improve their lot. Unfortunately, there is no assurance that indirect methods – methods that might be called non-race-based remedies – will have the effect of reducing racial inequality. Many of the policies that ought to work to reduce historical legacies of racial inequality – such as set-aside programmes, racial preferences in hiring and the like – fail an important new litmus test that many Americans consider to be reasonable: we should not make one group worse off in order to make another group better off.

There is no blueprint for resolving this dilemma. No one has discovered the magic bullet for solving the racial inequality problem. But the battle lines have been drawn, limiting us to a range of strategies that either offer little hope of actually reducing interracial inequality or promise to extend the hostility and ill-will between whites and non-whites in the United States.

ENDNOTES

1. According to the Gallup Poll, 7 per cent of whites and 29 per cent of non-whites supported affirmative action in 1981. See Gallup (1982). These figures changed little by 1991; nationally 11 per cent favoured affirmative action, 8 per cent of whites did, and 24 per cent of blacks did. Furthermore, 55 per cent of Americans believed the United States had enough laws aimed at reducing discrimination. See Gallup (1992).
2. Robert M. Solow (1992) believes that a source of doubt and discouragement regarding the current economy is the widening inequality in income distribution. Solow states that 'a policy of investment in human capital could choose to aim at bringing up the lower tail of that distribution. This would certainly reduce inequality and there is also a possibility that it might favor growth.'
3. Some argue that white females are the biggest gainers from affirmative action and that these gains are being made at the expense of black men. See Cortese (1992, pp. 77–89).
4. Lani Guinier (1989, p. 434) calls for 'new legal remedies to contradictions between American democratic ideology and minority disenfranchisement'. But the pragmatic centrist perspective prevents a strategy, such as cumulative voting, that holds promise of increasing black political power through reduction in the voting effectiveness of the majority. It runs against the basic democratic ideology positing not only one man, one vote but also majority rule.
5. Hill (1991) also makes the distinction between 'forward-looking, utilitarian' arguments in favour of race-based policies and 'backward-looking, reparations' arguments in favour of race-based policies.
6. One need only look at the cover story of *Nation's Business* and many other journals and periodicals to see that businesses are beginning to view diversity as an asset. See Sharon Nelton (1992, pp. 18–24). Businesses have become aware of the fact that they can recruit excellent employees by looking beyond the traditional white male candidates.
7. Dinesh D'Souza (1991, p. 231) writes: 'Universities show no interest whatsoever in fostering intellectual diversity But universities do take very seriously the issue of racial

underrepresentation. Here they are quite willing to consider goals, quotas ... whatever will rectify the tabulated disproportion. "What we're hoping ... is that racial diversity will ultimately lead to intellectual diversity" '.

8. Linda Greene (1990, p. 1531) writes: 'In the last decade of the twentieth century, the Court demands that the precious political capital of minorities seeking economic equality be spent determining the existence of racial economic discrimination rather than pursuing policies to insure minority participation in public economic programs.' The 'rights of whites' theory of the equal protection clause forces a strict scrutiny test requiring that special benefits to blacks do not necessarily come at the expense of making whites worse off.

8. Conclusions and policy directions

The questions we have addressed in this monograph are prompted in part by a concern that public policies designed to reduce or eradicate racial economic inequality have lost their moral and intellectual standing in past decades. Such policies as affirmative action, racial preferences and various forms of set-aside programmes are viewed by many as both unnecessary and unfair. Other policies, such as welfare expenditure programmes intended to reduce poverty generally, have lost political support in part because they appear not to work either in reducing general inequality or in reducing interracial inequality.

Current public policies on racial inequality are deeply rooted in a conceptual framework that points to the cultural and human capital deficiencies of blacks. These cultural and human capital deficiencies include lower educational attainment, lower labour force attachment, higher rates of female-headed families, and poorer skills that leave racial minority group members concentrated in certain occupations and industries that pay low wages. Conspicuously absent in recent discussions of how to address the widening economic gap between white and non-white families is the role of discrimination and continued barriers to advancement based on race. Also absent is recognition of the historic role of unequal wealth and ownership of productive resources. Instead, much is said about what needs to be done to improve the aspirations, the motivation and the moral behaviour of poor blacks, and conspicuously little is said about other determinants of social and economic position.

Our empirical analysis establishes that unequal pre-labour market and extra-labour market discrimination, along with continuing unequal treatment of equally qualified families, lies behind the persistent earnings gaps between black and white family heads. Our empirical analysis verifies that racially unequal incomes and earnings persisted into the 1990s despite substantial public policy interventions during the 1970s. Our empirical analysis reveals as well that widening gaps *within* racial groups coincide with widening interracial inequality. In essence, then, the problem to be remedied – widening between-group inequality – is exacerbated by widening within-group inequality.

We find that widening earnings gaps between black and white family heads cannot be due solely to rising female headship among black families. Only a small portion of the 5 per cent increase in the racial earnings inequality between 1976 and 1985 can be explained by the higher proportion of female heads among black as opposed to white families. Public welfare retrenchment policies – such as reduced benefits for additional children and requirements that teenage mothers live with a parent – designed to promote family stability cannot hope to solve the problem of racial earnings inequality. Even policies designed to increase the supply of marriageable mates – policies that offer greater hope for increasing two-parent families than do welfare retrenchment policies – will do little to reduce earnings inequality precisely because female family headship is not the central cause of the widening gap between black and white family earnings.

The range of remedies available for reducing the racial gap is narrowed, moreover, because of the widening gap between the top and the bottom. Remedies designed to reduce between-race inequality are far more likely to be accepted and acceptable when within-race inequality is not a pressing concern. Unfortunately, at precisely the point in our history when new and better remedies for reducing racial inequality are demanded, general inequality is increasing. How is it possible to promote and implement effective policies designed to improve the economic status of African Americans when the economic status of white middle-class Americans is deteriorating?

Our empirical conclusions are pessimistic. Pursuing the path already established offers little or no hope for near term equalization of incomes between races. Worse, our central conclusions suggest that the *cause* of the persistent inequality most probably lies in pre-labour market or extra-market forces, rooted most probably in historic discriminatory institutional forces. Thus, even if there are immediate remedies such as affirmative action that might hope to reduce current income inequality, it is uncertain that those efforts will necessarily yield permanent reductions in racial economic inequality.

Our focus has been on income and earnings. When the debate widens to embrace the fact that unequal wealth is far more pronounced than unequal income and to recognize the longer-term negative impacts of unequal wealth on pre-labour market and extra-labour market inequalities, then we believe wealth redistribution remedies will take on an increasingly central role in policy discussions of racial inequality. To understand how this policy shift must come about, recall the path that previous discussions have taken.

THE CHANGING PATH OF POLICY DEBATE ON RACIAL INEQUALITY

Policy debates on racial inequality are linked inextricably to policy research and social science knowledge. The most recent surge of policy retrenchment related to affirmative action, race-based remedies and antidiscrimination efforts is occurring at the same time that widely read works such as *The Bell Curve* and *The End of Racism* are forcing policy analysts and researchers to re-examine their data and their analyses. The policy changes are both influenced by and influencing the research and studies of scholars and academics.

Such studies designed to assess the course of black economic progress in the United States seem to occur at regular intervals. Two standard questions are commonly addressed in these studies: How much progress has there been and what are the sources of advance and retreat? The most prominent of these have been the study conducted by Charles Johnson in the 1920s, the Myrdal report in the 1940s and the National Academy of Sciences report in the 1980s organized by Gerald Jaynes and Robin Williams, *A Common Destiny*.[1]

Comparisons are often made between racial groups with respect to relative earnings, income, weeks worked, unemployment rates and the like – outcomes linked to the labour market. Interestingly, economists have devoted considerably less attention to comparing positions in terms of wealth, net worth or asset ownership – outcomes with a much weaker link to labour market experiences. With the measures utilized, black progress is gauged by how much closer the profile of black accomplishment converges towards that of whites.

Until recently an implicit assumption in such studies has been an idealization of a particular concept of racial economic equality as a goal – equality of economic results. From the perspective that seems to inform these studies, the race problem in the United States would be over if the black population exactly mimicked the pattern of stratification that exists in the white population. If 10 per cent of white Americans are poor, then only 10 per cent of black Americans should be poor, rather than 35 to 40 per cent. Blacks should own a share of Fortune 500 companies that matches the black share in the population, rather than less than 0.5 per cent.

Similarly, blacks should possess a share of the general wealth in the United States that matches the black share in the US population. Blacks should hold 12 per cent of science and engineering doctorates in the US rather than less than 2 per cent. Furthermore, if 30 per cent of whites hold professional managerial positions, then 30 per cent of blacks should hold comparable positions, instead of a mere 16 per cent. Perhaps, by the same token, 88 per cent of the players in the National Basketball Association should be non-blacks!

The goal of racial parity carries no philosophical connotations whatsoever of an attack on inequality in general. The distinction between racial equality and general equality as social objectives is made plain in the following passage from Sundaram and Shari's (1986, p. 8) study of the New Economic Policy in Malaysia:

> Despite the government's avowed commitment to poverty eradication, it should be emphasized that there is no official commitment to reducing economic inequality

between the rich and the poor. On the contrary, there have been pronouncements by prominent government leaders on the need to maintain economic inequality as an incentive for stimulating private enterprise. For example, Dr. Mahathir Mohamed [the present Prime Minister of Malaysia] once said that '...in trying to redress the imbalance it will be necessary to concentrate your efforts on the Malays, to bring out more Malay entrepreneurs and to make Malay millionaires, if you like, so that the number of Malays who are rich equals the number of Chinese who are rich, the number of Malays who are poor equals the number of Chinese who are poor, and the number of unemployed Malays equals the number of unemployed Chinese, then you can say that parity has been achieved.'

The ideal of racial economic parity based upon equal economic results directs us to look at the occupational and income profile of black America. If the profile looks the same as that of white America, then the American 'race problem' could be declared at an end. Blacks would have achieved representational parity with whites in the sphere of labour market activities, having attained identical outcomes.

Juxtaposed against the retrospective concept of equality of economic results is the prospective concept of racial equality in the sense of equal opportunity. The principle of equal opportunity dictates that the chance to compete for society's prizes should be independent of an individual's ascriptive characteristics. Ability and motivation alone should determine how preferred positions and status are to be distributed across a community, and not group status, family wealth, inherited assets or other 'unfair advantages'. Equal opportunity espouses the meritocratic ideal as the foundation of the good society. The allocation of society's rewards is to be governed strictly by individual worth and performance, calibrated by commonly understood and presumably fixed standards.

Racial equality in the sense of equal opportunity necessarily permits unequal economic results as a possibility, but it promotes an ostensibly fair environment for generating the outcomes. Distribution of population across hierarchical ranks should be solely a matter of merit – not nepotism, racial or ethnic preference, or the capricious choice of successors by those already in power. Equality of opportunity, as a guidepost for social organization, aims to produce a deserving élite.

Laws that promote redistribution of wealth, tax inheritance heavily and attempt to mute the impacts of unearned advantage are often promulgated with an equality of opportunity ideal in mind. One of the largest threats to the ideal of equal opportunity is the persistence of group advantage from one generation to the next via wealth accumulation. Young home buyers, for example, do not begin with equal access to credit. Those from families with assets are able to secure loans through down-payments obtained from family gifts and loans. Those from poor families must struggle to obtain down-payments through savings. Even white poor families are more likely to own assets than black poor families (Myers and Chung, 1996). This, we argue, is the result of white privilege.

Since equality of opportunity does not guarantee equality of results, to attain the alternative ideal racially equal results may require an environment with compensatory racial privilege. An environment of equal opportunity may not generate equal outcomes for many reasons: wealth inequality, cultural differences between the races, differences in culturally reinforced aptitudes and abilities between the races or, what is more likely, the persistent effects of historic discrimination directed against the group with inferior status.

Even if today's society could miraculously be purged overnight of discrimination as a factor affecting the distribution of rewards, past discrimination might continue to affect the competitive capacity of individuals who are from ascriptively differentiated groups.[2] Historical discrimination that excluded members of a particular ethnic or racial group from desirable options, or from resources they might otherwise have obtained, can disadvantageously affect their descendants' ability to engage in today's equal opportunity wars.

This notion is supported by the research of Francine Blau and John Graham, who found that the wealth of young black families (heads of households aged 24 to 34 years) is on average 18 per cent of the wealth of young white families, and that they tend to hold less of it in the form of net liquid and net business assets and more of it as equity in houses and cars (Blau and Graham, 1990, pp. 321–39). Edward Wolff reports, based upon data from the 1983 Survey of Consumer Finances (SCF) and the 1984 and 1988 Survey of Income and Program Participation (SIPP), that the mean net worth of all black families averaged only 23 per cent of that of white families, and black family median net worth was only 9 per cent of that of whites throughout the 1980s. The marked difference is attributable to 'the large number of black families with zero net worth' (Wolff, 1992, pp. 555–6).

The gap is not due to racial differences in savings rates, nor to racial differences in rates of return earned on comparable assets, according to Blau and Graham.[3] The racial disparity in net worth is linked most decisively to a gap in access to the major source of wealth in American society: inheritance (Blau and Graham, 1990, pp. 337–8; Wolff, 1992, p. 556). Black parents and grandparents of earlier generations simply had less wealth to pass on to their descendants, given the historical limitations confronting them. Intergenerational transfers of household wealth can only be made if there is wealth in the family to transfer. To the extent that blacks were themselves property, and after emancipation were systematically denied opportunities to accumulate property, their wealth was severely truncated.[4]

But why does it matter if the black–white ratio of wealth – yet another comparative economic measure in which the white profile sets the standard –

is low? The implications would be especially profound if a genuinely colour-blind, equal opportunity world actually came into existence.

For example, it has been remarked widely that native black Americans tend to have lower rates of self-employment than many other ethnic groups. Data from the General Social Survey for the years 1983 to 1987 indicate that a mere 5 per cent of Americans of primarily African ancestry are self-employed, while 25 per cent of Jewish Americans are self-employed, and more than 12 per cent of Americans of English, German or Asian ancestry are self-employed (Butler and Herring, 1991, pp. 84–5). Moreover, blacks who are self-employed earn less than each of the white ethnic groups represented in the survey: about $6000 less than Irish Americans, $5000 less than Italian Americans, $10 000 less than Polish Americans, and over $20 000 less than Jewish Americans (Butler and Herring, 1991, p. 90).

Why is this the case? Despite commonplace anecdotal data about cultural differences in attitudes toward entrepreneurship, and regulatory barriers that disproportionately inhibit 'minority' business participation, three factors of critical importance emerge in careful studies explaining the self-employment gap. These factors are differences in educational backgrounds, particularly with respect to professional credentials – a factor of growing importance in an era of small business activity geared increasingly towards provision of professional services; differences in social learning opportunities; and, most important, differences in wealth.[5]

The social learning hypothesis says exposure to a relative's self-employment activity, especially that of a father, raises the likelihood that individuals will themselves be self-employed. However, racial differences in wealth make it less likely that blacks, compared to whites, might have had a self-employed parent or relative. Such differences also lower the range of educational options.

The effects of historic deprivations are cumulative. Persistent economic deprivations in the past – born of exclusion, seizure of property and containment – reduce the average level of wealth in a population. Not only do lower levels of wealth adversely affect attainable levels of education and participation in small business activity for past generations, they also affect access to quality housing and the amenities associated with living in comfortable communities with safe and quality schools. And, in the context of self-employment activity, they affect the conditions for entry into the business environment for the present generation. Access to bank loans, for example, is greatly reduced if the potential applicant does not have sizeable equity capital (Bates, 1991, p. 35). It is a notorious complaint of aspiring black business persons that they are trapped in a Catch-22. Without adequate financial capital they cannot get their enterprise off to a proper start. Without equity capital they cannot get debt capital. Without both they cannot have adequate operating capital.

To compound matters, there is strong evidence of discriminatory lending practices by commercial banks toward blacks. Faith Ando found that the rate of bank loan application acceptances of short-term loan applications by black owners of established small businesses in the early 1980s was much lower than the rate for Hispanics, whites and Asians. In fact, she found that the rate was *highest* for Asians and virtually *identical* for whites and Asians. After controlling for various indicators of possible risk differentials, Ando still found that black firm owners had a significantly lower likelihood of having their loan application accepted (Ando, 1988).

That the sources of wealth differ substantially between blacks and whites further underscores the legacy of racial inequality. Among the 20 per cent most wealthy Americans, 94 per cent had income from interest, dividends, rent, royalties, estates or trust. In contrast, only 32 per cent of the poorest fifth had such property income, and most of those families where white.

In 1990, 46 million families received property income. Almost 42 million of them were white. Of the 2.8 million blacks who received any interest, dividends, rents, royalties or income from trusts or estates, most property income came from interest. Even among black families with incomes above $100 000, very little income derives from dividends or rents.

If racial differences in wealth lie at the core of the self-employment disparity and at the core of the income gap among mature households, and if it is viewed as desirable to close the self-employment gap and the household income gap, the obvious solution is to engineer a racial redistribution of wealth. On the face of it, such a step seems to be beyond the pale of the politically plausible. But in Malaysia, as part of the New Economic Policy (NEP) inaugurated in 1969, ownership of equity was shifted disproportionately towards the ethnic Malay population in an affirmative action programme on a scale never contemplated in the United States, except by advocates of reparations for slavery and Jim Crow. In the 20 years following the adoption of the NEP in Malaysia, the Malay share of ownership in Malaysian corporations rose from less than 2 per cent to 20 per cent.[6]

Still, there have been complaints by its proponents that the programme failed because it did not attain its target of 30 per cent Malay ownership. Supporters and opponents contend that it did not improve the degree of intragroup equality among the native Malays; while opponents complain the NEP violates the principle of equal opportunity.

There remain, however, some proponents of equal opportunity who would make a case for some form of compensatory actions on behalf of a group that has experienced historical deprivations. For example, the philosopher John Rawls has designed a social ideal that he refers to as a world of 'fair equal opportunity' (Rawls, 1971, p. 100).

To open the door to the possibility that procedural equality or equal opportunity can lead to equal outcomes, the participating groups in the social game must be sufficiently similar in average capacity and motivation to make an authentic contest. Therefore, Rawls argues, the equal opportunity principle must be modified by a fairness principle to prevent the emergence of 'a callous meritocratic society' (Rawls, 1971, p. 100). Rawls says that true fairness would require compensating persons for differential disadvantages they face due to 'birth' and 'natural endowment' – what he views as 'undeserved inequalities'. Consequently, 'to provide genuine equality of opportunity, society must give more attention to those with fewer native assets and to those born into the less favorable social positions ... greater resources must be spent on the education of the less than the more intelligent, at least over a certain part of life ...' (Rawls, 1971, pp. 100–101). Even an individual's personal 'character depends in large part upon fortunate family and social circumstances for which he can claim no credit' and may be the source of additional 'undeserved inequalities' in a society that provides rewards for personal character. Again, redress for an unfair initial advantage needs to be made to produce fair equal opportunity (Rawls, 1971, pp. 101–102).

Rawls thus appears willing to offset innate or genetic disadvantages with compensatory policies. He also seems receptive to ongoing or continuous dosages of compensatory measures for those faced with 'undeserved' disadvantages. Certainly the logic of his position would justify a racial redistribution of wealth or reparations of some sort for the descendants of enslaved Africans and victims of Jim Crow politics, who suffer inherited disadvantages as a consequence of their ancestors' experiences in America.

Indeed, one of the few white advocates of reparations, Charles Krauthammer, argues in favour of paying every African American a once-and-for all lump sum of, say, \$100 000 to close the door on alternative affirmative action schemes that look to him like employment or educational admissions reservations (Krauthammer, 1990, p. 18).

Rawls and Krauthammer are both attempting to cope with the tension between their preferred worlds of equal opportunity and the phenomenon of inherited disadvantage that would disproportionately limit the ability of particular groups to compete successfully. This conflict is very evident in the philosophical difficulty that Rawls's notion of fair equal opportunity runs into:

> Indeed, if initial differences across individuals are minimized to make the game fair, why have them run the social foot race at all? Is there not even in Rawls' fair equal opportunity, a cloven hoof of inegalitarianism? For running alongside the notion of 'undeserved inequalities' there must be 'deserved inequalities.' The more narrow the range of initial conditions that must be equalized before the social game is considered 'fair,' the closer we are to [pure equal opportunity, undiluted by Rawlsian 'fairness']. The wider the band of conditions that must be equalized before the social game is

considered 'fair,' the closer we are to a guarantee of equal results from the game. In short if 'undeserved inequalities' are identified in a limited sense, fair equal opportunity converges to pure procedural equality; if undeserved inequalities are identified broadly, fair equal opportunity converges with uniformity of outcomes. (Darity, 1987, p. 180)

The Malaysian-type policy is the antithesis of the pure equal opportunity principle, for it seeks in race-conscious fashion to redress the present-day consequences of past inequities. And, indeed, unless an environment of equal opportunity is inaugurated in conjunction with a major attempt to redress inherited inequalities, then equal opportunity is liable to seal in place unequal results by race. Uniform procedural conditions for social rivalry coupled with vast inherited disparities in resources is a recipe for perpetual disparity.

Moreover, equal opportunity as a social ideal presumes that social competition is desirable, supposedly from an incentive standpoint: that society should produce winners *and* losers. Those who tend to be proponents of equal results as the social ideal typically duck the question of whether there are potentially desirable effects from social competition at all, particularly with respect to incentives for achievement.

The expectation that American society has been on a trajectory towards racial parity is ideologically satisfying for those with somewhat uncritical, mainstream views of the opportunity structure afforded in the United States. The American Dream is or soon will be possible for all, even the descendants of enslaved Africans. At last the discrepancy between American beliefs and American racial practices would evaporate. Myrdal's famous 'dilemma' would be resolved at last.

WEALTH REDISTRIBUTION AS A REMEDY FOR RACIAL INEQUALITY

If we believe that inequalities in current economic prospects are rooted in unequal pre-labour market characteristics and/or historical inequalities in ownership and wealth, a case can be made for redistributing wealth in order to eliminate racial economic inequality. One controversial form of wealth redistribution is reparations. We define reparations as compensatory payment for an acknowledged grievous social injustice to a group. The social injustices visited upon African Americans would include the historical experiences of slavery, legally sanctioned apartheid or Jim Crow practices, and ongoing discrimination. These three facets constitute the particular pattern of injustice affecting African Americans and have led some to advocate a scheme of reparations as restitution for those wrongs (see, for example the essays in America, 1990).

These advocates have included black nationalist activists James Forman and 'Queen Mother' Audley Moore. In 1969 Forman, one of the founding members of the Student Nonviolent Coordinating Committee (SNCC), interrupted a Sunday morning service at Riverside Church in New York City and read a black manifesto that included a demand that churches and synagogues pay $500 million to black Americans as a *first* phase of reparations for historic oppression (see Forman, 1972; Bitker, 1973; Carson, 1981).

'Queen Mother' Audley Moore began a campaign in the 1950s for the same sum, again as partial compensation for slavery. She met President Kennedy at the White House in 1962 in an attempt to advance the cause, and her Reparations Committee of Descendants of US Slaves did file a legal claim in California. However, her efforts were largely viewed as idiosyncratic and were eclipsed in the public eye by the legislative successes of the Civil Rights Movement. Nevertheless, she never viewed the Civil Rights Act of 1964 or the Civil Rights Bill of 1965 as measuring up to the intent of her reparations claim (Bair, 1993, pp. 812–13; Sommerville, 1992, pp. 764–7).

In 1934 the National Movement for the Establishment of a 49th State, based in Chicago, called for the creation of a new state of the union 'wherein colored people in the United States can have the opportunity to work out their own destiny, unbridled and unhampered by artificial barriers ...'. The organization offered four main reasons for carving out a separate geographical area for black Americans who would choose to live there, the third of which included the observation that 'aid to the Negro in the establishment of his new state offers an opportunity for the nation to reduce its debt to the Negro for past exploitation' (Aptheker, 1992, pp. 84–90).

Realized instances of reparations in the United States include the Congressional agreement in the late 1980s to pay $20 000 to each living Japanese American subjected to internment during World War II. The same enabling legislation included a provision to make payments of $12 000 to 450 living Aleut Indian evacuees with supplementary funds provided to compensate them for their wartime losses (Dewar, 1988). Even earlier agreements were reached with the Passamaquody Indian tribe in Maine, inclusive of land and monetary compensation in settlements for abrogation of treaties by the US government (Liebman, 1983, p. 14). Similar land and gambling rights agreements have been made with other Indian tribes in the north-western United States.

There are also precedents elsewhere in the world. In 1988 the German industrial giant, Daimler-Benz, agreed to pay the equivalent of $11.7 million to victims of Nazi forced labour policies during the war, as well as to their families. On the basis of an agreement signed in Luxembourg in 1952 between West Germany and the World Jewish Congress, the West German government had paid close to $50 billion in reparations to Holocaust survivors by the end of the 1980s (Associated Press, 1988, p. 27A).

In May 1995 the Austrian Parliament passed a bill to compensate victims of Nazism there as well. The bill also provides compensation for 'those who fled Austria [due to Nazi persecution] and their children born before May 9, 1995'. Heinrich Neisser, deputy speaker of the Austrian Parliament, estimated that the cost of the reparations programme will range from $300 to $500 million (Cohen, 1995, p. 22).

And there are potential claims to be made elsewhere. In the early 1970s the West Indian economist, Norman Girvan (1974), argued that the comprehensive pattern of European exploitation of the Third World led to European economic development and, therefore, all Third World peoples should receive compensation. Girvan's estimate of the value of the exploitation attributable to the use of black slave labour during the period 1790–1860 alone, compounded to the time of his essay, ranged from $448 to $995 million.

In May 1993 at a summit of African and African American leaders held in Libreville, Gabon, Reverend Jesse Jackson proposed that slave reparations be 'paid' to the African nations in the form of debt relief. The collective total of African states' external debt was about $255 billion at the time of the summit, owed primarily to multilateral organizations, particularly the World Bank and the International Monetary Fund, and to foreign governments.

Patently restitution could be justified for the deleterious impact of slavery and the slave trade on the African continent. The 'killing fields' of Cambodia are another instance where the prospect of reparations appears to be appropriate.

But we are unaware of any instance in which compensatory payments were made to peoples of primary African descent for their subjugation to slavery – whether to emancipated slaves in the West Indies in the 1830s or emancipated slaves in the United States of America in the 1870s. In contrast, in the British West Indies, slave owners were paid for the loss of their human property by the British Parliament. The masters were paid £2 per slave, the total coming to £20 million in 1833, an extraordinary sum. But the ex-slaves themselves received nothing (Marx, 1974, p. 352 n. 12).

In the US South rumours abounded that the ex-slaves would receive the vaunted 40 acres and a mule. But with the end of radical reconstruction, prospects for any form of reparations for the ex-slaves evaporated in the US. On the other hand, Abraham Lincoln and the Republican Party had earlier proposed payment to slave owners as a means to emancipate the slaves and avoid civil war. Lincoln's proposal did not include a plan for compensation for the slaves themselves (Lincoln, 1976, pp. 328–9).

Indeed, no compensation has ever been paid to the relatives or descendants of slaves who died during the drive to the African coast from the interior of the continent, during the Middle Passage, during the 'seasoning' period in the

New World, or who lived to labour from sunup to sundown under a regime of forced labour over the course of more than 200 years.

The end of slavery in the United States came with war and when at last the war had ended 4 million largely illiterate ex-slaves were thrust into a ravished and economically battered region. No effort was made at restitution, nor even any significant effort at investment in the ex-slaves aside from the modest and short-lived activities of the Freedman's bureau and the short-lived political actions of the ex-slaves themselves in Southern state legislatures (DuBois, 1935).

The collapse of slavery and the demise of reconstruction gave way to a formal American system of apartheid in the US South that lasted roughly from 1873 to 1960, directly affecting the lives of four generations of African Americans beyond slavery. Thereafter the civil rights revolution launched a series of legislative initiatives that dismantled the formal structure of American apartheid. This included the adoption of federal anti-discrimination legislation and the adoption of affirmative action in the form of a Nixon administration executive order (Anderson, 1994).

Even with the formal structure dismantled, anti-black discrimination is still powerfully operative, particularly in dictating access to occupation and earnings (see the papers in Fix and Struyk, 1992; Darity, Guilkey and Winfrey, 1995). Ongoing discrimination is a persistent obstacle to racial equality.

Various economic rationales for reparations for African Americans can be considered: compensation for slavery; compensation for discrimination both in the Jim Crow and post-Jim Crow era; and compensation for a cumulative disparity in wealth. Estimates of the requisite payments range from $60 000 per African American to $266 667 per African American or a payment in excess of $1 million for a family of four.[7]

Total estimates of reparations for slavery and/or discrimination are in the range of trillions of dollars. These figures are astronomical, although the estimates fall in the range of those offered by reparations advocacy groups such as the Rockville, Maryland-based Black Reparations Commission that has placed the recommended total payment as high as $4 trillion. Other procedures used to compute the reparations due for enslavement of African Americans and the cumulative effects of discrimination produced estimates of $500 billion dollars in 1983. The 1995 figure would be closer to $650 billion.[8]

Historic patterns of control and repression have limited black wealth accumulation and the cross-generational consequences are present to this day. Swinton (1990) estimated that in 1983 the value of all private non-human assets in the United States was $7.1 trillion and that total black wealth amounted to no more than 2 per cent of that sum (also see Browne, 1974). At that time, for black wealth holdings to match non-black wealth holdings proportionately, black ownership of US non-human assets would need to have risen from approximately $142 billion to $800 billion, a more than fivefold increase.

Recently Swinton has proposed a level of reparations requiring payment to the African American population of $700 billion to $1 trillion motivated by the same analysis – as an avenue to redress inherited inequality between the races. This is indicative of the magnitude of the wealth redistribution that would be required to make the proportion of black ownership of the US capital stock equivalent to the black presence in the US population.

The question of allocative equity among blacks would have to be addressed if such a redistribution were pursued. Increased wealth customarily enhances maintenance of a secure income, access to advanced educational credentials, the capacity to form sustainable businesses, and, for that matter, the capability to overcome or bypass the adverse effects of anti-black prejudice.

It can be argued, of course, that blacks already have been compensated for historic injustices in the form of affirmative action. So, the argument goes, there is no need for a new reparations initiative; reparations already have been paid.

Historically, affirmative action has not rested on the goal of compensation for past injustices, nor has it provided a vehicle for redress of wealth disparity. Until recent Supreme Court decisions requiring strict scrutiny of race-based programmes, affirmative action programmes have largely been designed to address the question of present discrimination. Indeed, the courts as a whole have ruled that general societal discrimination or lingering impacts of segregation or slavery are not in and of themselves proof of current discrimination (Myers,1993).

The most favourable study of the benefits of affirmative action at the national level is the research of Jonathan Leonard on government contractors compared with non-contractors. Leonard demonstrates that government contractors have a higher rate of hiring blacks than non-contractors. But the study is weakened somewhat because the contractors' rate of hiring blacks was already significantly higher before affirmative action was inaugurated. Moreover, during the 1990–91 recession, blacks were the only racial group to suffer net job losses at 35 242 firms reporting to the Equal Employment Opportunity Commission (EEOC), government contractor firms (Sharpe, 1993).

More convincing is the Heckman and Payner (1989) study on textile manufacturing in South Carolina. This appears to be a case where affirmative action was pursued with some force, and the racial composition of South Carolina's manufacturing industry changed dramatically.

Regardless, affirmative action is now under heavy assault. Philosophically it is especially disturbing to those who idealize a colour-blind society, although how a society with sharp inequalities, historically generated by race, can close the gap without utilizing race conscious policies is not clear to us.

At least one vociferous opponent of affirmative action, Charles Krauthammer (1990, p. 18), endorses reparations as a substitute for affirmative action. We see the need for both. But, barring the collapse of the US economy, a programme of substantial reparations can have a greater effect. If forced to choose – and we hope the Krauthammer 'deal' is not a Faustian bargain – we would take substantial reparations and forego affirmative action. At minimum the resources from reparations could mitigate the effects on the life chances of those African Americans who are victims of racism.

ENTREPRENEURSHIP AND WEALTH REDISTRIBUTION

We would argue that there is really no substitute for continued and vigorous enforcement of existing anti-discrimination statutes. We would be remiss if we suggested that a direct redistribution of $1 trillion to African Americans without a government-backed, publicly supported anti-discrimination mechanism would suffice to eliminate racial economic inequality for all time. While we believe that such anti-discrimination enforcement efforts are required and essential for preventing further erosion of blacks' economic position, we doubt whether they are sufficient to assure equality.

But would direct redistribution of wealth, with anti-discrimination enforcement, be enough? What about the large portions of the incarcerated black population? What about the many poorly trained, unskilled young adults? What about young black males who have dropped out of the labour force and who have turned increasingly to illegal activities for their livelihoods? What happens to them in the redistribution scheme?

The answer may lie in enterprise and entrepreneurship. There is a long tradition of trying to translate the enterprising skills of the poor and the criminal talents of inner-city youth into productive entrepreneurial activity. It is a part of the literature on entrepreneurial training for the disadvantaged.

The academic community was introduced to this concept by Michael Piore, one of the originators of the concept of dual labour markets. Piore noted that there was a primary labour market with well paying, high-quality jobs, and a secondary labour market, in which most blacks were isolated, with low-paying, unpleasant jobs. He noted, however, that there was a segment within the secondary labour market that had many of the personal characteristics of managers and entrepreneurs and not of primary labour market workers. Programmes designed to train these persons as ordinary workers might fail because these persons were better suited to be entrepreneurs.

The strategy advocated was deceptively simple: train young disadvantaged blacks to be managers and entrepreneurs, not primary labour market workers. The strategy was to recognize the existing strengths of many young blacks who were all too frequently destined for lives of crime, drugs and ultimately imprisonment, or joblessness, unemployment and ultimately economic dependency, because traditional training programmes were focused on training these youths for industrial and manufacturing jobs when blue-collar jobs were disappearing and crime was becoming more and more attractive.

The strategy was to value the attributes of young teenage mothers, on welfare and out of school, with no skills and no hope of obtaining them, rather than condemn them for either their lack of initiative and motivation or for their immorality. In essence, this strategy gave the disenfranchised the hope of owning and running legitimate enterprises as an alternative to making babies or doing drugs. The strategy focused on black people's strengths rather than their failings.

In a wealth redistribution scheme, the poorest of blacks could become entrepreneurs, home owners, and small business owners. Black youth might apply their entrepreneurial skills learned in the booming and lucrative drug market to legal and viable economic activities with high long-run returns. Welfare mothers might receive training in accounting, tax law, finance and bookkeeping so that they could run their own businesses, even housekeeping and catering services. Efforts would be needed to redirect the phenomenal talents of young street hustlers so that they could produce and sell food and clothing products in the black community.

Moreover, there will be a need to invest the redistributed wealth and monitor the performance of the investment pool. Who will do this? Community controlled corporations or development councils? Expert advisers from the historically black colleges and universities or from the minority professional associations of lawyers, bankers and accountants? Will the money be put into a trust for education and home purchase?

One route towards assuring that the poorest of the poor within the African American community are the beneficiaries of strategies like reparations designed to redistribute wealth is to enhance their involvement in enterprise through training programmes now. Although it may seem unrealistic to suggest that a former drug dealer or welfare mother should be trained in the nuances of tax law, budgeting and accounting, it is certain that the poor will be disadvantaged again and again if even wealth redistribution occurs and the poor are shut out of decision making and policy making concerning what is to be done with the redistributed wealth.

Many of these ideas of empowering the poor, increasing ownership among the disadvantaged, and promoting entrepreneurship among inner city youth appeal to stark conservatives who resort to the power of the marketplace and self-help strategies for solving problems of poverty and race. Unfortunately, these self-help, market-oriented policies are of little use if a) discrimination continues to exist, and b) unequal wealth persists from one generation to the next. If we are to be successful in reducing racial economic inequality within our children's or children's children's lifetimes, wealth redistribution will have to be a central part of the overall agenda for change. As outrageous and unrealistic as it may sound at this moment to the vast majority of Americans, the astronomical debt to African Americans must be repaid once and for all.

ENDNOTES

1. Johnson (1930); (1944) and Jaynes and Williams (1989).
2. For a theoretical demonstration of this result see Ruhm (1988).
3. Indeed, several studies on consumption behaviour have shown that at any given level of income blacks have a lower propensity to consume and a higher propensity to save than whites on average. See Friedman (1957), pp. 79–85; Alexis (1971) and Hamermesh (1982). Only Marjorie Galenson's (1972) study is an exception, and Galenson found no racial differences in savings rates.
4. For a comprehensive statement of this argument see Swinton (1992) See also Higgs (1980).
5. The relevant studies are Bates (1991) and Butler and Herring (1991), passim. It is notable here that recent immigrant populations who have high rates of self employment typically have high rates of advanced educational credentials. The case of the Korean immigrants is of signal importance in this regard. See Steinberg (1981) p. 104, n. 48.
6. See Cait Murphy (1990). It should be noted, however, that over the 20-year period the ethnic Chinese share in Malaysian equity also rose slightly. The ethnic Malay gains were attributable to a sharp decrease in the foreign ownership share in Malaysian corporations and to the disproportionate allocation of the sharp rise in corporate valuation over the period to the ethnic Malays.
7. These estimates are based on calculations of James Marketti (1990) who has computed the potential income lost by Africans by being enslaved. Marketti used the average market price of slaves decade by decade from 1790–1860 as an estimate of the income Africans could have earned as free labourers in the United States. Compounded to 1995, using Marketti's procedure, one can estimate a total compensation for this 'diverted income' ranging from $1.8 trillion to $4.7 trillion, measured in 1983 dollars. The lower figure was based upon use of a 3 per cent interest rate for compounding, while the higher figure was based upon use of an interest rate of 5 per cent before 1860 and 3 per cent thereafter. An alternative calculation can be performed with a 5 per cent interest rate before 1860 and a 3 per cent interest rate thereafter that treats the horizon of diverted income as stretching from 1620 to 1860. In 1983 dollars the magnitude of reparations would reach the $8 trillion threshold, requiring a payment of $266 667 per African American or a payment in excess of $1 million for a family of four.
8. David Swinton (1990) estimates that 40–60 per cent of the gap in black–white median incomes is due to the *cumulative* effects of discrimination.

Bibliography

Acs, Gregory and Sheldon Danziger, *Educational Attainment, Industrial Structure and Male Earnings*. Working paper, Institute for Research on Poverty, 1989.

Adler, Paul, 'New Technologies, New Skills', *California Management Review*, **29** (1) (Fall 1986), 9–28.

Alexis, Marcus, 'Some Negro–White Differences in Consumption', in *The Black Consumer*, edited by George Joyce and Norman A.P. Govoni, pp. 257–74. New York: Random House, 1971.

Allport, Gordon W. *The Nature of Prejudice*, Cambridge: Addison-Wesley, 1954.

Altonjj, Joseph and David Card, 'The Effects of Immigration on the Labor Market Outcomes of Natives', in *Immigration, Trade, and the Labor Market*, edited by John M. Abowd and Richard B. Freeman, pp. 201–34. Chicago: University of Chicago Press, 1989.

America's Choice: High Skills or Low Wages. Rochester, NY: National Center on Education and the Economy, 1990.

America, Richard F. (ed), *The Wealth of Races: The Present Value of Benefits from Past Injustices*. Westport, CT: Greenwood Press, 1990.

America, Richard F., *Paying the Social Debt: What White America Owes Black America*. Westport, CT: Praeger, 1993.

Anderson, Bernard E., 'Affirmative Action Policy Under Executive Order 11246: A Retrospective View', in *Civil Rights and Race Relations in the Post Reagan-Bush Era*, edited by Samuel L. Myers Jr. Westport, CT: Greenwood Publishing Group, 1997.

Ando, Faith, *An Analysis of Access to Bank Credit*. Los Angeles: UCLA Center for Afro-American Studies, 1988.

Aptheker, Herbert (ed.), 'The National Movement for the Establishment of a 49th State', In *A Documentary History of the Negro People in the United States*, vol. 4. Secaucus: Carol Publishing, 1992.

Associated Press. 'West German Firm to Pay WWII Forced Laborers Nearly $12 Million', *Dallas Morning News*, 12 June 1988, p. 27A.

Atkinson, Anthony B., 'On the Measurement of Inequality', *Journal of Economic Theory*, **2** (3) (September 1970), 244–63.

Bailey, Tom, *Changes in the Nature and Structure of Work: Implications for Skill Requirements and Skill Formation*. Technical paper no. 9. Columbia University Project on the Conservation of Human Resources, 1989.

Bair, Barbara, 'Moore, Audley (Queen Mother)', in *Black Women in America: An Historical Encyclopedia*, edited by Darlene Clark Hine. Brooklyn: Carson Publishing, 1993.

Bamezai, Anil, 'Rising Earnings Disparity and Technological Changes', unpublished Ph.D. dissertation. The RAND Graduate School, 1989.

Bartel, Ann P. and Frank R. Lichtenberg, 'The Age of Technology and Its Impact on Employee Wages', in *Economics of Innovation and New Technology*. UK: Harwood Academic Publishers, forthcoming.

—————— and Frank R. Lichtenberg. 'The Comparative Advantage of Educated Workers in Implementing New Technology', *Review of Economic Statistics*, **69** (1) (February 1987), 1–11.

Bates, Timothy, 'Discrimination and the Capacity of New Jersey Area Minority and Women-Owned Businesses', unpublished manuscript, Graduate School of Management and Urban Policy, New School for Social Research 1991.

Bean, Frank, G. Lindsay Lowell and Lowell J. Taylor. 'Undocumented Mexican Immigrants and the Earnings of Other Workers in the United States', *Demography*, **25** (1) (February 1988).

Becker, Gary, *The Economics of Discrimination*. Chicago: University of Chicago Press, 1957.

Bell, Derrick, *Faces at the Bottom of the Well*. New York: Basic Books, 1993.

Bell, Linda and Richard Freeman, 'The Causes of Increasing Inter-Industry Wage Dispersion in the United States', in *Industrial and Labour Relations Review*, **44** (2) (January 1991), 275–87.

Berger, Mark C., 'The Effect of Cohort Size on Earnings Growth: A Reexamination of the Evidence', *Journal of Political Economics*, **93** (3) (June 1985), 561–73.

Berman, Eli, John Bound and Zvi Griliches, 'Changes in the Demand for Skilled Labor with U.S. Manufacturing: Evidence from the Annual Survey of Manufactures', *Quarterly Journal of Economics*, **109** (2) (May 1994), 367–97.

Bishop, John, 'Achievement, Test Scores and Relative Wages', AEI Conference, Wages in the 1980s, 1989.

Bitker, Boris, *The Case for Black Reparations*. New York: Random House 1973.

Blackley, Paul, 'Spatial Mismatch in Urban Labor Markets: Evidence from Large U.S. Metropolitan Areas', *Social Science Quarterly*, **71** (1) (March 1990).

Blalock, Hubert M., Jr, *Toward a Theory of Minority Group Relations*. New York: John Wiley & Sons, 1967.

Blau, Francine D. and John W. Graham, 'Black/White Differences in Wealth and Asset Composition', *Quarterly Journal of Economics*, May 1990, 321–39.

———— and Lawrence M. Kahn, 'The Gender Earnings Gap: Learning from International Comparisons', *American Economic Review*, **82** (2) (May 1992), 533–8.

———— and Lawrence M. Kahn, 'Rising Wage Inequality and the U.S. Gender Gap', *American Economic Review*, **84** (2) (May 1994), 23–28.

———— and Andrea Beller, 'Black-White Earnings Over the 1970s and 1980s: Gender Differences in Trends', *Review of Economics and Statistics*, **74** (1992), 276–86.

Bleakley, Fred R., 'Lenders' Gains.' *Wall Street Journal*, 12 February 1992.

Blinder, Allan S., 'Wage Discrimination: Reduced Form and Structural Estimates', *Journal of Human Resources*, **4** (Fall 1973), 436–55.

Bluestone, Barry, Mary Huff Stevenson and Chris Tilly, 'The Deterioration in Labor Market Prospects for Young Men With Limited Schooling: Assessing the Impact of "Demand" Side Factors', paper presented at the Eastern Economic Association Meeting, Pittsburgh PA, 1991.

Blumstein, Alfred, 'On Racial Disproportionality of United States Prison Populations', *Journal of Criminal Law and Criminology*, no. 73 (1982), 1259–81.

———— and Elizabeth Grady, 'On the Racial Disproportionality of United States Prison Populations', *Law and Society Review*, **16** (1982), 265–90.

Boozer, Michael A., Shari Wolkon and Alan B. Krueger, *Race and School Quality Since 'Brown vs. Board of Education'*, Princeton Industrial Relations Working Paper, no. 301, 1992.

Borjas, George J., 'Immigrants, Minorities, and Labor Market Competition', *Industrial and Labor Relations Review*, **40** (3) (April 1987), 382–92.

———— and Valerie Ramey, 'Foreign Competition, Market Power, and Wage Inequality: Theory and Evidence', unpublished manuscript. University of California–San Diego, 1993.

———— and Valerie Ramey, 'Time-series Evidence on the Sources of Trends in Wage Inequality', *American Economic Review*, **84** (2) (May 1992), 10–16.

Bound, John and Richard B. Freeman, 'The Gender Earnings Gap: Some International Evidence', In *Differences and Changes in Wage Structure*, edited by Richard B. Freeman and Lawrence Katz. Chicago: University of Chicago Press, 1994.

———— and Richard B. Freeman, 'The Impact of Wage Structure on Trends in U.S. Gender Wage Differentials: 1975–1987.' unpublished manuscript. University of Illinois, March 1993.

———— and Richard B. Freeman, 'What Went Wrong? The Erosion of Relative Earnings and Employment Among Young Black Men in the 1980's', *Quarterly Journal of Economics*, **107** (February 1992), 201–32.

———— and Harry J. Holzer, *Structural Changes, Employment Outcomes, and Population Adjustment Among White and Blacks, 1980–1990*. Madison, WI: Institute for Research on Poverty, University of Wisconsin–Madison, 1995.

Boyd, Robert, 'Black Business Transformation, Black Well-being and Public Policy', *Population Research and Policy Review*, **9** (1990).

Bridges, George S. and Robert D. Crutchfield, 'Law, Social Standing, and Racial Disparities in Imprisonment', *Social Forces*, **66** (3) (March 1988), 699–724.

Brooks, Roy L., *Rethinking the American Race Problem*. Berkeley: University of California Press, 1992.

Brown, Charles, 'Black–white Earnings Ratios Since Civil Rights Act of 1964: The Importance of Labor Market Dropouts'. *Quarterly Journal of Economics*, February 1984, 31–44.

Brown, Michael K. and Steven P. Erie, 'Blacks and the Legacy of the Great Society: The Economic and Political Impact of Federal Social Policy', *Public Policy*, **29** (Summer 1981), 299–330.

Browne, Robert S., 'Wealth Distribution and Its Impact on Minorities', *The Review of Black Political Economy*, **4** (1974), 27–38.

Burr, Jeffrey A., Omer R. Galle and Mark A. Fossett, 'Racial Occupational Inequality in Southern Metropolitan Areas, 1940–1980: Revisiting the Visibility-discrimination Hypothesis', *Social Forces*, **69** (3) (March 1991), 831–50.

Bush, Vanessa, 'Lessons Learned in 1986 Ease Today's Refinancing Wave', *Savings Institutions*, May 1991.

Butler, John S., *Entrepreneurship and Self-help Among Black Americans: A Reconsideration of Race and Economics*. Albany, NY: State University of New York Press, 1991.

———— and Cedric Herring, 'Ethnicity and Entrepreneurship in America', *Sociological Perspectives*, **34** (1) (1991), 84–5.

———— and James H. Heckman, 'The Government's Impact on the Labor Market Status of Black Americans: A Critical Review', In *Equal Rights and Industrial Relations*, edited by Leonard J. Hausman et al. Madison, WI: Industrial Relations Research Association, 1977.

Cancian, Maria, Sheldon Danziger and Peter Gottschalk, 'Working Wives and Family Income Inequality Among Married Couples', In *Uneven Tides: Rising Inequality in America*, edited by Sheldon Danziger and Peter Gottschalk. New York: Russell Sage, 1994.

Canner, Glen B., A. Gabriel Stuart and J. Michael Wooley, 'Race, Default Risk and Mortgage Lending: A Study of FHA and Conventional Loan Markets.' *Southern Economic Journal*, **58** (1991), 249–62.

Card, David and Alan B. Krueger, 'The Economic Status of Black Americans: What Can We Do About It?: Trends in Relative Black–white Earnings Revisited', *American Economic Review*, **83** (2) (May 1993).

—— and Alan Krueger, 'School Quality and Black–White Relative Earnings: A Direct Assessment', *Quarterly Journal of Economics*, **107** (1992), 151–200.

—— and Thomas Lemieux, 'Changing Wage Structure and Black–white Wage Differentials', *American Economic Review*, **84** (2) (May 1994), 29–33.

—— and Thomas Lemieux, *Wage Dispersion, Returns to Skill and the Black–white Wage Differential*. Working Paper no. 4365. Cambridge, MA: National Bureau of Economic Research, 1993.

Carr, James H. and Isaac F. Megbolugbe, 'The Federal Reserve Bank of Boston Study on Mortgage Lending Revisited', *Journal of Housing Research*, **4** (2) (1993), 277–313.

Carson, Clayborne. *In Struggle: SNCC and the Black Awakening in the 1960s*. Cambridge, MA: Harvard University Press, 1981.

Center for Human Resource Research, *NLS Users' Guide 1994*. Columbus, OH: Ohio State University Press, 1994.

Chachere, Bernadette, Richard America and Gerald Udinsky, 'An Illustrative Estimate: The Present Value of the Benefits from Racial Discrimination, 1929–1969', in *The Wealth of Races: The Present Value of Benefits from Past Injustices*, edited by Richard F. America. Westport, CT: Greenwood Press, 1990.

Chinhui, Juhn, Kevin M. Murphy and Brooks Pierce, 'Accounting for the Slowdown in Black–White Wage Convergence', in *Workers and Their Wages: Changing Patterns in the United States*, edited by Marvin Kosters. Washington, DC: American Enterprise Institute Press, 1991.

Clark, Stephen, Richard Hemming and David Ulph, 'On Indices for the Measurement of Poverty', *The Economic Journal*, **91** (June 1981), 515–26.

Cocheo, Steve, 'Affordable Housing: No Easy Answers', *ABA Banking Journal*, October 1992.

Cohen, Shawn, 'Austrians Provide Reparations to Holocaust Survivors', *Washington Jewish Week*, 29 June 1995, p. 22.

Conrad, Cecilia, 'The Economic Cost of Affirmative Action, in *Economic Perspectives on Affirmative Action*, edited by Margaret C. Simms. Washington, DC: Joint Center for Political and Economic Studies.

Conrad, Cecilia A., 'A Different Approach to the Measurement of Racial Inequality', *Review of Black Political Economy*, **22** (1) (Summer 1993), 19–31.

Conrad, Cecilia, 'A New Approach to Measurement of Racial Inequality', mimeo. Barnard College, 1986.

Cortese, Anthony J., 'Affirmative Action: Are White Women Gaining at the Expense of Black Men?', *Equity & Excellence*, **25** (1992), 77–89.

Cotton, Jeremiah, 'Opening the Gap: The Decline in Black Economic Indicators in the 1980s', *Social Science Quarterly*, **70** (4) (December 1989), 803–35.

――――, 'The Relationship Between Wage and Inequality and Trade', in *The Changing Distribution of Income in an Open U.S. Economy*, edited by J.H. Berstrand, T.F. Cosimano, J.W. Houck and R.G. Sheehan. New York: Elsevier, 1994.

Culp, Jerome and Bruce Dunson, 'Brothers of a Different Color: A Preliminary Look at Employer Treatment of White and Black Youth', unpublished manuscript.

Cutler, D.M. and E.L. Glaeser, 'Are Ghettos Good or Bad?' in *NBER Working Paper No. 5163*, 1995.

D'Amico, Ronald, and Nan Maxwell, 'The Continuing Significance in Minority Male Joblessness', *Social Forces*, forthcoming.

―――― and Nan Maxwell, 'The Impact of Post-school Joblessness on Male Black–white Wage Differentials', *Industrial Relations*, **33** (2) (April 1994).

Danziger, Sheldon and Daniel Feaster, 'Income Transfers and Poverty in the 1980's', in *American Domestic Priorities*, edited by John Quigley and Daniel Rubinfield. Berkeley: University of California Press, 1985.

―――― and Peter Gottschalk, 'Income Transfers: Are They Compensation for Past Debt?', in *The Wealth of Races: The Present Value of Benefits from Past Injustices*, edited by Richard F. America. Westport, CT: Greenwood Press, 1990.

―――― and Peter Gottschalk, 'Increasing Inequality in the United States: What We Know and What We Don't', *Journal of Post Keynesian Economics*, **VII** (2) (Winter 1988–9), 174–95.

―――― and Peter Gottschalk (eds), *Uneven Tides: Rising Inequality in America*. New York: Russell Sage, 1993.

―――― and Peter Gottschalk, 'Work, Poverty and the Working Poor', Testimony Before the Employment and Housing Subcommittee of the House Committee on Government Operations, mimeo, 1985.

――――, Peter Gottschalk and Eugene Smolensky, 'How the Rich have Fared, 1973–87', *American Economic Review*, **79** (2) (May 1989), 310–14.

Darity Jr, William A., 'Illusions of Black Economic Progress.' *Review of Black Political Economy* **10** (4) (Winter 1980), 154–68.

――――. 'Equal Opportunity, Equal Results and Social Hierarchy', *Praxis International*, **7** (2) (July 1987), 180.

――――, 'The Human Capital Approach to Black–white Earnings Inequality: Some Unsettled Questions', *Journal of Human Resources* (1982).

――――, 'The Political Economy of Uneven Development from the Slave(Ry) Times to the Managerial Age', paper presented at the 1991 Conference on Africology, University of Wisconsin at Milwaukee,1991.

————, 'Underclass and Overclass: Race, Class and Economic Inequality in the Managerial Age', In *Essays on the Economics of Discrimination*, edited by Emily P. Hoffman, pp. 67–84. Kalamazoo, MI: The Upjohn Institute, 1991.

———— and Samuel L. Myers Jr, 'Public Policy and the Conditions of the Black Family Life', *Review of Black Political Economy*, 1 & 2 (1984), 165–87.

————, David Guilkey and William Winfrey, 'Ethnicity, Race and Earnings', *Economic Letters*, **47** (March 1995), 401–8.

———— and Samuel L. Myers Jr, 'Black Economic Progress: A Case Against the Dramatic Improvement Hypothesis', Institute for Research on Poverty Discussion Paper #613–80, 1980b.

———— and Samuel L. Myers Jr, 'Black–white Earnings Gaps Have Widened: The Problem of Family Structure, Earnings Inequality and the Marginalization of Black Men', AASP Working Paper Series: *Policy Research, Analysis and Minority Communities*, **1** (5), University of Maryland at College Park, August, 1991.

———— and Samuel L. Myers Jr, 'Changes in Black–White Income Inequality, 1968–78: A Decade of Progress?', *Review of Black Political Economy*, **10** (Summer 1980), 355–79.

———— and Samuel L. Myers Jr, 'Does Welfare Dependency Cause Female Headship? The Case of the Black Family', *Journal of Marriage and the Family*, **46** (1984), 765–80.

———— and Samuel L. Myers Jr, 'Family Structure, Earnings Inequality and the Marginalization of Black Men', paper presented at the Western Economics Association Meetings, Lake Tahoe, July, 1989.

———— and Samuel L. Myers Jr, 'The Impact of Violent Crime on Black Family Structure', *Contemporary Policy Issues*, **8** (1990), 15–29.

———— and Samuel L. Myers Jr, 'Public Policy Trends and the Fate of the Black Family', *Humboldt Journal of Social Relations*, **14** (1 & 2) (1986–87), 134–64.

———— and Samuel L. Myers Jr, *Racial Earnings Inequality: Trends and Prospects*. Minneapolis: University of Minnesota, 1992.

———— and Samuel L. Myers Jr, 'The Vintage Effect and the Illusion of Black Progress', *Urban League Review*, **5** (1) (Summer 1980a), 54–65.

———— and Samuel L. Myers Jr, 'The Widening Gap: A Summary and Synthesis of the Debate on Increasing Inequality', prepared for the National Commission for Employment Policy, 1995.

————, Samuel L. Myers, Jr, Emmett D. Carson and William Sabol, *The Black Underclass: Critical Essays on Race and Unwantedness*. New York: Garland Publishing, 1994.

———— and Samuel L. Myers, Jr, 'Family Structure and the Marginalization of Black Men: Policy Implications', In *The Decline of Marriage Among African-*

Americans: Causes, Consequences, and Policy Implications, edited by M. Belinda Tucker and Claudia Mitchell-Kernan. New York: Russell Sage, 1995.

Dennis, Marshall, *Fundamentals of Mortgage Lending*. Reston Publishing Company, 1978.

DeParle, Jason, 'Sharp Criticism for Head Start, Even by Friends.' *New York Times*, 19 March 1993, pp. A1, A17.

Dewar, Helen, 'Senate Votes to Give Apology, Compensation to Interned Japanese Americans', *Washington Post*, 21 April 1988, p. A9.

Dhesi, Autar S. and Harbhajan Singh, 'Education, Labour Market Distortions and Relative Earnings of Different Religion–caste Categories in India (A Case Study of Delhi', *Canadian Journal of Development Studies* (1989).

DiNardo, John, Nicole Fortin and Thomas Lemieux, *Labor Market Institutions and the Distribution of Wages, 1973–1992: A Non-parametric Approach*, mimeo. University of Montreal, 1993.

D'Souza, Dinesh, *The End of Racism: Principles for a Multicultural Society*. New York: The Free Press, 1995.

———, *Illiberal Education*. New York: The Free Press, 1991.

DuBois, W.E.B. *Black Reconstruction in America, 1860–1880*. New York: Atheneum, 1935.

———, 'The Negro Criminal', reprint of article from the 1899 Kraus-Thomson Organization Limited, Millwood, NY, original edition of *The Philadelphia Negro*, In *The Economics of Race and Crime*, edited by M.C. Simms and Samuel L. Myers, Jr. New Brunswick, NJ: Transaction Books, 1973.

Duke, Lynn, 'Job Market Still Tilts to Whites', *The News and Observer (Raleigh, NC)*, 15 May 1991, pp. 1A, 11A.

Duncan, Otis D., 'Inheritance of Poverty or Inheritance of Race', in *On Understanding Poverty*, edited by Daniel P. Moynihan, pp. 85–110. New York: Basic Books, 1967.

Eichengreen, Barry, 'Experience and the Male–female Earnings Gap in the 1890s', *Journal of Economic History*, **44** (3) (September 1984), 822–34.

——— and Henry A. Gemery, 'The Earnings of Skilled and Unskilled Immigrants at the End of the Nineteenth Century', *Journal of Economic History*, **46** (2) (June 1986), 441–54.

Ellwood, David, 'The Spatial Mismatch Hypothesis: Are There Jobs Missing from the Ghetto?', in *The Black Youth Employment Crisis*, edited by Richard Freeman and Harry Holzer. Chicago: University of Chicago Press, 1986.

——— and Jonathan Crane, 'Family Change Among Americans: What do we know?', *Journal of Economic Perspectives*, **4** (4) (Fall 1990), 65–84.

Engle, Robert F. and Clive Granger, 'Co-integration and Error Correction: Representation, Estimation, and Testing', *Econometrica*, **55** (2) (March 1987), 251–76.

Ermisch, John and Robert Wright, 'Welfare Benefits and Lone Parents' Employment in the U.K.', *Journal of Human Resources*, **26** (Summer 1991), 424–56.

Fainstein, Norman, 'The Underclass/Mismatch Hypothesis as an Explanation for Black Economic Deprivation', *Politics and Society*, **15** (4) (1987), 403–51.

Farley, Reynolds, *Black and Whites: Narrowing the Gap?* Cambridge, MA: Harvard University Press, 1984.

——, 'Blacks, Hispanics, and White Ethnic Groups: Are Blacks Uniquely Disadvantaged?', *American Economic Review: Papers and Proceedings*, **80** (2) (May 1990), 237–41.

——, 'Three Steps Forward and Two Back? Recent Changes in the Social and Economic Status of Blacks', *Ethnic and Racial Studies*, **9** (1) (January 1985), 4–28.

Feinberg, Phyllis, 'Lower Interest Race Spark Surge: Insurance, Financing, Hybrid Deals Still Popular', *National Real Estate Investor*, October 1989.

Ferguson, Ronald F., 'Shifting Challenges: Fifty Years of Economic Change Toward Black–white Earnings Equality', *Daedalus: Proceedings of the American Academy of Arts and Sciences*, **124** (1) (Winter 1995).

Fix, Michael and Raymond J. Struyk (eds), *Clear and Convincing Evidence: Measurement of Discrimination in America*. Washington, DC: Urban Institute Press, 1992.

Forman, James, *The Making of Black Revolutionaries*. New York: Macmillan, 1972.

Fossett, Mark A., 'Community-level Analysis of Racial Socioeconomic Inequality: A Cautionary Note', *Sociological Methods and Research*, **16** (4) (May 1988), 454–91.

—— and K. Jill Kiecolt, 'The Relative Size of Minority Populations and White Racial Attitudes', *Social Science Quarterly*, **70** (4) (December 1989), 820–35.

Fosu, Augustin Kwasi, 'Occupational Mobility of Black Women, 1958–1981: The Impact of Post-1964 Antidiscrimination Measures', *Industrial and Labor Relations Review*, **45** (1992), 281–94.

Franklin, John Hope and Alfred A. Moss Jr, *From Slavery to Freedom: A History of African Americans*, 7th edition New York: Knopf, 1994.

Freeman, Richard B., 'Black Economic Progress After 1964: Who Has Gained and Why?', in *Studies in Labor Markets*, edited by Sherwin Rosen. Chicago: University of Chicago Press/National Bureau of Economic Research, 1981.

——, 'Changes in the Labor Market for Black Americans, 1948–1972', *Brookings Papers on Economic Activity*, (1), (1973).

——, 'Decline of Labor Market Discrimination and Economic Analysis', *American Economic Review: AEA Papers and Proceedings*, May 1973b, pp. 280–86.

————, 'How Much Has De-unionization Contributed to the Rise in Male Earnings Inequality', in *Uneven Tides: Rising Inequality in America*, edited by Sheldon Danziger and Peter Gottschalk. New York: Russell Sage, 1994.

Friedman, Milton, *A Theory of the Consumption Function*. Princeton, NJ: Princeton University Press, 1957.

Frisbie, W. Parker and Lisa Neidert, 'Inequality and the Relative Size of Minority Populations: A Comparative Analysis', *American Journal of Sociology*, **82** (5) (1976), 1007–30.

Gage, Theodore Justin, 'Firms Keep Vultures from Bank Loans with Restrictive Covenants', *Corporate Cashflow*, August 1992.

Galanter, Marc, *Competing Equalities: Law and the Backward Classes in India*. Berkeley: University of California Press, 1984.

Galenson, Marjorie, 'Do Blacks Save More?', *American Economic Review*, **62** (1) (March 1972), 211–16.

Gallup, George E. (ed.), *The Gallup Poll: Public Opinion 1981*. Wilmington: Scholarly Resources, Inc., 1982.

———— (ed.), *The Gallup Poll: Public Opinion 1991*. Wilmington: Scholarly Resources, Inc., 1992.

Galster, George C. and W. Mark Keeney, 'Race, Residence, and Economic Opportunity: Modeling the Nexus of Urban Racial Phenomena', *Urban Affairs Quarterly*, **24** (1) (September 1988), 87–117.

Garber, Steven, Steven Klepper and David Nagin, 'The Role of Extralegal Factors in Determining Criminal Case Disposition', in *Research on Sentencing: The Search for Reform*, edited by Alfred Blumstein et al. Washington, DC: National Academy Press, 1983.

Geshwender, James A. and Rita Carroll-Seguin, 'Exploding the Myth of African-American Progress', *Signs*, **15** (1990), 94–110.

Gibson, J., 'Race as a Determinant of Criminal Sentences: A Methodological Critique and a Case Study', *Law and Society Review*, **12** (1978), 455–78.

Girvan, Norman, 'The Question of Compensation: A Third World Perspective', *Race*, **16** (July 1974), 53–82.

Gittleman, Maury and David R. Howell, 'Changes in the Structure and Quality of Jobs in the U.S.: Effects by Race and Gender, 1973–1990', *Industrial and Labor Relations Review*, forthcoming.

Goldsmith, Arthur H., Jonathan Veum and William Darity Jr, 'The Impact of Psychological and Human Capital on Wages', *Economic Inquiry*, **35** (4) (October 1997), 815–29.

Gottschalk, Peter and Sheldon Danziger, 'Family Structure, Family Size, and Family Income: Accounting for Changes in the Economic Well-being of Children, 1968-1986', in *Uneven Tides: Rising Inequality in America*, edited by Sheldon Danziger and Peter Gottschalk. New York: Russell Sage, 1994.

Gramlich, Edward M., Richard Kasten and Frank Sammartino, 'Growing Inequality in the 1980s: The Role of Federal Taxes and Cash Transfers', in *Uneven Tides: Rising Inequality in America*, edited by Sheldon Danziger and Peter Gottschalk. New York: Russell Sage, 1994.

Granssano, Bill, 'Lenders Buy Down Rates to Boost Low Loan Volumes', *Savings Institutions*, June 1989.

Greene, Linda S., 'Race in the 21st Century: Equality Through Law?', *Tulane Law Review*, **64** (1990), 1515–41.

Grogger, Jeffrey, 'Arrests, Persistent Youth Joblessness and Black/White Employment Differentials', *Review of Economics and Statistics*, **76** (1992).

Guinier, Lani, 'Keeping the Faith: Black Voters in the Post-Reagan Era', *Harvard Civil Rights–Civil Liberties Law Review*, **24** (1989), 393–435.

Hagan, John and Kristin Bumiller, 'Making Sense of Sentencing: A Review and Critique of Sentencing Research', in *Research on Sentencing: The Search for Reform*, edited by Blumstein et al. Washington, DC: National Academy Press, 1983.

Hamermesh, Daniel, 'Social Insurance and Consumption', *American Economic Review*, **72** (1), March 1982, 101–13.

Hammar, Tomas G., 'Dual Citizenship and Political Integration', *International Migration Review*, **19** (1985), 438–50.

Harrison, Bennett, 'The Intra Metropolitan Distribution of Minority Economic Welfare', *Journal of Regional Science*, **12** (January 1972), 23–43.

——— and Barry Bluestone, *The Great U-turn*. New York: Basic Books, 1988.

Hashimoto, Munori and Levis Kochin, 'A Bias in the Statistical Estimation of the Effects of Discrimination', *Economic Inquiry*, July 1980, 478–86.

Hawkins, Darnell F., *Ethnicity, Race and Crime: Perspectives Across Time and Place*. Albany, NY: State University of New York Press, 1995.

Heckman, James J., and Brook S. Payner, 'Determining the Impact of Federal Antidiscrimination Policy on the Economic Status of Blacks: A Study of South Carolina', *American Economic Review*, **79** (1989), 138–77.

Heckman, James and Peter Siegelman, 'An Evaluation of the Methods and Findings of the Urban Institute Employment Audit Studies', unpublished manuscript. University of Chicago, 1991.

Hernstein, Richard and Charles Murray, *The Bell Curve*. New York: The Free Press, 1994.

Herzog, John P. and James S. Earley, *Home Mortgage Delinquency and Foreclosure*. New York: National Bureau of Economic Research, 1970.

Hewitt, Janet Reilley, 'Boardroom View', *Mortgage Banking*, April 1992.

Hicks, John Richard, *The Theory of Wages*. London: Macmillan, 1932.

Higgs, Robert, *Competition and Coercion: Blacks in the American Economy*. Chicago: University of Chicago Press, 1980.

Hill Jr, Thomas E., 'The Message of Affirmative Action', *Social Philosophy and Policy*, **8** (1991), 108–29.

Hindelang, Michael J., 'Equality Under the Law', *Law and Society Review*, **12** (1978), 455–78.

———, 'Race and Involvement in Common Law Personal Crimes', *American Sociological Review*, **43** (1) (February 1978), 93–109.

Hirsch, Barry T. and John T. Addison, *The Economic Analysis of Unions: New Approaches and Evidence*. Boston: Allen and Unwin, 1986.

——— and David A. McPherson, 'Union Membership and Coverage Files from the Current Population Surveys: Note', *Industrial and Labor Relations Review*, **46** (3) (April 1993), 574–8.

Holzer, Harry J., 'Black Employment Problems: New Evidence, Old Questions', *Journal of Policy Analysis and Management* (1995).

Horrigan, Michael W. and Ronald B. Mincy, 'The Minimum Wage and Warnings and Income Inequality', In *Uneven Tides: Rising Inequality in America*, edited by Sheldon Danziger and Peter Gottschalk. New York: Russell Sage, 1994.

Howell, David R., 'The Collapse of Low-skill Male Earnings in the 1980's: Skill Mismatch or Shifting Wage Norms?', unpublished paper, 1994.

Howell, David, 'Employment Restructuring Across Industry Segments', *Industrial and Labor Relations Journal*, Spring 1995.

——— and Susan Wieler, 'The Demand for Skills, Shifts in Wage Norms and Low-Skill Earnings: Implications for Education and Training Policy', paper presented at the Allied Social Sciences Association meeting, Boston, MA, December 1995.

Hughes, Michael and David H. Demo, 'Self-Perceptions of Black Americans: Self-Esteem and Personal Efficacy', *American Journal of Sociology*, **95** (1989), 132–59.

———, Mark Allen Hughes and Janice Fanning Madden, 'Residential Segregation and the Economic Status of Black Workers: New Evidence for an Old Debate', *Journal of Urban Economics*, **29** (1991).

Ihlanfeldt, Keith, 'Intra-Metropolitan Variation in Earnings and Labor Market Discrimination', *Southern Economic Journal*, **55** (1988), 123–40.

——— and David Sjoquist, 'Job Accessibility and Racial Differences in Youth Employment Rates', *American Economic Review*, March 1990.

Jacobe, Dennis, 'Get Fannie and Freddie Out of Refinancing', *American Banker*, 20 March 1992.

Jacobs, John, 'Black America 1991: An Overview', in *The State of Black America 1992*, 2–3. New York: National Urban League, Inc., 1992.

Jasen, Georgette, 'Homeowners Find It Pays to Refinance – yet Again', *Wall Street Journal*, 9 September 1993.

Jaynes, Gerald D. and Robin M. Williams Jr (eds), *A Common Destiny: Blacks and American Society*. Washington, DC: National Academy Press, 1989.

Jaynes, Gerald, 'The Labor Market Status of Black Americans: 1939–1985', *Journal of Economic Perspectives*, **4** (4) (Fall 1990), 24.

Jenkins, Stephen P., ''Lone Mothers' Employment and Full-time Work Probabilities', *Economic Journal*, **102** (March 1992), 310–20.

Johnson, Charles S., *The Negro in American Civilization: A Study of Negro Life and Race Relations in the Light of Social Research*. New York: Henry Holt, 1930.

Johnson, G. David and Marc Matre, 'Race and Religiosity: An Empirical Evaluation of a Causal Model', *Review of Religious Research*, **32** (1991), 252–66.

Johnson, Robert C., 'Black Underrepresentation in Science and Technology', *Trotter Institute Review*, Winter/Spring 1991, 13–18.

Juhn, Chinhui, Kevin M. Murphy and Brooks Pierce, 'Accounting for the Slowdown in Black–white Wage Convergence', in *Workers and Their Wages*, edited by M. Kosters, pp. 107–43. Washington, DC: American Enterprise Institute Press, 1991.

———, Kevin M. Murphy and Brooks Pierce. 'Wage Inequality and the Rise in Returns to Skill', *Journal of Political Economy*, **101** (3) (June 1993), 410–42.

Kain, John, 'Housing Segregation, Negro Employment and Metropolitan Decentralization', *Quarterly Journal of Economics*, **82** (May 1968), 175–97.

Karoly, Lynn A., 'The Trend in Inequality Among Families, Individuals and Workers in the United States: A Twenty-five Year Perspective', in *Uneven Tides: Rising Inequality in America*, edited by Sheldon Danziger and Peter Gottschalk. New York: Russell Sage, 1994.

Kasarda, John D., 'Urban Change and Minority Opportunities', in *The New Urban Reality*, edited by Paul E. Peterson. Washington, DC: Brookings, 1985.

Katz, Lawrence F. and Kevin M. Murphy, 'Changes in Relative Wages, 1963–87: Supply and Demand Factors', *Quarterly Journal of Economics*, **107** (1) (February 1992), 35–78.

Killingsworth, M.R. and J.J. Heckman, 'Female Labor Supply: A Survey', in *Handbook of Labor Economics, Volume 1*, edited by O. Ashenfelter and R. Layard. New York: Elsevier Science Publishers, 1986.

———, 'Female Labor Supply: A Survey', in *Handbook of Labor Economics*, edited by O. Ashenfelter and R. Layard. New York: North-Holland, 1986.

Kimenyi, Mwangi S., 'Rational Choice, Culture of Poverty, and the Intergenerational Transmission of Welfare Dependency', *Southern Economic Journal*, **57** (1991), 947–60.

Kirschenman, Joleen and Kathryn M. Neckerman, ' ''We'd Love to Hire Them, but . . . '': The Meaning of Race for Employers', In *The Urban Underclass*, edited by Christopher Jencks and Paul Peterson. Washington, DC: Brookings, 1991.

Klepper, Steven, 'Bounding the Effects of Measurement Error in Regressions Involving Dichotomous Variables', *Journal of Econometrics*, no. 37 (1988), 343–59.

―――― and Daniel Nagin, 'The Deterrent Effect of Perceived Certainty and Severity of Punishment Revisited', *Criminology*, **27** (4) (November 1989), 721–46.

Knight, Jerry, '25-year Low in Mortgage Rates Fuel Refinancing Rage', *Washington Post*, 28 August 1993.

Korenman, Sanders, Jennifer E. Miller and Sjaastad John, 'Long-term Poverty and Child Development in the United States: Results from the NLSY', *Children and Youth Services Review*, **17** (1/2) (1995), 127–55.

Krauthammer, Charles, 'Reparations for Black Americans', *Time*, 31 December 1990, p. 18.

Kulkosky, Edward, 'Fannie: A Refinancing Bust Won't End Mortgage Boom', *American Banker*, 13 December 1993.

―――― , 'Home Lenders Reached New Heights in 1993', *American Banker*, 13 December 1993.

Kuznets, Simon, 'Economic Growth and Income Inequality', *American Economic Review*, **45** (1) (1955).

LaLonde, Robert J. and Robert H. Topel, 'Labor Market Adjustments to Increased Immigration', in *Immigration, Trade and the Labor Market*, edited by John M. Abowd and Richard B. Freeman, pp. 167–99. Chicago: University of Chicago Press, 1989.

Land, Kenneth C., 'Models of Criminal Careers: Some Suggestions for Moving Beyond the Current Debate', *Criminology*, **30** (1) (1992), 149–55.

Lashbrook, Dusty, 'Controlling the Fluid Pipeline', *Mortgage Banking*, April 1992.

Lawlor, Julia and Jeffrey Pitts, 'Job Hunt: Blacks Face More Bias', *The USA Today*, 15 May 1991, p. 1.

Lazear, Edward, 'The Narrowing of Black–white Differentials is Illusory', *American Economic Review*, **69** (September 1979), 553–64.

Leake, Donald O. and Brenda L. Leake, 'Islands of Hope: Milwaukee's African American Immersion Schools', *Journal of Negro Education*, **61** (1992), 24–9.

Leonard, Jonathan, 'The Impact of Affirmative Action Regulation and Equal Employment Law on Black Employment', *Journal of Economic Perspectives*, Fall 1990.

―――― , 'The Interaction of Residential Segregation and Employment Discrimination', *Journal of Urban Economics* (1987).

Leonard, Jonathan S., 'Employment and Occupational Advance Under Affirmative Action', *Review of Economics and Statistics*, **66** (August 1984), 377–85.

Levy, Frank, *Dollars and Dreams: The Changing American Income Distribution.* New York: Russell Sage, 1987.

—— and Richard J. Murnane, 'U.S. Earnings Levels and Earnings Inequality: A Review of Recent Trends and Proposed Explanations', *Journal of Economic Literature*, **30** (3) (September 1992), 1333–81.

Lewin-Epstein, Noah, 'Neighborhoods, Local Labor Markets, and Employment Opportunities for White and Nonwhite Youth', *Social Science Quarterly*, **66** (1) (March 1985) 163–71.

Liebman, Lance, 'Anti-discrimination Law: Groups and the Modern State', in *Ethnicity and Public Policy: Achieving Equality in the United States and Britain*, edited by Nathan Glazer and Ken Young. London: Heinemann Educational Books, 1983.

Lincoln, Abraham, *The Annals of America*. Vol. 9 of *1858–1865 the Crisis of the Union*. Chicago: Encyclopedia Britannica, Inc., 1976.

Lipin, Steven, 'GAF Refinancing Package Faces Difficult Sell in Secondary Market', *American Banker*, 13 August 1990.

Listokin, David and Stephen Casey, *Mortgage Lending and Race: Conceptual and Analytical Perspectives of the Urban Financing Problem.* New Brunswick, NJ: Rutgers University, Center for Urban Policy Research, 1980.

Lizotte, A. J., 'Extra-legal Factors in Chicago's Criminal Courts: Testing the Conflict Model of Criminal Justices', *Social Problems*, **25** (5) (1977), 564–80.

Lobov, W. and W.A. Harris, 'De Facto Segregation of Black and White Vernaculars', in *Diversity and Diachrony*, edited by David Sankoff, pp. 1–24. Philadelphia: John Benjamins, 1986.

Lusar, Robert, Jr, 'The Mechanics of Economic Development', *Journal of Monetary Economics* (1988).

Lynch, Lisa M., 'The Youth Market in the 80s: Determinants of Re-employment Probabilities for Young Men and Women', *Review of Economics and Statistics* (1989).

Manski, Charles, 'Anatomy of the Selection Process', *Journal of Human Resources*, **24** (1989), 343–60.

Mare, Robert and Christopher Winship, 'The Paradox of Lessening Racial Inequality and Joblessness Among Black Youth: Enrollment, Enlistment, and Employment, 1964–1981', *American Sociological Review*, **49** (1984).

Margo, Robert A. *Race and Schooling in the South, 1880–1950: An Economic History*. Chicago: The University of Chicago Press, 1990.

Marketti, James, 'Estimated Present Value of Income Diverted During Slavery', In *The Wealth of Races: The Present Value of Benefits from Past Injustices*, edited by Richard F. America. Westport, CT: Greenwood Press, 1990.

Marshall, F. Ray, *Rural Workers in Rural Labor Markets*. Salt Lake City: Olympus Publishing Company, 1974.

Marx, Karl, 'The Civil War in the United States', in *Surveys from Exile: Political Writings*, vol. 2. New York: Vintage Books, 1974.

Mason, Patrick, 'Decomposing the Unobservable: Educational Attainment and Wage Discrimination Among African-Americans, Latinos and Whites', unpublished paper. Wayne State University, 1994.

Massey, Douglas, 'American Apartheid: Segregation and the Making of the Underclass', *American Journal of Sociology*, **96** (2) (1990), 329–57.

Mattera, Philip, *Prosperity Lost*. UK: Addison-Wesley, 1990.

Maume Jr, and David J., A. Silvia Cancio and T. David Evans, 'Cognitive Skills and Racial Inequality: Reply to Farkas and Vicknair', *American Sociological Review*, **61** (August 1996), 561–4.

Maxwell, Nan, 'The Effect on Black–white Wage Differences of Differences in the Quantity and Quality of Education', *Industrial and Labor Relations Review*, **47** (January 1994), 249–64.

McCall, Patricia L., Kenneth C. Land and Lawrence E. Cohen, 'Violent Criminal Behavior: Is There a General and Continuing Influence of the South?', *Social Science Research*, no. 21 (1992), 286–310.

Megbolugbe, Isaac F. and Man Cho, 'An Empirical Analysis of Metropolitan Housing and Mortgage Markets', *Journal of Housing Research*, **4** (2) (1993), 191–224.

Michel, Richard C., 'Economic Growth and Income Equality Since the 1982 Recession'. Washington, DC: The Urban Institute, 1990.

Miller, Herman P. (ed.), *Poverty American Style*. Belmont, NH: Wadsworth, 1966.

Miller, Mark J., 'Dual Citizenship: A European Norm?', *International Migration Review*, **23** (1989), 945–50.

Montgomery, Edward, Kathryn Shaw and Mary Ellen Benedict, 'Pensions and Wages: An Hedonic Theory Approach', *Journal of International Economic Review*, **33** (1) (February 1992), 111–28.

——— and William Wascher, 'Race and Gender Wage Inequality in Services and Manufacturing', *Industrial Relations*, **26** (1987), 284–90.

Morris, Norval and Marc Miller, 'Predictions of Dangerousness', In *Crime and Justice: An Annual Review of Research*, vol. 6, edited by Michael Tonry and Norval Morris, pp. 1–50. Chicago: University of Chicago Press, 1985.

Mortgage Bankers Association of America. *Financial Statements and Operating Ratios for the Mortgage Banking Industry*,1987 (December).

Moss, Phillip and Chris Tilly, *Why Black Men Are Doing Worse in the Labor Market: A Review of Supply-side and Demand-side Explanations*. New York: Social Science Research Council, 1991.

Munnell, Alicia H., Lynn E. Browne, James McEneaney, and Geoffrey M.B. Tootbell, 'Mortgage Lending in Boston: Interpreting HMDA Data', Federal Reserve Bank of Boston Working Paper, 1992.

Murphy, Cait, 'The Grandest Affirmative Action Failure of All', *Wall Street Journal*, 27 December 1990.

Murphy, Kevin M., Mark Plant and Finis Welch, 'Cohort Size and Earnings in the United States', in *Economics of Changing Age Distributions in Developed Countries*, edited by Ronald D. Lee, W. Brian Arthur and Gerry Rodgers, pp. 39–58. Oxford: Clarendon Press, 1988.

—————— and Finis Welch, 'Industrial Change and the Rising Importance of Skill', in *Uneven Tides: Rising Inequality in America*, edited by Sheldon Danziger and Peter Gottschalk. New York: Russell Sage, 1994.

—————— and Finis Welch, 'The Structure of Wages', *Quarterly Journal of Economics*, **107** (1) (February 1992), 285–326.

Murray, Charles A., *Losing Ground: American Social Policy, 1950–1980*. New York: Basic Books, 1984.

Myers Jr., Samuel L., '"The Rich get Richer and..." The Problem of Race and Inequality in the 1990s', *Law and Inequality: A Journal of Theory and Practice*, **XI** (2) (June 1993), 369–89.

——————, 'Black–white Differentials in Crime Rates', *Review of Black Political Economy*, **10** (Winter 1980), 133–52.

——————, 'Measuring and Detecting Discrimination in the Post-Civil Rights Era', in *Race and Ethnicity in Research Methods*, edited by John H. Stanfield II and Rutledge M. Dennis, pp. 172– 97. Newbury Park, CA: Sage Publications, 1993.

——————, 'Estimating the Economic Model of Crime: Employment Versus Punishment Effects', *Quarterly Journal of Economics*, **48** (February 1983), 157–66.

——————, 'The Rehabilitation Effect of Punishment', *Economic Inquiry*, **18** (July 1980), 353–66.

——————, 'How Voluntary Is Black Unemployment and Black Labor Force Withdrawal?', in *The Question of Discrimination: Racial Inequality in the U.S. Labor Market*, edited by Steven Shulman and William A. Darity, Jr, pp. 81–108. Middletown, CT: Wesleyan University Press, 1989.

——————, 'The Incidence of Justice', in *Of Crime and Delinquency*, edited by C.M. Gray. London: Sage Publications, November, 1979.

—————— and Kenneth E. Phillips, 'Housing Segregation and Black Employment: Another Look at the Ghetto Dispersal Strategy', *American Economic Review*, **69** (1979), 298–302.

——————, 'Measuring and Detecting Discrimination in Punishment', *Journal of Quantitative Criminology* (1985).

———, 'Racial Disparities in Home Mortgage Refinancings', Western Economics Association meetings. Vancouver, British Columbia, July 1994.

——— and Chanjm Chung, 'Racial Differences in Home Ownership and Home Equity among Preretirement-Aged Households', *The Gerontologist*, **36** (3) (1996), 350–60.

———, Andriana Abariotes, Lekha Subaiya and Nathan Tiller, 'Disparities in Mortgage Lending in the Upper Midwest: Does Discrimination Exist?', Western Economics Association meetings. Vancouver, British Columbia, July 1994.

——— and Tsze Chan, 'Racial Discrimination in Housing Markets: Accounting for Credit Risk', *Social Science Quarterly* (1995).

Myrdal, Gunnar, *An American Dilemma: The Negro Problem and Modern Democracy*. New York: Harper, 1944.

National Science Foundation, *National Patterns of r & d Resources: 1990*. NSF 90-316. Washington, DC: National Science Foundation Press, 1990.

Neal, Derek and William Johnson, 'The Role of Premarket Factors in Black–white Wage Differences', In *NBER Working Paper no. 5124*, 1995.

Neal, Larry, 'A Calculation and Comparison of the Current Benefits of Slavery and an Analysis of Who Benefits', In *The Wealth of Races: The Present Value of Benefits from Past Injustices*, edited by Richard F. America. Westport, CT: Greenwood Press, 1990.

Neckerman, Kathryn M. and Joleen Kirschenman, *Hiring Strategies, Racial Bias, and Inner-city Workers: An Investigation of Employers Hiring Decisions*, mimeo. Department of Sociology, University of Chicago, 1990.

Neckopulos, James M., 'Mortgage Lenders Should Get Ready to Change Course', *American Banker*, 14 December 1992.

Nelton, Sharon, 'Nurturing Diversity', Nation's Business, **83** (6) (June 1995), 25 (3).

O'Neill, June, 'The Role of Human Capital in Earnings Differences Between Black and White Men', *Journal of Economic Perspectives*, **4** (1990), 25–46.

——— and Solomon Polachek, 'Why the Gender Gap in Wages Narrowed in the 1980s', *Journal of Labor Economics*, **11** (1) (January 1993), 205–28.

Oaxaca, Robert, 'Male–female Wage Differentials in Urban Labor Markets', *International Economic Review*, **14** (1973), 693–709.

Ong, Paul M., and Janette R. Lawrence, 'Race and Dislocation in California's Aerospace Industry', *Review of Black Political Economy*, forthcoming.

——— and Janette R. Lawrence 'Race and Post-displacement Earnings Among High-tech Workers', *Industrial Relations: A Journal of Economy & Society*, **30** (3) (Fall 1991).

Payton, Brenda, 'Looking for a Post-Gulf Role: The Black Antiwar Movement', *The Nation*, 1 July 1991, pp. 8–11.

Perry, Bruce, 'Neither White Nor Black.' *Ethnic Groups*, **6** (1985), 293–304.

Petersilia, Joan, 'Criminal Career Research: A Review of Recent Evidence', in *Crime and Justice: An Annual Review of Research*, edited by Michael Tonry and Norval Morris. Chicago: University of Chicago Press, 1980.

———, *Racial Disparities in the Criminal Justice System*. Santa Monica, CA: The Rand Corporation, 1983.

Peterson, Mark A. and Harriet B. Braiker. *Doing Crime: A Survey of California Prison Inmates*. Washington, DC: US GPO, 1980.

Peterson, Ruth and John Hagan, 'Changing Conceptions of Race: Toward an Account of Anomalous Findings of Sentencing Research', *American Sociological Review*, 47 (February 1984), 56–70.

Price, Richard and Edwin Mills, 'Race and Residence in Earnings Determination', *Journal of Urban Economics* (1985).

Rawls, John, *Theory of Justice*. London: Oxford University Press, 1971.

Reed, William, 'The African, African-American Summit', *The Baltimore Afro-American*, 12 June 1993, p. A11.

Reynolds, Morgan and Eugene Smolensky, 'Welfare Economics: Or When Is a Change an Improvement?', in *Modern Economic Thought*, pp. 447–66. Philadelphia: University of Pennsylvania Press, 1977.

Rodgers III, William M., 'The Relationship Between Macroeconomic Conditions and Male Black–white Earnings Ratios: The 1980 in an Historical Context', unpublished paper. College of William and Mary, October 1994.

——— and William E. Spriggs, 'What Does the AFQT Really Measure? Race, Wages, and Schooling And the AFQT Score', *Review of Black Political Economy*, **24** (4) (Spring 1996), 13–46.

Rose, Stephen J., 'Declining Family Incomes in the 1980s: New Evidence Form Longitudinal Data', *Challenge*, November–December 1993.

———, 'On Shaky Ground: Rising Fears About Incomes and Earnings', Research Report No. 94-02. National Commission for Employment Policy, October 1994.

Rountree, Pamela Wilcox, Kenneth C. Land and Terence D. Miethe, 'Macro–micro Integration in the Study of Victimization: A Hierarchical Logistic Model Analysis Across Seattle Neighborhoods', *Criminology*, **32** (3) (August 1994): 387–414.

Ruhm, Christopher J., 'When "Equal Opportunity" Is Not Enough: Training Costs and Intergenerational Inequality', *Journal of Human Resources*, **23** (2) (Spring 1988), 155–72.

Saenger, Gerhart, *The Social Psychology of Prejudice*. New York: Harper & Bros, 1953.

Sanford, Rose, 'Demystifying Mortgage Banking', *Journal of Retail Banking*, Spring 1991.

Schneider, Gregory D., 'Round Two for Refinancing', *ABA Banking Journal*, October 1992.

Sen, Amartya, *On Economic Inequality*. Oxford: Clarendon Press, 1973.

———, 'Poverty: An Ordinal Approach to Measurement', *Econometrica*, **44** (2) (March 1976), 219–31.

Sharpe, Rochelle, 'Losing Ground: In Latest Recession Only Blacks Suffered Net Employment Loss; Firms Added Whites, Asians and Hispanics Overall, But They Deny Any Bias', *The Wall Street Journal*, 14 September 1993, A1, A12–13.

Shin, Eui-Hang and Young Hwan Lee, 'Relative Size of Black Population and Occupational Differentiation in Metropolitan Areas', *Journal of Black Studies*, **21** (1) (September 1990), 52–71.

Shulman, S. and William Darity Jr (eds), *The Question of Discrimination: Racial Inequality in the US Labor Market*, Middleton, CT: Wesleyan University.

Simms, Margaret (ed.), *Economic Perspectives on Affirmative Action*. Washington, DC: Joint Center for Political and Economic Studies, 1995.

——— and Myers Jr. Samuel L. (eds), *The Economics of Race and Crime*. New Brunswick, NJ: Transaction Books, 1988.

Slottje, Daniel J., Kathy J. Hayes and Joyce Shackett, 'Labour Force Participation, Race and Human Capital: Influence on Earnings Distributions Across States', *Review of Income and Wealth*, **38** (1992), 27–37.

Smith, James P., 'The Convergence to Racial Equality in Women's Wages', RAND Paper Series P-6026, 1978.

———, 'The Improving Status of Black Americans', RAND Paper Series P-6055, 1978.

——— and Finis R. Welch, 'Black Economic Progress After Myrdal', *Journal of Economic Literature*, **27** (1989), 519–64.

——— and Finis R. Welch, 'Black-White Male Wage Ratios: 1960–1970', *American Economic Review*, June 1977.

——— and Finis R. Welch, *Closing the Gap, Forty Years of Economic Progress for Blacks*. Santa Monica, CA: The Rand Corporation, 1986.

——— and Finis R. Welch. *Race Differences in Earnings: A Survey and New Evidence*. Santa Monica, CA: The Rand Corporation, 1978.

Solow, Robert M., 'Growth with Equity Through Investment in Human Capital', lecture given for the George Seltzer Distinguished Lecture. University of Minnesota, Industrial Relations Center, 1992.

Sommerville, Raymond R., 'Queen Mother Audley Moore', in *Notable Black American Women*, edited by Jessie Carney Smith. Detroit: Gale Research, Inc., 1992.

Sowell, Thomas, *Civil Rights: Rhetoric or Reality?* New York: W. Morrow, 1984.

Squires, Gregory D., *From Redlining to Reinvestment*. Philadelphia: Temple University Press, 1992.

Steele, Claude, 'Race and the Schooling of Black Americans', in *Race and Gender in the American Economy: Views from Across the Spectrum*, edited by Susan F. Feiner. Englewood Cliffs, NJ: Prentice Hall, 1994.

Steele, Shelby, *The Content of Our Character*. New York: St. Martins Press, 1990.

Steinberg, Stephen, *The Ethnic Myth: Race, Ethnicity and Class in America*. Boston, MA: Beacon Press, 1981.

Struyk, R. J., M. A. Turner and M. Fix. *Opportunities Denied, Opportunities Diminished: Discrimination in Hiring*. Washington, DC: Urban Institute, 1991.

Sundaram, Jomo Kwame and Ishak Shari, *Development Policies and Income Inequality in Peninsular Malaysia*. Kuala Lumpur, Malaysia: Institute of Advanced Studies, University of Malaysia, 1986.

Swinton, David H., 'The Economic Status of African Americans: Limited Ownership and Persistent Inequality', in *The State of Black America 1992*, pp. 61–118. New York: The National Urban League, Inc., 1992.

Swinton, David, 'Racial Inequality and Reparations', In *The Wealth of Races: The Present Value of Benefits from Past Injustices*, edited by Richard F. America. Westport, CT: Greenwood Press, 1990.

Tilly, Chris, 'Understanding Income Inequality', *Sociological Forum* (1991).

Topel, Robert H., 'Regional Labor Markets and the Determinants of Wage Inequality', *American Economic Review*, **84** (2) (May 1994), 17–22.

———, 'Wage Inequality and Regional Labor Market Performance in the United States', in *Savings and Bequests*, edited by Toshiaki Tachibanaki. Ann Arbor: University of Michigan Press, 1994.

US Bureau of the Census, *The Black Population in the United States: March 1991*. Table 11, 57. Washington, DC: US GPO, 1991.

———, Current Population Reports, Series P60. *Money Income of Households, Families and Persons in the United States: 1990*. Washington, DC: US Government Printing Office.

US Department of Commerce, *The Black Population in the United States*, Washington, DC: US GPO, 1991.

———, *Current Population Survey*. Washington, DC: US GPO, 1985.

———, *Current Population Survey*. Washington, DC: US GPO, March 1976.

———, 'Families Maintained by Female Householders 1970–1979', Current Population Reports, Special Studies Series P-23, 1980.

US Department of Justice, Bureau of Justice Statistics, *Sourcebook of Criminal Justice Statistics, 1985*. Washington, DC: US GPO, 1986.

———, *Sourcebook of Criminal Justice Statistics, 1990*. Washington, DC: US GPO, 1991.

United States Congress, *Discrimination in Home Mortgage*. Senate Committee on Banking, Finance and Urban Affairs. Washington, DC: US Government Printing Office, 1990.

———, *Hearings on a Bill to Amend the Truth in Lending Act to Establish Additional Disclosure and Advertising Requirements for Home Equity Loans*. House Committee on Banking, Finance and Urban Affairs. Washington, DC: US Government Printing Office, 1987.

———, *Home Equity Loan Consumer Protection Act of 1987*. House Committee on Banking, Finance and Urban Affairs. Washington, DC: US Government Printing Office, 1987.

———, *Mortgage Discrimination*. Senate Committee on Banking, Finance and Urban Affairs. Washington, DC: US Government Printing Office, 1990.

———, *The Mortgage Refinancing Reform Act of 1992*. House Committee on Banking, Finance and Urban Affairs. H.R. 5170. Washington, DC: US Government Printing Office, 1990.

———, *Trends in Family Income*. Congressional Budget Office. Washington, DC: US Government Printing Office, 1988.

———, P.L. 100-383, 100th Congress, 1988.

United States General Accounting Office, *Federal Financial Institutions Examination Council Has Made Limited Progress Toward Accomplishing Its Mission*. Washington, DC: GAO, 1984.

———, *Home Equity Financing*. GAO/GGD-93-63. Washington, DC: GAO, 1993.

Vedder, Richard, Lowell Gallaway and David C. Klingaman, 'Black Exploitation and White Benefits: The Civil War Income Revolution', in *The Wealth of Races: The Present Value of Benefits from Past Injustices*, edited by Richard F. America. Westport, CT: Greenwood Press, 1990.

Vroman, Wayne, 'Changes in Black Workers' Relative Earnings: Evidence for the 1960's', in *Patterns of Racial Discrimination*, edited by George von Furstenburg et al. Lexington, MA: Lexington Books, 1974.

———, 'Transfer Payments, Sample Selection, and Male Black–White Earnings Differences', *American Economic Review*, 76 (May 1986), 351–4.

Washington, Booker T., 'Negro Crime and Strong Drink', an article in the *Journal of the American Institute of Criminal Law and Criminology*, in *The Booker T. Washington Papers*, edited by Louis R. Harland and Raymond W. Smock, pp. 21–30. Chicago: University of Illinois Press, 1912.

Welch, Finis R., 'Affirmative Action and Discrimination', in *The Question of Discrimination: Racial Inequality in the U.S. Labor Market*, edited by Steven Shulman and William A. Darity, Jr, pp. 153–89. Middletown, CT: Wesleyan University Press, 1989.

———, 'Black–white Differences in Returns to Schooling', *American Economic Review*, (December 1973), 893–907.

Welch, Finis, 'The Employment of Black Men', *Journal of Labor Economics*, **8** (1) (1990): 226-74.

Wilcox, Walter F., 'Negro Criminality', in *The Economics of Race and Crime*, edited by Margaret C. Simms and Samuel L. Myers, Jr, pp. 33–45. New Brunswick: Transaction Books, 1988.

Williams, Robin, *The Reduction of Intergroup Tensions*. New York: Social Science Research Council, 1947.

Willis, R.J., 'Wage Determinants: A Survey and Reinterpretation of Human Capital Earnings Functions', in *Handbook of Labor Economics, Vol. 1*, edited by O. Ashenfelter and R. Layard. New York: Elsevier Science Publishers, 1986.

Wilson, William Julius, *The Declining Significance of Race*. Chicago: University of Chicago Press, 1982.

————, *The Truly Disadvantaged: The Inner City, the Underclass and Public Policy*. Chicago: University of Chicago Press, 1987.

———— and Robert Aponte, 'Urban Poverty', *Annual Review of Sociology*, **2** (1985), 231–58.

———— and Katherine Neckerman, 'Poverty and Family Structure: The Widening Gap Between Evidence and Public Policy Issues', in *Fighting Poverty: What Works and What Doesn't*, edited by Sheldon Danziger and D. Weinberg. Cambridge: Harvard University Press, 1986.

Wolff, Edward N., 'Changing Inequality of Wealth', *American Economic Review: Papers and Proceedings*, **82** (2) (May 1992), 555–6.

Wolfgang, Marvin E. and Bernard Cohen, *Crime and Race: Conceptions and Misconceptions*. New York: Institute of Human Relations Press, American Jewish Committee, 1970.

————, Robert M. Figlio and Thorsten Sellin, *Delinquency in a Birth Cohort*. Chicago: University of Chicago Press, 1972.

Woodbury, Stephen, 'Earnings of Black Immigrants: Implications for Racial Implications', in *New Approaches to Economic and Social Analyses of Discrimination*, edited by Richard Cornwall and Phanindra Wunnava, pp. 295–330. New York: Praeger, 1991.

Zenner, Walter P., *Minorities in the Middle: A Cross-Cultural Analysis*. Albany, NY: State University of New York Press, 1991.

Zimmerman, David J., 'Regression Toward Mediocrity in Economic Stature', *American Economic Review*, **82** (1992), 409–29.

Zweig, Ronald, *German Reparations and the Jewish World: A History of the Claims Conference*. Boulder, Colorado: Westview Press, 1987.

Index

marriageable males 30, 101, 129, 132, 147
married couple families 48
Marx, Karl 156
Mason, Patrick 55–6
Massey, Douglas 55
Mattera, Philip 14
Maume, David J. Jr 56
Maxwell, Nan 41, 53, 57
Metropolitan Statistical Areas (MSAs) 49
middle classes, squeezing of 1, 2, 5, 6, 11–12, 14, 21, 23, 25–7, 29–30, 31–2, 39, 58, 63
migration, South-North 43, 45, 42
Miller, Mark J. 141
'minority conservative' school 135
minority voting 136
monopolies legislation 139
Montgomery, Edward 122 n.1
Moore, Audley 155
Moss, Phillip 8, 54, 70
Murnane, Richard J. 38, 39, 41, 42
Murphy, Cait 161 n.6
Murphy, Kevin M. 41, 59 n.7, 69, 70, 123 n.9
Myers, Samuel L. Jr 30, 43, 54, 57, 59 n.5, n.6, 75, 83, 102, 123 n.7, n.10, n.11, 129, 150, 158
Myrdal, Gunnar 139, 148, 154

National Academy of Sciences 148
National Institute of Drug Abuse 50
National Longitudinal Survey of Youth (NLSY) 53, 56
National Movement for the Establishment of a 49th State 155
Nation of Islam 141
Nation's Business 144
Nazis 155–6
Neal, Derek 41, 53
Neisser, Heinrich 156
Nelton, Sharon 144 n.6
New York Stock Exchange 38
NLSY *see* National Longitudinal Survey of Youth (NLSY)
non-cash benefits 14
non-earners 47, 72–5 *passim*, 84–7, 90–95, 113, 126

non-race based strategies 134–5, 137–9, 140–41, 144, 146
non-whites 15, 17
North Central region, female-headed families in 48

O'Neill, June 41, 53, 57
operatives, decline in 33–4, 36, 47–8, 51, 58, 160

Pand Study of Income Dynamics (PSID) 53
Pareto-efficiency 140, 141, 142
part-time working 25, 61, 83
Passamaquody Indians 155
Payner, Brook S. 158
per capita incomes, black-white ratio 125–6
Pierce, Brooks 59 n.7, 69, 123 n.9
Piore, Michael 159
Pitts, Jeffrey 51
Polish Americans 151
population changes *see* baby boom effect; demographic changes; immigration
power, access to 136
preferential scoring 137, 146
prisoners 126, 136, 141, 159
professional/managerial occupations 70–72, 76, 126, 127, 128, 148, 151
property income 152
PSID *see* Pand Study of Income Dynamics (PSID)
public office, representation in 136
public sector, black employment in 143, 158

quotas 1, 133, 137

race based strategies 1, 135–42, 147
opposition to 133–4, 142–4, 146
see also affirmative action programmes; preferential scoring; quotas; set-asides
race-neutral strategies 134
racial economic equality 148–54
wealth redistribution to obtain 154–9
Rawls, John 152–4
Reagan, Ronald Wilson 5, 14, 95, 128
recession, effects of 39, 41–2, 128, 129